W9-CEU-869

Charles Taylor

Philosophy Now

Series Editor: John Shand

This is a fresh and vital series of new introductions to today's most read, discussed and important philosophers. Combining rigorous analysis with authoritative exposition, each book gives clear and comprehensive access to the ideas of those philosophers who have made a truly fundamental and original contribution to the subject. Together the volumes comprise a remarkable gallery of the thinkers who have been at the forefront of philosophical ideas.

Published

Thomas Kuhn
Alexander Bird

John Searle
Nick Fotion

Charles Taylor
Ruth Abbey

Charles Taylor

Ruth Abbey

PRINCETON UNIVERSITY PRESS
PRINCETON AND OXFORD

Published in 2000 in North America, Central America,
South America,the Caribbean, and the Philippines by
Princeton University Press, 41 William St., Princeton,
New Jersey 08540. All rights reserved.

Copyright © Ruth Abbey, 2000

First published in 2000 by Acumen
Acumen Publishing Limited
17 Fairfax Road
Teddington
TW11 9DJ, UK

ISBN: 0-691-05713-3 (hardcover)
ISBN: 0-691-05714-1 (paperback)

Library of Congress Card Number: 00-107365

Designed and typeset in Century Schoolbook
by Kate Williams, Abergavenny.
Printed and bound by Biddles Ltd., Guildford and King's Lynn.

www.pup.princeton.edu
10 9 8 7 6 5 4 3 2 1

Contents

Acknowledgements

More than half of this book was written, and the whole of it revised, while I was a member of the School of Social Science at the Institute for Advanced Study, Princeton. The Institute provided a wonderfully conducive atmosphere for academic work. I am also grateful to the University of Notre Dame, Australia, for giving me a leave of absence to visit the Institute. I want to thank Charles Taylor for his assistance in the preparation of this work. I also remain indebted to those who taught me at McGill University: James Booth, Charles Taylor and James Tully.

For miscellaneous reasons, several others have earned my gratitude during the writing of this book. They are Clifford Ando, Fredrick Appel, Sue Ashford, Adam Ashforth, Aube Billard, Natalie Brender, Simone Chambers, Douglas J. Den Uyl, Leo Falcone, Steven Gerrard, Gabriella Hoskins, William Hughes, Ian Malcolm, John Shand, Ian Thompson and Marcia Tucker.

But most of all I owe thanks to my husband, Jeremy Moon, for helping me keep faith in myself.

Introduction

The very breadth of subject matter is . . . what will first strike the "Anglo-Saxon" philosopher . . . It is the combination of the desire for synthesis and the recognition of diversity which makes many of [his] analyses both penetrating and (necessarily) inconclusive. One becomes acutely conscious reading his work of the fact that philosophy is both an endless discussion and a source of clarification and understanding.

(Taylor 1968a: 402)[1]

The Canadian philosopher Charles Taylor is one of the most influential and prolific philosophers in the English-speaking world today. The fact that he sometimes writes in French or German, combined with the translation of some of his works into Swedish, Japanese, Spanish, Greek, Portuguese, Italian, Polish, Chinese, Dutch, Norwegian and Turkish, means, moreover, that his influence extends far beyond an English-language audience. Perhaps the most striking feature of Taylor's *oeuvre* is its breadth (cf. Miller 1995: 26); his work ranges from reflections on artificial intelligence to analyses of contemporary multicultural societies. Also notable is the scope of his approach to philosophical questions, for he typically brings his knowledge of Greek, Christian, Renaissance and modern thought as well as his appreciation of the arts to bear on such questions.

1

This book provides an introduction to and overview of Taylor's thought. As a work of this size could not convey the scope and depth of Taylor's thought in its entirety, the focus is on his contributions to some of the more enduring debates within western philosophy. Taylor's reflections on the topics of moral theory, selfhood, political theory and epistemology are surveyed, with these four areas providing the main chapter divisions for the book. As the movement from one chapter to the next shows, however, these divisions are somewhat arbitrary, for Taylor's contribution to one field of inquiry usually has connections with and ramifications for his contributions to others. To accommodate those wanting an outline of Taylor's thinking in just one of these areas, each chapter is presented as a relatively self-contained unit. Connections across chapters are signalled for those interested in pursuing the links among Taylor's positions.

Taylor's approach to morality is explored in Chapter 1. It discusses his distinctive brand of pluralism, his dissatisfactions with the dominant approaches to morality and his concepts of strong evaluation, moral frameworks, narrative, hypergoods and constitutive goods. Taylor's particular type of moral realism, which I call falsifiable realism, is also examined. This chapter concludes with an account of the role he accords to articulation in moral philosophy. Along the way, the question of what a moral theory is and does is addressed.

Chapter 2 attributes a two-dimensional approach to selfhood to Taylor, arguing that his analysis of the self draws on ontological and historicist aspects. The chapter begins with an overview of the ontological features of selfhood; those that do not change. These include the self's moral orientation, the centrality of self-interpretation, the fact that humans are animals with language, the dialogical nature of selfhood and the significance of embodiment. The chapter then moves into a description of Taylor's historicist reading of the modern self, charting the changing conceptions that have emerged over the centuries from Plato to postmodernism. Most of the depiction of Taylor's historicist approach to selfhood is drawn from his largest work so far, *Sources of the Self*.

Political theory is the topic of Chapter 3, which begins by outlining the communitarian elements of Taylor's thought. Following Taylor's own advice, these are divided into two levels: ontological and advocacy. His long-standing critiques of negative freedom and of atomism feature prominently in this discussion of the communitarian elements of his work. An account of the role of shared goods in politics is given and his attempt to revive the republican tradition in western politics explained. The second part of the chapter examines Taylor's complicated relationship to liberalism. It covers his defence of individual rights, the value he accords civil society and his critique of the idea of state neutrality. The challenges posed to traditional conceptions of liberalism by the politics of recognition are also considered.

Taylor's ongoing insistence on a distinction between the natural and the human sciences opens the chapter on epistemology. His admiration for and application of Gadamer's concept of the fusion of horizons emerges in this context. The discussion then moves into Taylor's conception of practical reason, which is also informed by the hermeneutical tradition. Why he sees these arguments as necessary becomes evident in the light of his interpretation of the scientific revolution of the seventeenth century and its enduring legacy. Taylor believes that this legacy extends beyond epistemology in particular and philosophy in general to touch the whole of modern western culture. The chapter then describes arguments about how to overcome this epistemological legacy, discussing his theory of engaged, embodied agency and his related emphasis on the tacit background or pre-understanding of ordinary life. It concludes by referring to those elements of his view of language not covered in the previous chapters.

The absence of a chapter devoted to Taylor's philosophy of language might seem anomalous, given the great importance he attributes to language in human life. However, precisely because of its importance, language is discussed in each of the four major chapters. It is, for example, hard to separate Taylor's theory of language from his account of personhood, both in his claim that humans are language animals and in his discussion of how expressivism has shaped the modern western identity. Articulation plays a major role in Taylor's moral theory and the ability of language to open up a public space appears in his political theory. To separate Taylor's discussions of language from these other domains of his thought would, therefore, be artificial.

But artificial separations between the different departments of Taylor's thinking cannot be avoided altogether. As noted at the beginning of Chapter 1, in dividing Taylor's analysis of moral life from his account of selfhood, I am trying to sever themes that resist separation. This is just one example of a recurrent dilemma: time and time again Taylor's thoughts on one topic veer readily into another. Yet notwithstanding the many connections and coherences that unite his arguments across a range of topics, Taylor is no system builder. On the contrary, his characteristic impulse is to complicate, rather than simplify and streamline problems. For example, he repeatedly reminds us of plurality. He draws attention to the plurality of goods that appear in most individuals' lives, to the multiple strands that have forged the modern identity, to the different traditions that shape democratic politics. He refuses the temptation to reduce complexity to single principles or to offer pre-packaged theoretical solutions to practical problems that must be worked out by the participants themselves.

Yet while Taylor promotes the recognition of diversity – of goods, worldviews, approaches to knowledge – diversity does not always presage disintegration or incommensurability for him. He maintains the hope that the horizons of quite different modes of life or tables of values might be permeable and capable of some integration. This attempt to mediate unity and diversity highlights a central feature of Taylor's thought; his attempt to reconcile solitudes.[2] He is often described as a thinker who integrates the themes and approaches from continental philosophy with those from the Anglo-Saxon analytical tradition of thought (Ignatieff 1985: 63; Scialabba 1990: 534; Dauenhauer 1992: 211). Yet this is just one of many manifestations of his quest for points of convergence between seemingly antagonistic beliefs, outlooks or streams of thought. His approach to selfhood, for example, attributes immense importance to changing self-interpretations and the way these are influenced by cultures, yet he does not accept that selves are interpretation "all the way down". He insists, rather, that there are enduring and universal features of selfhood, even while acknowledging that these are interpreted differently at different times by different groups and cultures. Likewise, as a political theorist, he rejects the supposed antagonism between liberalism and communitarianism and strives to retain the best features of both approaches to social life and politics. And, as Chapter 4 shows, Taylor's arguments about epistemology combine criticisms of foundationalism with a realist approach to the natural sciences.[3]

This reluctance to accept as given the binary structures that shape the terms of so much philosophical inquiry is closely related to another characteristic of his thought: his attempt to recover the excluded middle ground between two extremes. This desire to chart a course between Scylla and Charybdis is evident in his moral theory, where he sketches a realist position that falls between the Platonic idea that goods exist independently of humans and the projectivist idea that humans impose moral meanings on the world. His moral theory also steers a course between irreducible pluralism on the one hand and reductionism on the other. His analysis of modernity tries to persuade both the champions and the critics of modernity that they are wrong by presenting modernity as a more subtle and complex achievement than either side permits.

Just as Taylor takes a dialogical approach to the self, so his own position is worked out in conversation and contest with some of the major figures of the western philosophical tradition. I try to convey a sense of Taylor's immersion in the history of western thought by providing, where relevant, brief discussions of his interpretation of previous thinkers who have had a major impact on his thinking. These include Aristotle, Hegel, Rousseau, Herder, Heidegger and Wittgenstein. Taylor's hope that seeming antitheses might be reconciled is, for example, one reflection of the influence of Hegel on his thinking.

Taylor's work has attracted its share of criticism, both for the way he has interpreted other thinkers and for his own substantive claims. Because this book's primary goal is to outline Taylor's thought in a clear, coherent and accessible way without reducing its richness and depth too greatly, criticisms of Taylor's work are usually reserved for the notes. At times, however, references to the secondary literature appear in the body of the text, particularly when the interpretations offered by other commentators differ markedly from my own. My hope is that when my claims appear controversial compared to the readings of others, these disputes will drive readers back to Taylor's writings to determine for themselves the "best account" of his thought. To facilitate this return I have tried to make the sources and grounds for my expositions as clear as possible. When an idea recurs in several of his writings, I indicate this too. This also makes it more likely that readers coming to this book from different disciplines and knowing different areas of Taylor's thought will find some familiar point of reference.

The breadth and depth of Taylor's knowledge and interests are combined with an accessible, almost conversational writing style and use of everyday examples. As Isaiah Berlin observes, Taylor's work enjoys "an authenticity, a concreteness, and a sense of reality" (Tully & Weinstock 1994: 1). I see Taylor's approachability as a philosopher as intimately connected to his work as a teacher – for many years he taught the introduction to political theory course at McGill University – and to his role as a political activist and public intellectual in Quebec and Canada. Taylor has been the vice-president of the federal New Democratic Party (NDP) and president of its Quebec branch. Between 1962 and 1968 he ran four times, all unsuccessfully, for federal parliament as an NDP candidate. In one of the elections he even ran against Pierre Trudeau, who became the Canadian prime minister. Reflecting on what he learned from his career as an aspiring politician, Taylor referred to the sense of reality and responsibility that had to inform his thinking about policy. He also valued the variety of people he met during these campaigns; this broadened his understanding of politics, as well as of what makes people "tick".[4] In fact, the distance between political theory and the practice of politics is another of the gulfs Taylor has sought to bridge. He recalls that as a student of political theory:

> we studied major authors and principles, but we said nothing about such relevant issues as the corruption of democracy in major bureaucratized societies, a theme I later addressed with Tocqueville. I intended to bring both sides together, to relate this intellectual tradition to current problems.   (1998b: 104)

He continues to this day to attack approaches to politics that proceed as if "the socio-historical world comes simply packaged" as well as those that are oblivious to political realities, dwelling instead in "a dissociated world of self-enclosed theory" (Taylor 1995c: 103–4).

Despite his failed parliamentary ambitions, Taylor's political activism has continued. He advocates tirelessly in Quebec for recognition of the province as a distinct society but against secession from Canada. He has been a major contributor to magazines and journals in Quebec and Canada. He served on the provincial government's *Conseil de la Langue Française* (French Language Council) and was one of the experts consulted by the Belanger-Campeau commission on the future of Quebec.[5] His theories of politics are, moreover, dialectically related to his experiences of politics, for developments in Quebec influence his thinking about politics just as his thinking about political philosophy shapes his interpretation of Quebec.[6] This connection is particularly evident in his account of the politics of recognition, which is discussed in detail in Chapter 3. Illustrating the symbiotic relationship between his thought and practical politics, Taylor writes that "Philosophy is important in this struggle lest this dimension of recognition be forgotten. If it is only discussed in terms of redistribution, of institutional equality, the problems of recognition will re-emerge in a perverse way" (1998b: 108).

Living in Quebec has, however, influenced more than just Taylor's thinking about politics. He is deeply attached to the expressivist theory of language and selfhood that he traces to Herder, and suggests that his experience of living in Canada helped to forge this attachment. As he says:

> My attraction to Herder was prepared long ago by my situation in Quebec, where two languages as well as two philosophies of language, came face to face: while English speakers considered language as an instrument and did not understand why someone would refuse to adopt the most widely used instrument . . . for French speakers language constitutes a way of being in the world. Having belonged to a mixed family for several generations, it always seemed obvious to me that language is more than an instrument, that each language carries with it its own sense of humour, conception of the world etc. Hence my interest for language and for the Romantic philosophy of language, which criticized the instrumentalist philosophy of Hobbes, Locke or Condillac.
>
> (1998b: 109; cf. 1998d: 253)[7]

Taylor's biography is another factor contributing to his aspiration to mediate between seemingly rival positions. He describes himself as having "lived astride these two worlds [Quebec and Canada] which do not understand each other" (1998b: 107).[8]

This book concludes by pointing to some of the future directions of Taylor's work, outlining his recent reflections on what it means to live in a secular age. The contours of an argument presented as part of the Gifford lecture series are identified and points of continuity with his published works noted. The secularity project, which seems to be of comparable magnitude to *Sources of the Self,* is a work in progress for Taylor, and when dealing with such an engaged and energetic thinker it is only appropriate to "conclude" an overview of his work by showing where it is heading. The concluding chapter also illustrates one of this book's recurrent themes: that even Taylor's most theoretical writings have a practical purpose, one that reaches back to the roots of western philosophy. Taylor hopes that his large-scale analyses of modern western culture will contribute to the self-knowledge of its members and influence the way people think about themselves and others.

Chapter 1

Explaining morality

Introduction

This chapter and the next are premised on a rather artificial division between Taylor's moral theory and his account of selfhood. This division is artificial because, as both chapters show, Taylor's view of the self is closely connected with his analysis of moral life and *vice versa*. Their close connection is posited very early in *Sources of the Self*; at the end of its first paragraph we read that "Selfhood and the good, . . . or selfhood and morality, turn out to be inextricably intertwined themes" (Taylor 1989a: 3; cf. x, 33, 41, 105). So in these first two chapters, I am trying to disentangle themes that resist separation.

In this chapter's presentation of Taylor's moral theory, the focus is on what he takes to be the universal or permanent features of moral life. A major part of the account in Chapter 2 of his views on selfhood traces the shifts that he posits in conceptions of the self from the ancient to the modern western world. This distinction between things that change and those that stay the same in Taylor's depiction of identity and moral life corresponds loosely with the structure of *Sources of the Self*. In Part I of that work, Taylor identifies what he takes to be the permanent structures of moral life, while from Parts II to V he charts the changing notions of the self from Plato to postmodernism.[1]

So notwithstanding his sensitivity to historical changes in notions of the self that have a powerful influence on the sort of goods valued by individuals and societies, Taylor does not think that ethics is history "all the way down". From a meta-ethical viewpoint, he discerns certain structural features that are common to the moral life of all human beings. The focus of this chapter is these enduring features of moral life. It discusses Taylor's distinctive brand of pluralism, his critiques of other approaches to morality such as relativism, subjectivism and projectivism and his concepts of strong evaluation, moral frameworks, narrative, hypergoods and constitutive goods. Taylor's particular type of moral realism, which I call falsifiable realism, is also considered. This chapter concludes with an account of the place he accords to articulation in moral philosophy. Along the way, the question of what a moral theory is and does will be addressed.

Morality's domain

Before looking in detail at the various components of Taylor's moral theory, it is necessary to ask what this is a theory of; what does he see the domain of morality to be? As his belief in the tight relationship between morality and selfhood intimates, Taylor construes the moral realm in a broad way. It includes the issues normally associated with morality, such as questions about the individual's relationships to others. In this sort of inquiry, debates arise about what is the correct thing to do in situations involving others and responses typically revolve around ideas of rights, duties, obligations and justice. However, along with these questions about the right way to conduct one's relationships with others, Taylor takes morality to encompass questions about what it is good to be. This second range of questions asks about a person's sense of dignity and self-respect and the provenance of these ideas. The issues of dignity and respect point, in turn, to the more amorphous area of an individual's sense of meaning or fulfilment in life. Of course the concerns in this latter cluster are often quite particular, either to cultures or to groups within them or to individuals, and this further separates Taylor's approach to morality from much modern moral philosophy that focuses on the universal.

The breadth of Taylor's conception of morality is partly a reaction against the limitations he perceives in most modern moral philosophy. Its shortcoming are twofold. Firstly, much modern moral philosophy is concerned with obligations to others, with what it is right to do in other-regarding actions. Taylor is critical of this stripped-down approach, which equates morality exclusively with questions about what it is right to do. He complains that in most modern moral philosophy:

> The focus is on the principles, or injunctions, or standards which guide *action,* while visions of the good are altogether neglected. Morality is narrowly concerned with what we ought to *do,* and not with what is valuable in itself, or what we should admire or love.
>
> (1995b: 145, original emphasis; cf. 135, 152; 1996d: 3)

Secondly, modern moral philosophy typically provides universalist responses to these questions about what it is right to do to and for others. These universalist answers are premised upon an ideal of human equality. Yet as Taylor sees it, this approach tends to neglect questions about what it is good to be that are susceptible to more personal and particular responses. By construing morality in a fuller way, he is trying to remind us that "there are also other moral ideals and goals – e.g. of less than universal solidarity, or of personal excellence – which cannot be easily coordinated with universalism, and can even enter into conflict with it" (1985b: 233).

Some thinkers use the terms morality and ethics to refer respectively to this distinction between what it is right to do and what it is good to be. They see morality as being about universalizable rules and codes of conduct that should govern other-regarding actions, while ethics is concerned with questions about the self, meaning and fulfilment in life.[2] Although sympathetic to the outlook that underlies this (Taylor 1996d: 4, 10, 12), Taylor does not adopt this distinction in any systematic way. Instead, he goes on using the term morality to cover both dimensions. A major reason for using the term morality in this more comprehensive way is his belief that questions about right action and meaning or fulfilment in life both involve strong evaluation (1989a: 3–4, 14, 15). This important term is explained below.[3]

WHAT IS IT GOOD TO BE?
WHAT IS IT GOOD TO LOVE?

Charles Taylor

Pluralism

Along with its wide focus, another key feature of Taylor's moral thought is its pluralism. As indicated, he insists that the domain of the moral includes quite different goods: some are universal, others obtain within a more limited collectivity such as the nation while yet others are more particular and specific to cultures or groups (1985b: 244; 1997a). As this suggests, he believes that in any person's life there is always a multiplicity of goods to be recognized, acted upon and pursued. These goods are not only plural in the numerical sense but they are plural in an ontological sense; they are of qualitatively different types from one another and, because of this, cannot always be harmoniously combined, rank-ordered or reduced to some more ultimate or foundational good. Aristotle is an important source of inspiration for Taylor's ontological pluralism, for his insistence, *contra* Bentham's utilitarianism, that there are qualitatively different yet valuable things to be incorporated in a good or fully human life.[4]

Yet Taylor's awareness of the potential for rivalry among the qualitatively different goods distances his outlook from Aristotle's. While Aristotle acknowledged that there were qualitatively different goods available to humans, he believed that these goods could be combined, at least in the lives of some (Taylor 1988e: 813). For Aristotle, living a good life involved realizing all the goods in their proper proportion and order. A good life should include the pursuit of philosophy, participation in politics, virtue friendship and family affection. These are all different goods and they realize different human capacities but there is no necessary conflict among them (1989a: 25). One of the problems for individuals in the modern world is that, according to Taylor, we face a wider array of different goods. Indeed, one of his aims in the later parts of *Sources of the Self* is to show how these new goods, such as expressivism and the affirmation of ordinary life, developed. But modern individuals are not just faced with more goods; we are also confronted with the fact that some of the things worthy of affirmation are irreconcilable with others. As Taylor says, "There is no guarantee that universally valid goods should be perfectly combinable, and certainly not in all situations" (*ibid.*: 61). This means that individuals need to choose from a range of goods that vie for their allegiance or attachment in the knowledge that the things not chosen are none the less worthy of affirmation. From this pluralist point of view, moral choices are hard and necessarily entail sacrifice and loss. Taylor describes modern human beings as:

> always in a situation of conflict between moral demands, which seem to them to be irrecusable, but at the same time uncombinable. If this conflict is not felt, it is because our sympathies or horizons are too narrow, or we have been too easily satisfied with pseudo-solutions. (1994d: 213)

Although pluralism is often associated with secularism,[5] Taylor implies that the monotheism of Judaism, Christianity and Islam provides, paradoxically perhaps, another source of ontological moral pluralism. The belief that the world was created by an omnipotent deity who saw that this creation was good means that there is much in the world to affirm. This also means that in forgoing some of these things, the believer is facing the loss of something genuinely good. Taylor contrasts this with the Stoic outlook, which tries to transvalue or reappraise those goods that cannot be realized as not worth having anyway. He provides a dramatic illustration of the contrast between the Stoic and monotheistic outlooks by comparing the death of Jesus with that of Socrates. What Jesus's passion in the garden communicates is that his imminent death will bring not only suffering but also the loss of something valuable: his mortal life. Socrates' rationalism in prison conveys the opposite; dying is a relief and a release and the loss of mortal life is not worth mourning. At a more general level, Taylor describes the difference thus:

> The great difference between Stoic and Christian renunciation is this: for the Stoic, what is renounced is, if rightly renounced, ipso facto not part of the good. For the Christian, what is renounced is thereby affirmed as good – both in the sense that the renunciation would lose its meaning if the thing were indifferent and in the sense that the renunciation is in furtherance of God's will, which precisely affirms the goodness of the things renounced: health, freedom, life. Paradoxically, Christian renunciation is an affirmation of the goodness of what is renounced. For the Stoic, the loss of health, freedom, life does not affect the integrity of the good. On the contrary, the loss is part of a whole which is integrally good and couldn't be changed without making it less so. (1989a: 219)

Whatever its provenance, this emphasis on moral pluralism brings Taylor's thinking into line with modern and postmodern outlooks, which stress the myriad goods facing individuals. However, in Taylor's thought this pluralism does not have the consequences it often does in other schools of thought. He does not, for example, advocate relativism, the belief that all goods are theoretically of equal value and that it is impossible to argue rationally for the superiority of some to others. He finds the relativist idea that what the individual faces in the moral world is a dazzling array of equally appealing and equally arbitrary goods to be an utterly implausible account of moral life. As he explains:

> The point of view from which we might constate that all orders are equally arbitrary, in particular that all moral views are equally so, is just not available to us humans. It is a form of self-delusion to think that we do not speak from a moral orientation which we take to be right. That is a condition of being a functioning self, not a metaphysical view we can put on or off.
>
> (*ibid.*: 99; cf. 100)

As well as illustrating Taylor's rejection of moral relativism, this passage expresses his belief in the close link between a person's identity and moral commitments. It also points toward his belief that for a moral philosophy to be credible it must make some contact with how people actually experience their moral lives.

However, this rejection of relativism as an account of how individuals experience their moral lives is not tantamount to a critique of cultural relativism, the idea that different cultures might have quite different worldviews and moral outlooks and that it is impossible to find a fair and rational way of arbitrating among them. It is quite conceivable to argue that within a culture individuals are always already orientated towards some values but that among cultures there is no impartial way of deciding which moral outlook is superior or more compelling. A relativist outlook might be inappropriate at the individual level but necessary when comparing cultures. Although Taylor is alive to the different outlooks and specific goods of diverse cultures, he is not ultimately a cultural relativist either. He believes that it is possible to either reconcile or at least argue rationally about the value of different cultural traditions (*ibid.*: 61).[6]

Another response to the pluralism of moral life that is often related to relativism is subjectivism. Subjectivism involves the belief that the choice among goods can only be justified according to individual preferences or inclinations. This idea has been articulated by thinkers such as Thomas Hobbes in the seventeenth century and Friedrich Nietzsche in the nineteenth century. According to Hobbes:

> whatsoever is the object of any man's appetite or desire, that is it which he for his part calleth good: and the object of his hate and aversion, evil . . . For these words of good, evil, and contemptible are ever used with relation to the person that useth them: there being nothing simply and absolutely so: nor any common rule of good and evil, to be taken from the nature of the objects themselves; but from the person of the man.
>
> (Hobbes 1974 [1651]: 90)

Nietzsche claims that as the world is inherently meaningless, humans must give meaning to their own lives. An individual's values matter not because they are inherently laudable but because that person has chosen to affirm them (Taylor 1976a: 289; 1985a: 29). This Nietzschean view has, in turn, been an important influence on the twentieth-century movements of existentialism and postmodernism. As we shall see when discussing his brand of moral realism, Taylor also rejects subjectivism, believing it to be a flawed account of how humans experience moral goods.

Nor does Taylor follow many modern philosophers and lodge his faith in the idea that in the face of a conflicting array of goods we can have recourse to a single principle or procedure that will tell us how to order them, thereby removing the troublesome consequences of pluralism. Calling this general approach formalism (1985b: 231), he places a number of approaches to ethics under its rubric. For example, when faced with a moral dilemma, a Kantian would say that I should choose in accordance with the categorical imperative by selecting the good that, if chosen universally, could be affirmed. A Benthamite would say that I should choose the good that will maximize my pleasure and minimize my pain, and would recommend the felicific calculus to determine which good best achieves this outcome. Many liberals would say that I should choose whichever good I like, in so far as its pursuit brings no harm to others. Although these principles are quite different from one another, the general idea is the same: in a situation of moral choice, individuals can appeal to some general principle or procedure that will enable them to steer their way through the uncertainty. As Taylor sees it:

> There has been a tendency to breathtaking systematization in modern moral philosophy. Utilitarianism and Kantianism organize everything around one basic reason. And, as so often happens in such cases, the notion becomes accredited among the proponents of these theories that the nature of moral reasoning is such that we ought to be able to unify our moral views round a single base. (1995b: 149; cf. 1989a: 76, 79, 89)

In attacking the formalism of modern moral theory, Taylor is echoing and extending Hegel's attack on Kant. As Hegel sees it, the price Kant paid for the achievement of organizing moral life around the criterion of the right was emptiness; his general principle became so abstract as to have nothing substantive to say about moral life (Taylor 1975a: 370; 1979a: 77–8). So for Taylor, the formalism of modern moral theory is achieved at the expense of ontological pluralism. The formalist outlook assumes that all the goods can be reasoned about or calculated in the same way, which effectively denies any qualitative differences among them. This approach also prematurely circumscribes the domain of morality by requiring that only goods that can be thought about in this homogeneous way be included among the moral. As Taylor sees it then, formalism's basic premise – that all the goods can be reasoned about in the same manner – is faulty. And by positing that only goods that can be thought about in the same manner qualify as moral, it produces distortion and reductionism, artificially limiting the range of things that can count as goods (1994f: 39; 1996d: 17; 1997a: 172, 175). Taylor responds to the pluralism of moral life in a quite different way from the approaches canvassed here, insisting instead on the recognition of qualitative distinctions among goods (1985b: 230–47; 1994d: 250).

Formalism in moral theory is, moreover, simply one manifestation of what Taylor sees as a wider trend toward reductionism in modern western philosophy. He associates this general movement with an aspiration to emulate the natural sciences, describing the ambition to understand human life in terms of a single principle of explanation as a:

deeply entrenched intellectual habit or outlook characteristic of our kind of society . . . Single principle explanations work against complex, multi-faceted understandings of human life, but they benefit from association with the tremendous prestige of natural science explanations that . . . seem to reduce complex phenomena to single principles and laws.

(1994e: 177)

Strong evaluation

The concept of "strong evaluation" is the key to understanding Taylor's distinctive response to moral pluralism. Taylor derives his idea of strong evaluation from Harry Frankfurt's arguments about second-order desires. Second-order desires are desires we have about our own desires. Although we experience a range of desires, we do not view them all equally; some are seen as higher or more admirable than others. Frankfurt contends that this ability to value desires differently contributes to the human distinction; it is one of the things that separates humans from animals (Frankfurt 1971). Although Frankfurt does not use the term strong evaluation, his argument that individuals can see some of their desires as qualitatively different from others informs Taylor's concept of strong evaluation (Taylor 1985a: 15–16, 102).

So the idea of strong evaluation emerges from a picture of humans as creatures with multiple desires. The term "strong evaluation" captures Taylor's belief that individuals rank some of their desires, or the goods that they desire, as qualitatively higher or more worthy than others. The term refers, therefore, to distinctions of worth that individuals make regarding their desires or the objects of their desires. One of the entailments of strong evaluation is that although there are always multiple goods clamouring for attention in a person's life, they do not all appear in the same light. Some are recognized as being inherently more worthy, more valuable, more meaningful or more importuning than others (*ibid.*: 3, 16, 19; 1989a: 4, 20, 47). As this suggests, Taylor's conception of strong evaluation is inherently contrastive and hierarchical. It involves emotions, desires or judgements that could be plotted on a vertical axis: as strong evaluators, humans are moved by a sense of what is higher or lower, noble or base, better or worse, worthy or mean, courageous or cowardly, and so on (1976a: 283). Taylor conveys the hierarchical judgements involved in strong evaluation when he says that "A good test for whether an evaluation is 'strong' in my sense is whether it can be the basis for attitudes of admiration and contempt" (1989a: 523 n.2; cf. 1985b: 239–40).

Taylor takes strong evaluation to be a fact of moral life:

> the qualitative distinctions we make between different actions, or feelings, or modes of life, as being in some way morally higher or lower, noble or base, admirable or contemptible . . . are central to our moral thinking and ineradicable from it.
> (1985b: 234; cf. 1989a: 42).

He sees this capacity for evaluating or judging desires to be a distinctively and universally human one. As he says, "I think this is something like a human universal, present in all but what we would clearly judge as very damaged human beings" (1994d: 249; cf. 1985a: 16, 28, 33). Although these remarks suggest that Taylor is simply employing the concept of strong evaluation to describe the way humans are, Owen Flanagan's observation that this concept has a dual function in Taylor's moral theory is helpful here. Strong evaluation is both descriptive and normative: Taylor believes that it both describes how people are as well as outlining what is required for full personhood (Flanagan 1996: 147).

To understand just what Taylor means when he claims that strong evaluation is a necessary part of the moral identity of human beings, four areas require clarification. Firstly, and most straightforwardly, Taylor is not suggesting that each and every choice an individual makes is the subject of strong evaluation. Some choices do not imply or invoke any sense of higher or lower value. Decisions employing strong evaluation are qualitative, and can be contrasted with non-qualitative choices (Taylor 1976a: 282–5). In some instances, the image of choosing as simply weighing alternatives is the appropriate one for describing an individual's decisions. For example, whether I take the train or bus into town might just depend on what mode of transport is more convenient in light of my other plans and obligations. What I eat for lunch might depend on my degree of hunger, how much money I have with me, whether I got up early enough to make my own lunch, and so on. I might have a yearning to dine in an expensive restaurant, but budgetary constraints result in my eating a sandwich on a park bench. Choices like these need not play the sort of powerful role in constituting identity that strong evaluation implies.

Yet there is nothing to suggest that such quotidian decisions could never become the subject of strong evaluation. If I become a vegetarian for ethical reasons, for example, what I eat for lunch can be seen in terms of a good that is strongly valued by me. If I am an environmentalist who believes that travelling by train generates less pollution or is a more socially responsible or collectively rational mode of transport, then my choice of transport can become part of my moral identity. So Taylor is not proposing that strong evaluation necessarily comes into play in every decision an individual makes. Yet nor is there anything in his treatment of this idea that precludes certain things from coming to be seen by some individuals as involving distinctions between higher and lower, noble and base.

Secondly, although Taylor uses the term evaluation and although this involves individuals recognizing some goods as qualitatively higher than others, it should not be inferred that individuals are always fully cognizant of the fact that they order or evaluate their desires in this hierarchical way. The meaning of evaluation in this context is closer to an intuitive judgement or response than to the outcome of a reasoned, reflective process. As we shall see, Taylor does believe that the underpinnings of strong evaluation can be articulated to some extent, but this is neither a necessary nor sufficient condition of strong evaluation. He contends that individuals always make these sorts of qualitative judgements even if they are unaware that they are doing so and even if they are oblivious to the bigger moral picture that forms the background to their distinctions of worth.

Many of Taylor's commentators have interpreted his concept of strong evaluation as requiring a reflective stand towards one's ethical commitments. And it is easy to see how some of his early formulations of strong evaluation created the impression that it requires reflection on and articulation of moral priorities. In one essay he writes that "Our strong evaluations may be called contrast articulations . . . they are attempts to formulate what is initially inchoate, or confused, or badly formulated" (1976a: 295). Taylor's interpreters have tended to be critical of this, charging him with excessive rationalism. They also point out that the neo-Socratic approach to strong evaluation is at odds with Taylor's ambition to give an account of how people actually live their moral lives, for it is hard to claim that awareness of, reflection on and analysis of one's values really is a universal feature of human life.[7]

The neo-Socratic flavour of some of Taylor's early formulations of strong evaluation has, however, disappeared from his more recent work. His references to strong evaluation in *Sources of the Self* carry no requirement for reflection on, or articulation of, one's qualitative moral distinctions. As he says there, "It is this level of inarticulacy, at which we often function, that I try to describe when I speak of the 'sense' of a qualitative distinction" (1989a: 21; cf. 307). In another work, he makes this point more explicitly:

> I don't consider it a condition of acting out of a strong evalua-tion that one has articulated and critically reflected on one's framework ... I mean simply that one is operating with a sense that some desires, goals, aspirations are qualitatively higher than others. (1994d: 249; cf. 1995b: 140)

It would, however, be misleading to infer from this that the association of strong evaluation with reflection and awareness of one's judgements of higher and lower goods is something that was present in Taylor's earlier works but that has disappeared from his later ones. Rather, perhaps in response to some of the criti-cisms that have been levelled at this association, his later works have become less ambiguous about the relationship between strong evaluation and reflection. To illustrate that the later posi-tion can be considered a clarification, rather than a revision of, the earlier position, consider a passage from one of Taylor's earliest and most detailed discussions of strong evaluation. There he writes that:

> The strong evaluator can articulate superiority just because he has a language of contrastive characterization. So within an experience of reflective choice between incommensurables, strong evaluation is a condition of articulacy, and to acquire a strongly evaluative language is to become (more) articulate about one's preferences. (1976a: 288)

The first sentence of this passage seems to support the neo-Socratic interpretation by suggesting that strong evaluation goes hand in hand with an awareness of one's judgements of higher and lower. However, the following lines modify this, for Taylor introduces the qualification that this obtains in a situation of reflective choice. He also says that strong evaluation is a condition of articulacy, not that articulacy is a condition of strong evaluation. Strong evaluation itself is then distinguished from a strongly evaluative language. So rather than there being a substantive shift in his conception of strong evaluation, I think it is more correct to see him as making his argument clearer in his later formulations.[8]

In one of his earlier discussions of strong evaluation, Taylor associates this with the notion of taking responsibility for oneself. Because a human being is not simply hostage to his desires but can make qualitative, hierarchical distinctions among them, he can have some say in the sort of person he is (*ibid.*: 280–82; cf. 1985a: 28). However, this connection between strong evaluation and self-responsibility does seem to repose on an image of strong evaluators as cognizant of their values and judgements. If a person is motivated by what is only an implicit or intuitive sense of right and wrong, higher and lower, can he really be held responsible for the decisions made or actions taken on that basis? It seems to me that the attribution of self-responsibility and some degree of choice about who a person is can only be made when reasoning about these values has occurred, or could reasonably have been expected to occur. So there seems to be a tension between Taylor's concession that individuals can be moved by moral judgements that they are not fully aware of and his claim that one of the ways in which the capacity for strong evaluation distinguishes humans from animals is by according them some responsibility for who they are. It is interesting to note here that the nexus between strong evaluation and self-responsibility does not receive similar attention in Taylor's later discussions of strong evaluation. This suggests that as the neo-Socratic flavour of his formulations of strong evaluation diminished, so did the association between strong evaluation and self-responsibility.

Ultimately, Taylor's position on strong evaluation is that while individuals can be conscious of the moral judgements that underpin their strong evaluations, they need not be. Strongly valued goods need not be explicit or articulated in order to exercise a powerful influence on a person's actions and sense of morality and purpose. Nor do these judgements have to be part of the person's awareness to be valuable in explaining moral life. Instead, strongly valued goods can exist as part of the tacit background of their understanding.[9, 10]

The third caveat necessary for understanding what Taylor means by strong evaluation comes from the fact that although he uses the adjective "strong" to describe these evaluations, he is really trying to capture their quality rather than their force or power. I might, for example, have a very strong desire to humiliate my political opponent in public. But because I admire the ideal of magnanimity in public life and believe that petty, adversarial *ad hominem* politics is destructive, I have a sense that this powerful desire is base; I would like to think of it as beneath me, that in succumbing to it I would be unleashing my lower self. So I struggle against this strong desire on the basis of my strong evaluation that it is better to show magnanimity than contempt for those who disagree with me.

Finally, although Taylor believes that all individuals are strong evaluators, he does not believe that we all value the same things strongly. The fact of strong evaluation might be a human universal, but the goods thus valued vary across cultures and among individuals (1985a.: 3, 8; cf. 1989a: 42). Yet notwithstanding this sensitivity to the diversity of moral values among individuals and across cultures, Taylor believes that some goods do feature in all moral codes and are strongly valued by all cultures. These revolve around the idea of the value of human life and the dignity of the person. They carry injunctions against killing or maiming people, treating them cruelly and even failing to assist them in need. As he says:

> Every moral system has a conception of what we might call human dignity, . . . of the quality which, in man, compels us to treat him with respect, or . . . a conception which defines what it is to have respect for human beings.
> (1986a: 53; cf. 1989a: 4, 11, 14; 1985b: 232; 1995a: 35, 53, 56).

Many of these injunctions are, of course, honoured more in the breach than in the observance, but Taylor's response would be that even those who violate them would claim to be respecting them in some way. So advocates of capital punishment say that it is their respect for innocent life that leads them to urge death for murders. Historically, certain groups of people have been abused and disrespected on the pretext that they are somehow less than fully human. The category of who counts as a person worthy of respect has widened in the modern era and what respect means or demands has changed, but Taylor believes that the general moral idea that persons should be respected is a universal and strongly valued one.

It would seem that this claim about strong evaluation, that individuals always feel the pull of some goods as incomparably higher than others, represents Taylor's own resolution of the problem of moral pluralism. Isn't he simply saying that, in the face of multiple goods, always act in accordance with your strongly valued ones? Doesn't this provide a principle or procedure for deciding what to do in different situations and therefore represents the sort of formalist moral decision-making that he claims to be rejecting? Sadly, the situation is not this simple. Although Taylor claims that individuals necessarily value some goods more strongly than others, there is usually more than one of these strongly valued goods on any person's moral horizon. Moreover, these strongly valued goods can come into conflict with one another, so the problem of moral pluralism is not erased by the recognition of strong evaluation (1985b: 236).

To illustrate this, imagine a person who puts a strong premium on family life, loving to spend time with her partner and children. A fulfilling family life is clearly a strongly valued good for her. However, the same person is also dedicated to the pursuit of knowledge. As a professional scientist she loves to spend hours poring over a microscope. This pursuit does not just bring her pleasure; understanding even a tiny corner of the universe in a fuller way seems to her to be an admirable thing for a human being to do. Advancing scientific knowledge is unquestionably one of her strongly valued goods. Yet notwithstanding her passion and respect for science, she likes nothing more than to spend time away from the lab and the city as a whole to get back to nature. A week away from technology, communing wordlessly with the natural world is bliss, and she scorns her friends who couldn't survive an afternoon without their microwaves and mobile phones. This person is clearly a strong evaluator: spending time with her family, pursuing her career as a scientist and solitary communion with nature are all things that she values highly. A life without them would seem to her almost not worth living; she couldn't imagine herself not doing these things. However, it is not hard to see that these goods come into conflict; there might not be enough time in any month to fit them all in. How can she commune with nature and spend time with her children while also dedicating herself to the advancement of learning? She will be forced to forfeit or compromise some of her strongly valued goods. Taylor's point is that in such a situation of moral choice, which is very common, there are no guidelines telling individuals how to reconcile these demands; they may well be irreconcilable, not just in terms of the time each consumes but also in terms of the good each affirms. In making such forced choices, Taylor contends that individuals know that they are sacrificing something or things that are valuable in their own right.[11]

However, this sort of conflict is not the only reason why strongly valued goods fail to be realized. Taylor acknowledges that individuals do not always act in accordance with the objects of their strong evaluation (1989a: 62). However, he contends that in such cases individuals feel that they have let themselves down, have failed to live up to their higher or better selves. Failing to act in accordance with one's strongly valued goods will incur a sense of loss, weakness or frustration, and Taylor maintains that individuals cannot be indifferent to this failure. Or they may feel themselves to be in transition from one good to another. As this suggests, Taylor holds not only that some goods are strongly valued in people's lives but also that these goods provide important yardsticks of personal success or failure, development or decline. Part and parcel of something being a strongly valued good is that acting in accordance with or furtherance of it brings a sense of pride, satisfaction and achievement whereas acting against or ignoring it leaves one with a sense of failure or dejection (1995b: 142).

It is clear then that on Taylor's analysis, a person's identity is closely bound up with the goods he or she affirms, no matter how unselfconsciously this is done. He declares that "Our identity is therefore defined by certain evaluations which are inseparable from ourselves as agents. Shorn of these we would cease to be ourselves" (1985a: 34; cf. 1989a: 30). As indicated, this close relationship between the self and its strongly valued goods is not a static one; individuals experience themselves, he believes, as moving closer to or falling away from, their strongly valued goods (1989a: 42, 45, 47). However, as the need for choice indicates, it is possible and indeed common to do both at once; to feel that one is realizing one strongly valued good or set of goods while at the same time feeling like a failure with regard to others. Nor is Taylor's view of the tight relationship between the self and its strongly valued goods static in that it prohibits the possibility of an individual changing their strongly valued goods. His thesis that strongly valued goods inform individual identity does not rule out the acquisition of new goods and the abandonment of old ones. Such a process would, however, result in an important change in that person's identity and self-interpretations.[12]

Taylor's argument about the centrality of strong evaluation strikes a blow at relativism in moral theory; he insists that individuals do not see all their values or desires as being of potentially equal worth. This concept is wielded against the relativism of Bentham's utilitarianism in particular, with its desire to eliminate distinctions of worth among desires and goods and to place them on an equal footing (1985a: 17, 21, 23; cf. 1989a: 22–3, 383).[13] This concept of strong evaluation also challenges the notion of radical choice among values that was propounded by Jean-Paul Sartre. Taylor provides a refutation of Sartre's picture of the individual in a moral dilemma being forced to choose without criteria or priorities to guide the decision. While Taylor concedes that this can be a dramatic rendering of what happens when strongly valued goods collide, it cannot be inflated into an account of all moral choice (1976a: 291; 1985a: 29–33). He argues further that the idea of a moral dilemma turns out to be incomprehensible if the idea of radical choice is taken seriously, because goods that have been thus chosen can just be "unchosen" and the conflict dissolves. In contrast to the idea that individuals see things as having value because of their choice to endorse them, Taylor contends that strong evaluation prevents us from experiencing all our choices equally. In most cases, we sense that a desire or good of greater worth is at stake.

Taylor believes that in insisting on the reality and centrality of strong evaluation in moral life, he is actually stating the obvious. The need to labour the obvious in this way comes from what he takes to be the narrowness of much modern philosophy with its focus on obligations to others and procedural reasoning about these. Taylor accuses modern moral philosophy of being mute about the place of qualitative distinctions in moral life (1989a: 84, 90, 1995b: 146).[14] He argues, moreover, that these philosophies suppress the role of qualitative distinctions in moral life while at the same time being underpinned by them. Because of this failure or refusal to acknowledge strong evaluation, much modern moral philosophy is silent about the conditions of its own possibility and the vision of the good that inspires it (1989a: 88, 93; 1995b, 150). To take one example, Bentham famously denies the existence of qualitative distinctions among the goods valued by individuals. Yet the idea of being rational is, for him and for most subsequent utilitarians, a strongly valued one; it expresses, in Taylor's terms, "a qualitative contrast; it is the basis of moral admiration and contempt; it is a goal worthy of respect" (1985b: 244; cf. 1976a: 285–6). As we shall see, Taylor maintains that these hidden motivations can be unearthed by articulating the moral frameworks that underlie these philosophies.

Moral realism

Taylor's conception of strong evaluation also poses a challenge to subjectivism. He believes that when individuals experience some goods as inherently more worthy than others, they are responding to their sense that the good is valuable independent of their choice of it. As he says:

> I want to speak of strong evaluation when the goods putatively identified are not seen as constituted as good by the fact that we desire them, but rather are seen as normative for desire. That is, they are seen as goods which we ought to desire, even if we do not, goods such that we show ourselves up as inferior or bad by our not desiring them.   (1985b: 120)

Taylor claims that strongly valued goods command the respect of individuals because of their intrinsic value; they are experienced as making calls or demands upon individuals, rather than being freely or arbitrarily chosen by them (1989a: 4, 20; 1991a: 36–7). This claim, that when individuals strongly value goods, they do so with a sense that the good is intrinsically worthy of affirmation rather than being good because they have affirmed it, brings us to the question of Taylor's moral realism.

At the most general level, realists argue that there is a world that is independent of humans' interpretations and understandings of it. This means that human knowledge can be measured as more or less true according to its ability to given an accurate account of this independently existing world. In contrast to the quintessential anti-realist pronouncement by Nietzsche that "there are no facts, only interpretations" (Nietzsche 1968: 481), realists maintain that there are facts and interpretations, and that the interpretations that come closer to explaining the facts are better or truer than others.

There are three possible ways of interpreting Taylor's moral realism, which fall along a continuum of realist approaches to moral life. The first is weak realism. The third position is at the furthest extreme from this – strong realism. The second lies closer to, but is not the same as, strong realism. To describe this second position, which I attribute to Taylor, it is necessary to introduce the seemingly oxymoronic notion of falsifiable realism. While the weaker realist approach would be more readily acceptable to more of his readers,[15] it is ultimately the falsifiable approach, which carries forward elements of its weaker cousin, that Taylor wants to defend. However, some of his readers have misconstrued his falsifiable moral realism as strong moral realism; as the insistence that moral values do exist independently of human beings.[16]

The weak conception of moral realism would relate it to Taylor's claim to be offering a phenomenology of moral life, to be giving an account of how individuals experience the goods in their lives. As he says, "What we need to explain is people living their lives" (1989a: 58; cf. 32, 74; 1995a: 39). Taylor's realism could be simply depicting individuals' perceptions that the goods they value strongly exist independently of them; their feeling that they are responding to something inherently worthy in these goods when they affirm them. The fact that individuals may feel that these goods derive their worth not merely from being valued by them but believe, rather, that they are valued because they are worthy, need commit Taylor neither to the proposition that these goods actually do exist nor that they are valuable in themselves. On this weak reading of his moral realism, he can be seen as simply describing the way individuals experience their moral life. Some of his formulations support this interpretation; consider the following passage, which emphasizes the way individuals feel about the goods they pursue or admire:

> We sense in the very experience of being moved by some higher good that we are moved by what is good in it rather than that it is valuable because of our reaction. We are moved by seeing its point as something infinitely valuable. We experience our love for it as a well-founded love. (1989a: 74; cf. 341)

The strong interpretation of Taylor's moral realism shares these phenomenological features of the weak approach but interprets him as saying that these goods actually do exist independently of human beings; that people are right in feeling themselves to be responding to something outside and independent of them when they admire and pursue certain goods. On this reading, humans' perception that these goods exist independently of them is not just a feature of moral life but also a true depiction of the moral world. However, from Taylor's apparent defence of this stronger realist line it emerges that it is really falsifiable realism that he is promoting. He proceeds with an argument about necessity. He contends that in trying to explain moral life, we need to take seriously the fact that humans experience their moral world as he says they do. The best account of morality must be one that incorporates the fact that individuals experience goods as being worthy of their admiration and respect for reasons that do not depend on their choice of them (1989a: 58).[17] From the necessity of explaining morality in these realist terms, Taylor believes we can infer the reality of these goods. As he asks rhetorically, "How else to determine what is real or objective, or part of the furniture of things, than by seeing what properties or entities or features our best account of things has to invoke?" (1989a: 68). A little further on he rephrases the question but repeats the point:

> What better measure of reality do we have in human affairs than those terms which on critical reflection and after correction of the errors we can detect make the best sense of our lives? "Making the best sense" here includes not only offering the best, most realistic orientation about the good but also allowing us best to understand and make sense of the actions and feelings of ourselves and others. (*ibid.*: 57; cf. 1995a: 39)

This is not the sort of realist argument familiar to us from the natural sciences. In the natural sciences, realists typically contend that even without a population of human beings to know it, the natural world would continue to possess the forces it does in the presence of humans. Gravity, for example, is not something that derives its properties from the fact that humans know about it or understand it in a certain way. Conversely, for humans to properly understand gravity requires that they minimize the intrusion of their subjectivity into their attempts to understand it. This was the approach to the natural world adopted in the scientific revolution of the seventeenth century and it proved phenomenally

successful in furthering scientific knowledge and then in developing technology (see Chapter 4).

Although Taylor is a realist when it comes to the natural
sciences, his moral realism is defended in a different way. This
difference comes as no surprise, given his repeated attacks on the
belief that humans can be understood through the terms and
methods employed in the natural sciences (1989a: 80; see Chapter
4). He does not suggest that in trying to explain morality we imagine a moral world devoid of humans and attempt to separate its
subject-dependent properties from its objective or real properties
(1989a: 56, 257). Instead, his defence of moral realism begins with
humans and their experience of morality. It would make no sense
to him to try to explain moral life in abstraction from one of its
central forces; that is, humans (*ibid.*: 59, 68; cf. 1991d: 245, 247–8).
Beginning with humans and the way they experience morality, he
claims that the most plausible explanation of morality is one that
takes seriously humans' perception of the independence of the
goods. He believes, therefore, that his moral theory is superior to
all forms of projectivism, which explain morality away as meaning
imposed by humans on a morally neutral world (1989a: 53–62).

> The best accounts we can give of our own actual use of moral
> terms, in deliberating, or in describing, judging, explaining
> our own and others' actions, will all treat these goods as not
> projection-dependent.   (1994c: 207; cf. 1989a: 257).

Taylor concludes that unless and until a moral theory emerges
that can explain why the human urge to respond to goods as if they
had an independent existence is unconnected to reality, realism is
the most persuasive approach to moral life. Hence my designation
of it as falsifiable rather than strong: Taylor concedes that an
explanation of moral life could appear that showed his to be erroneous. This is clear from an important passage in *Sources of the
Self*, where he posits that the best account of moral life does
include reference to transcendent moral sources. However,
whether these sources are necessarily non-anthropocentric is not
so clear; Taylor's hunch is that they are "but all this remains to be
argued out" (1989a: 342).

One way of describing the difference among these three types of
realism is to consider the different significance each accords to the
experience of moral life. Weak realism, for example, could accept

Taylor's proposition that people react to their valued goods as if they had an independent existence, but see this as a myth. Weak realism takes realism as a description of how people experience their moral life but does not accept this as a true description of the moral world. This feature of moral experience has no bearing on its interpretation of reality. From the strong realist perspective, interpretations of moral life can also be misleading. Even if people didn't experience their moral life in this way and even if everyone adhered to projectivism, they would be wrong because moral goods are objective and real. Falsifiable realism lies between these two, albeit closer to strong realism, because it takes this fact about human moral experience seriously and imputes ontological significance to it. Because it starts from what it takes to be a feature of ordinary moral experience, it could not get going if people did not experience their moral life in this way. It will go on arguing in this way until a convincing account can be made as to why this experience is erroneous. So falsifiable realists accord the ordinary experience of moral life more significance than do weak realists or strong realists; from this standpoint, people's perceptions of their moral life cannot be so easily dismissed as illusory.

Some interpreters mistake Taylor's moral realism for what I have called strong realism; for the insistence that the goods individuals perceive as higher really do exist independently of them. They detect in this stance a form of neo-Platonism. Plato believed that the good did exist independently of human beings; its reality was not dependent upon human interpretations of it. Rather, one of the purposes of philosophy was to bring philosophers to an awareness of the good (Taylor 1989a: 122). Given that one of Taylor's techniques for criticizing modern moral theory is to return to ancient approaches to the good life to appreciate what has been eclipsed or denied by the modern mind-set, it seems plausible that he could be interested in resurrecting a Platonic approach to the good. However, Taylor rejects the assimilation of his type of realism to Plato's. One reason for this is his admission that Platonism is now irrelevant as a moral source. This is because Plato's ethics and metaphysics were so closely intertwined; his understanding of goodness was inseparable from his theory of the forms. As modern science has discredited the latter, so the power of the former has atrophied too (*ibid.*: 56, 73). However, this is not reason enough to quash the criticism that Taylor is a neo-Platonist, for as his criticisms of other moral theories indicate, the repudiation of something at the theoretical level is no guarantee that it does not influence one's thinking in some deeper, more tacit way.

The more substantive reason for Taylor's rejection of the assimilation of his moral realism to Plato's is the excessive polarization of this approach. The logic behind it is that one is either a Platonic moral realist or a projectivist. Taylor, in his characteristic way, wants to occupy the excluded middle ground between these two extremes. Unlike Plato, he does not think that it makes sense to see these moral goods as existing without human beings to know them. Unlike projectivists, he thinks it is wrong to construe these goods as existing solely through human artifice. As we have seen, he believes that human beings experience the goods that command their respect in a non-anthropocentric way, as not deriving solely from human will or choice nor depending only on the fact of individual affirmation for their value (*ibid.*: 342; 1994c: 208–11).

Religion

Others critics see in Taylor's moral realism the influence of his theism. Taylor is a Catholic of ecumenical outlook: he describes himself as "a Christian [who] finds greatness in some facets of Islam, Judaism, Buddhism" (1991d: 241; cf. 1994d: 226, 229; Morgan 1994: 65).[18] As a Christian, Taylor believes that God is the source of goodness. He does not conceal his theism; rather he identifies it as one of the forces that drives him to question anthropocentrism. Deep ecology is another of these forces (Taylor 1989a: 102, 342; 1994c: 213). By the term "deep ecology" Taylor is referring to the idea that the natural world has value in its own right and makes corresponding demands on humans for its preservation. This is in contrast to the view that has dominated modern western culture that the natural world has an instrumental value only, that it exists to satisfy human wants and can be used in whatever way is deemed necessary for this (1995a: 100). (This aspect of Taylor's thinking has been heavily influenced by Heidegger's critique of the idea of nature as "standing reserve".) As this suggests, Taylor is critical of moral outlooks that insist upon subjectivism, excluding all notions of non- or trans-human sources of goodness (1989a: 506). But he tries not to make his personal religious beliefs foundational to his moral theory, aiming instead to develop an explanation that is acceptable to people of different religious persuasions as well as to those unpersuaded by religion. However, some of his critics contend that he has failed in this endeavour, believing that his moral realism is only explicable by reference to his Catholicism, that his belief in God is the hidden foundation of his moral theory. His claim that humans experience their moral life in a non-subjectivist manner builds in the need for some transcendent source of goodness, and the most likely transcendent source, in western culture at least, is the Christian God. According to this line of criticism, those who do not share Taylor's theism will not be persuaded by his moral theory either.[19]

There is, however, some confusion surrounding the claims Taylor makes about the relationship between religion and morality. Skinner (1991: 147) and Lane (1992: 48, 55), who quotes Skinner's article, impute to Taylor the belief that only theism can be experienced as an adequate moral source. In reply, Taylor denies that this is his view. And the passage in *Sources of the Self* cited by Skinner and Lane does say something different. There Taylor writes that "no one doubts that those who embrace it [theism] will find a fully adequate moral source in it" (1989a: 317). A possible reason for the confusion could be that Taylor runs two points together here. One is about how theists experience their religious belief as a moral source – that is, as a fully adequate one. The second is about how this experience is viewed by non-theists. The first, that those who embrace theism will find in it a fully adequate moral source, might or might not be correct. Some commentators on Taylor have pointed to the problem of evil that has plagued Christianity from the time of St Augustine onwards as posing a challenge to this claim (Larmore 1991: 161; Schneewind 1991: 426).[20] Taylor's second tenet, that no one doubts that this is how theists experience it, is even more contestable, for many non-believers do think that religion is inadequate as a moral source, for many reasons.[21] Taylor clarifies that he was only making the first point: "It was a claim about how different views are understood by their protagonists, and not about the value of one view somehow being recognized by all" (1991d: 241; cf. 1994a: 125). However, it is clear that Taylor is not saying here that theism is the only adequate moral source. I think that he comes closer to claiming this in his argument about constitutive goods, which is laid out below.

Taylor's views about the relationship between morality and religion come in for criticism from theists too. Fergus Kerr, for example, takes him to task for failing to challenge Isaiah Berlin's depiction of Christianity as determinist and allowing no real role for human autonomy in the unfolding of history (Kerr 1997: 154–5). George Marsden criticizes Taylor for being too veiled about his Catholicism in *Sources of the Self*. Marsden discerns a tension between the fact that this work was "clearly controlled by questions shaped by a Christian agenda" and the way that its arguments appealed to a detached readership, interested in exploring the questions of modernity in a non-religious way (Marsden 1999: 87).[22] Taylor offers a dual explanation of the fact that, with the exception of *A Catholic Modernity?*, his religious commitments have not been accentuated in his works. The first has to do with the practice of philosophy. As he sees it, "the nature of philosophical discourse . . . has to try to persuade honest thinkers of any and all metaphysical or theological commitments" (1999a: 13). Secondly, he claims that academic culture in the western world is predominantly secular, making it inhospitable to arguments based on theistic premises (*ibid.*: 118–19).

Inescapable frameworks

Taylor believes that another enduring feature of moral life is the presence of what he calls moral frameworks or horizons (he uses these terms interchangeably). The idea of a moral framework refers to a series of beliefs that gives overall shape and direction to a person's values and moral outlooks. We are familiar with this sort of idea from religion; notwithstanding the very real debates among members of the same denomination about what sort of actions their faith enjoins or forbids, it makes some sense to think of Christianity or Islam as providing moral frameworks for their members. We can even think of some secular movements as providing moral frameworks; Marxism was one, feminism may be another and environmentalism a third. Again, although there is room for debate about what allegiance to such a perspective requires morally, it is conceivable that such allegiance provides members with a moral framework. So, if someone claimed to be a feminist and happily exploited their foreign female nanny, we could identify a contradiction between their moral framework and their action. The same could be said of the environmentalist who drove a gas-guzzling car and flatly refused to recycle household waste. These actions might not ultimately be incompatible with their moral framework but the onus would be on them to justify this seemingly hypocritical behaviour.

Although the secularity, pluralism and individualism of modernity have thrown the idea of moral frameworks into disrepute, Taylor believes that all individuals have a moral framework, whether they realize it or not. These frameworks give shape and meaning to individuals' lives and provide answers, no matter how tacitly, to the existential questions that he believes face all individuals about the purpose, conduct and direction of their lives. One's framework provides guidance about moral questions in the broad sense; that is, about what it is right to do *vis-à-vis* others and about what it is good to be; about what is meaningful and rewarding for an individual. As Taylor says:

> I want to defend the strong thesis that doing without frameworks is utterly impossible for us; otherwise put, that the horizons within which we live our lives and which make sense of them have to include these strong qualitative discriminations. Moreover, this is not meant just as a contingently true psychological fact about human beings . . . Rather the claim is that living within such strongly qualified horizons is constitutive of human agency, that stepping outside these limits would be tantamount to stepping outside what we would recognize as integral, that is, undamaged human personhood.
>
> (1989a: 27; cf. 31, 78)

Whether he uses the metaphor of framework or horizon, Taylor's point is that moral frameworks are indispensable, because they orient people in moral space. He sees this as another necessary feature of moral life; individuals feel themselves to exist within a space of moral questions about what is the right thing to do, what goods should be pursued and what is the right direction for their lives to take. Moral frameworks help them to answer these questions. Just as individuals orient themselves in physical space and find it hard to function if disorientated, so we orient ourselves in moral space: we usually have a sense of where we stand on moral questions and we feel ourselves as either moving towards or failing to move towards the goods in our lives (*ibid.*: 29–31, 33, 42). Taylor's conviction about humans' need to feel oriented in moral space does not deny that some individuals can feel themselves as lacking these reference points or as totally confused about moral matters or as having no sense of moral direction. What matters for him is that such situations are considered anomalous, as problematic, as stages to be worked through. As he says, "To begin to lose one's orientation is to be in crisis, and to lose it utterly is to break down and enter a zone of extreme pathology" (1994c: 209; cf. 1989a: 27–8, 30–31).[23] That these feelings of uncertainty, of flailing around morally, typify a situation of moral and of identity crisis, indicates again how closely intertwined the self and morality are for Taylor.

Strong evaluation and moral frameworks are not only both necessary parts of the structure of human life according to Taylor, but they interact. Although he sometimes implies that moral frameworks and strong evaluations are synonymous (1989a: 26), it makes more sense to think of one's moral framework as consisting of a series of strong evaluations, of judgements about which goods are of higher importance. At one point he writes of "having an identity which is defined in terms of certain essential evaluations which provide the horizon or foundation for the other evaluations one makes" (1985a: 39). However, moral frameworks can be adjusted to accommodate new strongly valued goods. And in the case of both strong evaluations and moral frameworks, individuals can be quite unaware of their role in orienting their moral life. As Taylor says, "We have to be rightly placed in relation to the good. This may not be very obtrusive in our lives if things go well and if by and large we are satisfied with where we are" (1989a: 44).

Hypergoods

Some moral frameworks include what Taylor calls a hypergood. Hypergoods are supreme among strongly valued goods and provide a way of rank-ordering the other less strongly valued goods in an individual's moral framework. As this suggests, hypergoods command even more respect and admiration than strongly valued goods and because of this become hegemonic in a person's life. One illustration of the presence of a hypergood in a person's moral framework appears when her dedication to wilderness preservation inspires her to spend extended periods perched in a redwood forest to protest against logging. Food and other supplies are hauled up to her by rope, she sleeps on a wooden platform and bathes from a bucket. This dedication does not deny the person's other strongly valued goods; she might strongly value education, world peace, individual liberty and socioeconomic justice. However, the overweening good for her is forest preservation: it is her hypergood. It does not expunge all the other goods but it does allow her to accord lower priority to other strongly valued goods. Another example of a hypergood shaping someone's life comes with the young, western human rights campaigner who has been jailed several times in a repressive, non-western country. Having been deported in the past for breaking the law, he declares that he would return and assist the people in their struggle for freedom and human rights. This time he is given a 17-year jail sentence. His commitment to the good of freedom dominates his entire life and brings him immense personal suffering and deprivation, to say nothing of the effect on his family.[24] As these real-life examples indicate, hypergoods go some way to mitigating pluralism, for they provide a way for individuals to rank-order their goods. Moreover, given Taylor's belief in the close relationship between identity and the good, his claim that the hypergood is the central feature of an individual's identity comes as no surprise. This supreme good provides the central point against which individuals measure their direction in life (*ibid.*: 63).

Yet Taylor seems to vacillate about whether hypergoods feature in all moral frameworks or only some. Introducing this concept, he suggests that hypergoods are not a necessary feature of moral frameworks; he writes of "*some* people [living] according to a higher-order contrast between such [strongly valued] goods" and refers to "people who understand their lives this way" (*ibid.*: 62–3; emphasis added). Shortly afterwards, he hypothesizes about their role in moral life, counselling that we should not be deterred from hypergoods "*if* these turn out to be really ineliminable from our best account [of the moral life]" (*ibid.*: 69; emphasis added). However, as his exposition of hypergoods unfolds, they imperceptibly become necessary properties of moral life. Consider the way he applies his necessity defence of moral realism to hypergoods:

> perhaps we will find that we cannot make sense of our moral life without something like a hypergood perspective, some notion of a good to which we can grow, and which then makes us see others differently.   (*ibid.*: 71).

A similar shift occurs in one of his criticisms of subjectivism. Taylor moves from the claim that humans see their strongly valued goods as independent of them, to the suggestion that the goods that move them and that seem infinitely valuable in this way are hypergoods (*ibid.*: 74) Again, at the conclusion of Part 1 of *Sources of the Self* he writes that "We have to search for a way in which our strongest aspirations towards hypergoods do not exact a price of self-mutilation" (*ibid.*: 106–7). With this move, hypergoods seem to have become a feature of all people's moral lives.

Hypergoods incur the risk of self-mutilation both because of the imperious demands they make on a person's allegiance and the concomitant fear that one might fail to live up to these demands. Such threats help to explain why some moral theorists have rejected them altogether and why they depict this rejection as an act of liberation. An illustration Taylor offers is Christianity, which is felt by some to lay a crushing burden on its adherents (*ibid.*: 81; 1995b: 142). Yet while cognizant of the dangers that can accompany hypergoods, he still wants to affirm their importance in moral life, which derives from their power to move people, to command love and respect (1989a: 73).

However, whether all moral frameworks, or only some, include hypergoods remains unclear from his analysis. Many of Taylor's interpreters impute the second position to him, that which depicts hypergoods as universal features of moral life.[25] I would advocate, however, the latter reading whereby only some people's moral frameworks include a hypergood. If hypergoods were experienced by all, the challenges of pluralism would not be as piquant as Taylor frequently suggests they are. His attempt to provide a phenomenology of moral life is also significant here, for many people do live their lives devoid of any sense of such a preponderant good. For these reasons, it makes more sense to think of hypergoods as contingent, rather than essential, elements of moral frameworks.

Narratives

Taylor's image of the self in moral space, moved by love and admiration for its strongly valued goods and wanting to move closer to them, is closely connected with the role he attributes to narrative in moral life. He believes that individuals necessarily interpret their lives in narrative terms; they make sense of their lives as an unfolding story in a way that gives meaning to their past and direction to their future (1989a: 47, 50–52). According to Taylor, the way we make sense of any particular moment or experience is by situating it in the longer context of our lives. It is impossible to give meaning to something without locating it in relation to past events or future hopes or fears. Underpinning this argument seems to be Taylor's adherence to the Heideggerian notion of humans as being-in-time (1998d: 255). It would seem that this ontological property of selfhood necessarily structures our self-interpretations for Taylor.

Given his belief in the close connection between morality and identity, it comes as no surprise that Taylor sees individuals' sense of their movement toward moral goods as providing an important way of structuring these narratives. Moral goods therefore play a central role in the stories individuals construct and reconstruct about their lives. These stories might include the discovery of a new good, the recovery of an old one, the sudden or dawning realization of an ongoing one, the need to choose among goods or a period of bewilderment and loss of orientation (1989a: 288–9).[26]

This idea that individuals interpret their lives in narratives terms was not originated by Taylor; he cites the work of Alisdair MacIntyre, Paul Ricoeur and Jerome Bruner as well as Heidegger as influencing his ideas on this topic (*ibid.*: 527 n.24).[27] However, Taylor's claims about the necessary structure of moral life, that it involves orientation towards strongly valued goods, the desire for their realization and an animating concern with one's place in relation to them, grounds the role of narrative more solidly in moral theory (*ibid.*: 47–51, 105). Of course narratives exist at the wider cultural level too, giving meaning to the histories, present and future of groups. Thus nations tell stories about themselves, and these dominant stories are often contested by different groups within the nation's boundaries. Ethnic groups, too, can construct stories about themselves. Religious traditions also develop narratives about their founding and their progress from there. So narratives function at different levels to give layers of meaning in individual lives,[28] and this point illustrates again Taylor's ontological pluralism or recognition of the qualitatively different sorts of goods that exist in people's lives.

Closely connected to Taylor's claim about the role of narrative in moral life is his discussion of what it means to "lead a life". He claims that when people think about how to balance the disparate goods in their lives, they combine a sense of diversity with one of unity. The many goods that claim one's allegiance do so within the context of a single life. When a person's life is viewed as a whole, it becomes easier to see that seemingly different and even incommensurable goods can be combined in practice. Taylor further maintains that people have a sense of themselves as leading a life, and that what this common-sense notion conveys is the idea of movement combined with an attempt to guide or control that movement (1997a: 179–80). While any person's life might move at different speeds at different times, there is none the less a sense of one's life being in motion, in process, in flux. Yet this movement is not undirected or uncontrollable, despite the occasional sense that some individuals have that events have overtaken them or that their lives are out of control.

The diversity of goods in any person's life can, moreover, be conceived of in a diachronic as well as a synchronic way. Within the context of a single life, individuals not only balance different goods but embrace new ones and shed others. Yet Taylor would argue that even a person who underwent a radical moral makeover could still forge a narrative about himself that married the diversity of goods with the unity of a life, for his narrative could tell a story about and make sense of his personal revolution. So a person's narrative doesn't have to be relentlessly linear; it can be a story about change, twists and turns. Notwithstanding the dramatic turns of speech that are often used to describe such radical personal change, such as "the new me" and "becoming a different person", Taylor would contend that people who undergo these changes still see themselves as the same person. The unity in this balance is provided by the single life led by that person and his continuing sense of personhood.

Taylor also concludes that we can get some insight into practical reasoning about morality by just looking at how people lead their lives. What we find is that moral reasoning combines "inescapable diversity and [a] continuing struggle for unity" (*ibid.*: 171; cf. 175). He traces this insight about moral life necessarily combining the reality of diversity with an aspiration to oneness back to Aristotle, indicating again the Stagirite's influence on his thought (*ibid.*: 183).

So the practices of ordinary moral life play a dual role in Taylor's thinking about moral theory. They can, as just indicated, offer guidance about how to think about morality; in this case how to balance the diversity of goods with the narrative unity of a life. Conversely, ordinary moral life is what moral theory should explain. At a very basic level, moral theory is no different from a theory of anything; it should explain its object. In this case of moral theory, it is people's moral lives that are to be explained. However, Taylor suggests that moral theory should explain people's attitudes, values and behaviour in ways that either do, or could be brought to, make sense to the people themselves. Moral theory should connect with the way people actually live their lives. He maintains that an explanation of moral life that takes no heed of the way people actually experience or relate to the goods in their moral life is inferior to one that builds into its explanation people's experience of the goods, one in which people could come to recognize themselves. As he speculates:

> Suppose I can convince myself that I can explain people's behaviour as an observer without using a term like "dignity". What does this prove if I can't do without it as a term in my deliberations about what to do, how to behave, how to treat people, my questions about whom I admire, with whom I feel affinity, and the like? (1989a: 57)

This conviction that a theory of morality has to make some contact with the way people experience their moral lives represents yet another of Aristotle's influences on his thinking. From Aristotle, Taylor learned that "Ethical theory has to comprehend given practice; it cannot just abstract from it" (1994f: 31).

One reason for this requirement of moral theory comes from Taylor's distinction between the human and the natural sciences.[29] It is also related to Taylor's view of the self (as explored in Chapter 2). In this context, it suffices to say that Taylor believes that human beings are self-interpreting animals; our understandings of ourselves play a crucial, albeit not exhaustive, role in shaping who we are and what we do (1985a: 202; 1989a: 34). This is not the case with the objects of natural science. What this means for Taylor is that any theory of human behaviour must take into account the way the humans under discussion understand themselves (1985a: 121, 177–8, 189). Any meaningful theory of morality must, as a consequence, take into account the way individuals experience their moral lives.

Articulation

As we have seen, Taylor maintains that many of the strongly held values, and even moral frameworks, by which people live often go unacknowledged, remaining in the background of their awareness. It is typically only in times of conflict or crisis that one is forced to spell out and defend the assumptions and presuppositions that underlie one's moral values and practices (1989a: 9).[30] For the most part, these goods, and the beliefs and insights that underpin them, go unarticulated by individuals themselves and also by modern moral theories. Because of this silence about the underlying sources of moral values, practices and attitudes, one of the important roles Taylor accords to moral theory is articulation, bringing into the light of awareness that which is unspoken but presupposed. Indeed, one of the things he sees his own work as doing is articulating both the most important goods by which modern individuals live and the various sources of these goods (*ibid.*: 3–4, 8, 10, 26). Taylor's preferred way of expressing this is to talk about what is morally moving, what it is that moves people to cleave to a particular moral outlook, what goods they are moved by in this process (*ibid.*: 203).[31]

In general the practice of articulating the tacit background of moral life requires eliciting the ideals that draw people to a particular moral outlook and that inspire them to act in accordance with it. In particular there are six separate but related functions for articulation in Taylor's moral philosophy. Its first function is to deepen understanding of moral values and responses by showing what underpins them. As he explains:

> To articulate a framework is to explicate what makes sense of our moral responses. That is, when we try to spell out what it is that we presuppose when we judge that a certain form of life is truly worthwhile, or place our dignity in a certain achievement or status, or define our moral obligations in a certain manner, we find ourselves articulating inter alia what I have been calling here "frameworks".   (1989a: 26; cf. 80)

Of course, given Taylor's belief in the close connection between morality and selfhood, when one understands more fully the background of one's values and commitments, a deeper self-knowledge is thereby attained. As such, the process of articulation fosters

41

one of philosophy's traditional goals – that of promoting self-understanding. As Taylor says, "The retrieval of suppressed goods is . . . valuable on the Socratic grounds that if we are going to live by the modern identity, it better be by an examined version of it" (*ibid.*: 504; cf. 498).

Articulating the background of moral values and responses also heightens awareness of the complexity of moral life and the diverse range of goods to which modern individuals adhere. Taylor believes that this second function of articulation, bringing to light the various goods by which modern individuals live, will show their plurality and different sources (*ibid.*: 105, 502). He hopes that one of the consequences of articulating this plurality will be to reduce the appeal of simplistic and reductionist normative theories that try to artificially harmonize different goods or that deny the reality of conflicting goods (*ibid.*: 107).

Because articulation deepens knowledge of moral values, Taylor suggests that articulating the multiple goods in the modern moral world has a third function: it increases the chances of rational debate about values. Understanding the underpinnings of moral responses in a fuller and clearer way makes it easier to debate their merits. Articulation's third function – to foster rational evaluation of goods – provides Taylor with further ammunition against the relativist idea that individuals just choose goods on the basis of preferences, desires or interests and that these choices cannot be rationally defended or criticized. As he says, "If you do convince your interlocutor by your discourse about a good, it will be because the good so articulated moves him, i.e., he comes to recognize it as an expression of *his* ethical intuitions" (1995b: 138, original emphasis; cf. 1991a: 31–2).

As this suggests, Taylor's distinctive brand of pluralism tries to chart a course between the Scylla of homogenizing reductionism and the Charybdis of radical or irreducible pluralism. He wants to draw attention to the plurality of and conflict among the goods that are denied by much modern moral philosophy. However, he also argues that it is wrong to assume *a priori* that seemingly divergent goods cannot be reconciled. As he says, "conflicts by themselves don't refute. But this doesn't mean that they are unarbitratible, or insurmountable" (1994c: 204; cf. 1989a: 61, 105, 107, 502, 1997a: 171). How compatible particular goods are can only be determined through the process of reflection, debate, discussion and possible recontextualization. As he says:

Conflicts can be resolved, but does this mean that all conflicts must find resolution? This doesn't seem to me to follow either. An a priori answer either way seems misplaced. This is the line I am trying to defend. We have to recognize the full stretch of goods which have a claim to our allegiance, and not artificially shorten the lost through bogus "refutations." Then we have to face the conflicts that arise, without the a apriori [*sic*] certainty either of resolvability or of irresolvability.

(1994c: 205)[32]

This process of discerning which goods are combinable and which are in conflict is fostered and strengthened by the awareness that comes from articulating the sources of morality.

The fourth function of articulation fuels Taylor's critique of rival approaches to morality. He believes that the process of articulation provides a corrective to "the [self-]enforced inarticulacy" of much modern moral philosophy, for these theories are dumb when it comes to the fact of qualitative discriminations that Taylor posits as essential to moral life (1995b: 153). Moreover, as indicated above, he claims that articulating the usually unspoken background of moral values allows him to bring to light the underlying moral motivations of these rival theories. Taylor insists that there are such motivations, despite the fact that the theories themselves are either blind to, or suppress, them because the existence of these motives, which typically embody a form of strong evaluation, is disallowed by the theory itself. Consider, for example, Bentham's claim that there are no higher goods in human life; that "pushpin is as good as poetry". From this standpoint there are only different pleasures and pains – or utilities – and it is up to individuals to maximize their pleasures and minimize their pains according to their personal tastes and interests. It is impossible to judge some pleasures as being intrinsically or qualitatively higher than others; all that can be compared is how successful individuals are in calculating their utilities. As a proponent of strong evaluation, Taylor finds this relativism totally unpersuasive and Benthamites would, no doubt, find Taylor's position equally incredible.

However, instead of simply arguing about whether strong evaluation is or is not a necessary feature of moral life, Taylor's practice of articulating the tacit, underlying moral sources of moral philosophies allows him to shift the level of debate. It enables him to argue that Bentham's denial of qualitatively higher goods is itself inspired by moral convictions that cannot plausibly be redescribed as subjective pleasures. These include commitments to rationality, equality, to respect for individuality and autonomy, hostility to paternalism and more generally the affirmation of ordinary life (1989a: 81, 332–3; 1995b: 142–4).[33] While these strong evaluations may not always feature explicitly in utilitarian theory, Taylor believes that it is incomprehensible without them. Paradoxically, these moral values, which are based on qualitative discriminations, converge to make Bentham deny the existence of qualitative discriminations in moral life.[34] If Taylor's analysis is correct, it means that classical utilitarianism denies the existence of qualitative discriminations that are the very condition of its own possibility as a moral outlook (1985b: 266; 1989a: 332–3, 337, 340). This sort of move explains Taylor's belief that because his approach to morality makes possible a fuller and clearer account of rival approaches, it is superior to them. He insists on what utilitarianism denies; that strong evaluations are a necessary feature of moral life. Because he can show that utilitarianism is driven by unacknowledged strong evaluations, his moral theory provides a more robust and comprehensive account of moral life than that offered by utilitarians.

Articulation serves a fifth important role, one that goes beyond simply understanding moral life or assessing the plausibility of different moral theories. Taylor proposes that because the articulation of a moral framework or source identifies what is moving about it, this can strengthen commitment to it. This is what he means when he says that articulation empowers: bringing a good to light, raising awareness of what usually remains tacit, brings its adherents into closer contact with this good and its ideals, which can invigorate their allegiance to it. Taylor writes that:

> Philosophers . . . have specific contributions to make to moral philosophy that can help us all realize that understanding why something or someone is good can empower one to love it more . . . a moral source is something that when turned toward and articulated can empower one to act in a way prescribed by the full moral view.
>
> (1994e: 184; cf. 1989a: 96–7, 504, 520; 1996d: 14)

Conversely, the failure to articulate or even attempt to express these underlying goods can contribute to their attrition. Taylor asserts that "Without any articulation at all, we would lose all contact with the good, however conceived. We would cease to be human" (1989a: 97). This link between articulation and allegiance points to another of the dangers of the self-enforced inarticulacy of much modern moral theory. Refusing to talk about or even acknowledge the existence of the strong evaluations that actually nourish these moral outlooks not only makes these theories cramped and self-deluded but can also weaken adherence to their essential, underlying goods.[35]

However, Taylor concedes that spelling out the goods underlying a moral value or outlook in philosophical vocabulary is not the only form of articulation that empowers these goods and inspires motivation for them. Indeed, when it comes to this fifth function, philosophical analysis is one of the weakest modes of articulation (1994c; 1994d: 212). Other ways in which the goods can be expressed or conveyed include poetry, literature, the visual and performing arts, music, prayer and ritual. All of these media have, in Taylor's view, the ability to bring an underlying good to awareness and to deepen its adherents' commitment to it. Illustrating this point, he writes that "A Bach cantata articulates a certain mode of Christian piety, in a way that cannot be substituted for by treatises on theology" (1997a: 179; cf. 1995a: 111). As this suggests, we need to distinguish between articulation in its broad and narrow senses to understand this function of articulation (1991d: 253). Articulation in the narrow sense means putting something into philosophical language, while articulation in the broad sense covers all these forms of expression. Yet while identifying the variety of media that can express an underlying good, Taylor acknowledges that not all forms of articulation are appropriate to all moral outlooks: some have a bias in favour of articulation through language (1989a: 21). Consider the Socratic tradition in western philosophy with its emphasis on the higher human life involving the ability to give a rational account of one's moral values.

However, returning to the original sources of a moral outlook need not always strengthen allegiances to the practices and life goods it has spawned. A return can also show that the way in which a particular good or ideal has evolved in modern culture is not its only possible configuration (*ibid.*: 513; 1991a: 58). Returning to the original vision or source of a moral outlook makes immanent critique possible, for the ways in which this good has become distorted or limited in practice become apparent, and other possible forms of its realization become visible. Debates about the place of technology in modern life provide an example of this. As Taylor writes:

> We can't see the development of technological society just in the light of an imperative of domination. Richer moral sources have fed it. But . . . these moral sources tend to get lost from view, precisely through the hardening of atomist and instrumentalist values. Retrieving them might allow us to recover some balance, one in which technology would occupy another place in our lives than as an insistent, unreflected imperative.
> (1991a: 96; cf. 72–3, 75, 79, 103)

So this represents the sixth and final function of articulation: immanent critique. From this point of view, ethical debate and change involve not simply repudiating some of the modern goods like individualism and technological control over nature but reconfiguring them. By making contact with the vision of the good that originally inspired them, it is possible to appreciate either how current practices or values have distorted this vision or that there are other possibilities that this vision could nourish.

Although one of the reasons why Taylor so values articulation is its ability to provide a fuller and richer understanding of a moral outlook, he does not believe that the articulation of a living ethical outlook can ever be complete. As the fullness of a moral view can never be brought to the fore all at once (1989a: 29, 34),[36] the quest to articulate its moral sources must be an ongoing process. This process is also one of dispute, revision and correction, because the formulation of the underlying sources of a moral outlook is often controversial. Departing from his usual emphasis on self-interpretation and moral theory making contact with the way people experience their moral lives, Taylor claims that practitioners of a certain morality or adherents to a certain value are not always best qualified to judge the accuracy of an articulation of its underlying sources. "The agent himself or herself is not necessarily the best authority, at least not at the outset" (*ibid.*: 9). This means that the process of articulation can see the interpreter claiming a superior knowledge of moral sources; the interpreter can propose a better account of what is actually going on than the agent himself. However, presumably Taylor would build into this scenario the requirement that the agent could eventually be brought to concede the superiority of the interpreter's understanding to his own. This is suggested by his proviso "at least not at the outset". Otherwise, Taylor would be in the anomalous position of claiming that the interpreter of underlying moral sources can use a vocabulary or explanation that the agent does not recognize while criticizing other moral theories for taking this third-person stance. As he says when outlining the importance of self-interpretations, "things have significance for me, and the issue of my identity is worked out, only through a language of interpretation which I have come to accept as a valid articulation of these issues" (*ibid.*: 34). Moreover, given that one of the functions of articulation is to bring to the foreground of awareness the goods that move individuals, it would be a strange outcome if the individuals supposedly moved by these goods could never come to recognize them in this articulation.

Constitutive goods

This image of individuals being moved by goods brings us to the final major concept in this overview of what Taylor believes are the structural features of moral life. Moral outlooks or worldviews operate at two levels. Most accessible are the things they deem to make life worth living or the virtues they advocate – Taylor calls these "life goods". Familiar examples of life goods include freedom, reason, piety, authenticity, courage and benevolence. Yet underlying a life good is its deeper, less obvious, but fundamental constitutive good. He contends that a morality's constitutive good serves as a powerful and empowering source for that outlook; indeed, it provides the source of strong evaluations.[37] Articulating a moral source requires the identification of its constitutive good. Along with the central and fundamental role it plays in a moral framework, which can, none the less, remain latent, a constitutive good also commands the love of its adherents. There is a sense in which knowing a constitutive good means loving, admiring or respecting it. Because of this, one is moved by it and wants to move ever closer to it: loving the good and wanting to act in accordance with it are inextricably linked for Taylor (*ibid.*: 533–4 n.2). So the usually discrete categories of knowledge, action and emotion must be fused when it comes to appreciating the role and power of constitutive goods in moral life. Another, but related feature of constitutive goods, which connects them directly to Taylor's brand of moral realism, is their adherents' sense that these goods have value independently of their being affirmed by them as particular individuals.

Perhaps the best way of explaining constitutive goods is through Taylor's own examples. In the case of theists, an understanding of God is the constitutive good; this is at the centre of their moral framework and gives meaning to all the other life goods therein. In Plato's moral theory the Idea of the Good is constitutive. This form is supreme over all others and imparts value to them. This ultimate good provides the goodness for the other goods; hence its designation as constitutive. For Plato this is the highest good, and knowing this good necessarily involves loving it and the desire to approach it. Taylor insists that constitutive goods play a pivotal role in humanist outlooks too. In Kantian ethics for example, the constitutive good is the image of the autonomous human agent and her ability to act out of respect for the moral law. The dignity conferred by acting in this way sets up a virtuous circle; individuals are moved by respect for the moral law to act in accordance with it and the consequence of such action is a dignity that itself commands awe.

All of these examples propose the existence of a moral source that transcends human beings.[38] Constitutive goods might, therefore, be a necessary part of some moral frameworks but not all. In the face of this objection, Taylor reasserts his belief that all moral frameworks or outlooks have a constitutive good (1996d: 13). In some, such as theism and Platonism, the reality and force of this good are manifest. In others they are more concealed, and it becomes necessary to disclose the existence and nature of the constitutive good (1994e: 184). Thus Taylor argues that even secular ethics repose on a constitutive good. A good that often commands respect and the desire to approach it among atheists, for example, is the image of the lone individual in a disenchanted world facing with lucidity and courage the abyss of meaninglessness or absurdity. She defies her condition by conferring meaning on her life and finding much to affirm and celebrate in this metaphysically barren universe. To illustrate this point, as well as the earlier one about articulation operating in a broad sense, Taylor turns to the character of Dr Rieux in Albert Camus's novel *The Plague*. The doctor's constitutive good is the demand he feels to respond to the ambient death and suffering with courage and compassion but without illusions. He is inspired in this by an image of the good humans can do in an inherently meaningless world. As Taylor says, to be moved by this image "is to see the point of the ethic which Camus proposes, both the understand better [*sic*] what it requires, and possibly to be empowered to act on it" (1994c: 212; cf. 1989a: 496).[39]

Taylor is the first to admit that there is something anomalous, and even presumptuous in him being the one to begin the process of articulating the constitutive goods of secular outlooks (1994e: 185). This also seems to be at odds with his emphasis elsewhere on the importance that should be attributed to self-interpretations when seeking to understand human behaviour. However (as the fuller discussion of this issue in Chapter 4 indicates), recognizing the significance of self-interpretations does not commit one to accepting them as beyond question or improvement. Taylor would argue that the silence of modern moral outlooks about sources and constitutive goods prevents these outlooks from fully understanding themselves. He would have to hope, though, that adherents to these secular ethics could be brought to see that the general shape of his depiction of their positions was useful or meaningful, even if corrigible on some matters.

However persuasive one finds Taylor's arguments about constitutive goods, it is important to recognize the erotic dimension of his moral theory. His arguments about the necessity of constitutive goods and the power of articulation to inspire restores the dimension of love to the centre of moral theory. Students of the Platonic and Augustinian approaches to moral life will know what a pivotal and explicit force love is there in explaining moral motivation.[40] Yet the idea of loving goodness has disappeared from most modern moral philosophy, probably because of its relativist and secular temperament. As one of Taylor's previously cited criticisms of modern moral theory claimed, in these outlooks "Morality is narrowly concerned with what we ought to *do*, and not with what is valuable in itself, or what we should admire or love" (1995b: 145, original emphasis; cf. 1996d: 5, 15; 1999a: 11, 120). By underscoring the need to articulate moral sources, or constitutive goods that empower humans because they are worthy of love and respect, Taylor is trying to restore the old idea of loving goodness to moral philosophy. For him it is love that moves people towards goods and love that leads them to value strongly some of the goods in their lives. And, as intimated in the discussion of his falsifiable realism, when individuals feel this love for the things they value, they feel as if they are loving something because it is worthy of their love. Taylor says in this context that:

> We sense in the very experience of being moved by some higher good that we are moved by what is good in it rather than that it is valuable because of our reaction . . . We experience our love for it as a well-founded love. (1989a: 74)

Yet the same good or moral source can spawn quite different ethical values, standards, strong evaluations or life goods. Taylor traces, for example, several quite different modern western moral outlooks back to the constitutive good of theism. The ideal of disengaged reason, for example, which he believes is powerful in many moral outlooks, sprang from Christian roots (*ibid.*: 245). The same is true of the belief in the value of scientific inquiry in general (*ibid.*: 310, 320). It is also true of the Romantic aspiration to make contact with nature. This means that moral outlooks can be parasitic on sources they do not acknowledge and may even repudiate (*ibid.*: 339). This also creates the potential for slippage between moral values and their ultimate moral source. For example, while the values of freedom, individualism, reason, equality and benevolence might enjoy widespread acceptance in modern western societies, and while we can say that there is an overlapping consensus about their importance, Taylor's thesis is that they all ultimately find their moral source or constitutive good in Christianity (*ibid.*: 495–6, 498).

In insisting on the need to return to these constitutive goods in order to understand our contemporary moral condition, Taylor is clearly according considerable power to Christianity. It is here, I think, that critics of his theism would be better advised to direct their claim about the necessary connection between his religious faith and his moral theory. Once it is argued that modern moral values can be fully understood only by reference to their history, the deck is stacked in favour of religion as a, if not the, constitutive good. As Michael Morgan writes:

> if Charles Taylor is right, the complexity of these narratives converges on a common conclusion, that the modern identity . . . cannot be properly comprehended without reference to its religious history. To understand who we are and what matters most to us necessarily involves retrieving the religious elements of our identity. (Morgan 1994: 49; cf. 54)

While Morgan welcomes this aspect of Taylor's thought, it should pose problems for non-theists, for Taylor is not just saying that Christianity has been an important moral source, but that making contact with such a constitutive moral good empowers, inspires and commands love. In this regard, his genealogy of morals differs markedly from that of Nietzsche, who claimed that tracing the history and returning to the wellsprings of current moral outlooks or standards can reveal how far they have mutated from their origin. Taylor, by contrast, suggests that such genealogical practice has the potential to inspire by reconnecting modern moral values to their constitutive source in theism.

Just how important Taylor takes religious beliefs to be in modern western culture emerges most clearly in Part IV of *A Catholic Modernity?*. There he contends that the modern emphasis on universal benevolence makes immense demands on humans' sense of solidarity with, and commitment to justice for, others. These values form part of western culture's strong evaluation: by failing to live up to them its denizens feel diminished as human beings. Yet Taylor worries about how the motivation for this colossal and never-ending philanthropic enterprise will continue to be generated. He has a related fear that this ethos can quickly flip over into its opposite, to engender a sense of the futility of trying to help others precisely because the demand appears insatiable and the project interminable. Religious faith becomes salient here, for Taylor proposes that the experience of and desire to emulate God's divine and unconditional love for the humans forged in his image can continue to power such universal solidarity and benevolence (1999a: 30–37; cf. 120; 1994e: 183–4). So in this work Taylor is expressing in a more direct and explicit way some of the ideas gestured at in the conclusion of *Sources of the Self*. There he made the general claim that "High standards need strong sources". He ventured that the things humanists take to foster universal benevolence and justice were not as fecund as the Christian notion of *agape*, the "love that God has for humans which is connected with their goodness as creatures" (1989a: 516). In the absence of a divine source for *agape*, Taylor wondered whether moderns were "living beyond our moral means" (*ibid.*: 517). While these concerns are very similar to those aired in *A Catholic Modernity?*, the major difference is that what in *Sources of the Self* appears as a "hunch ... that great as the power of naturalist sources might be, the potential of a certain theistic perspective is incomparably greater" (*ibid.*: 518; cf. 1998b: 112), seems to have solidified into an expression of religious faith in this more recent work. So the suggestion that *A Catholic Modernity?* represents the missing, final chapter of *Sources of the Self* (Marsden 1999: 89) is a plausible one, and points again to the important place of Christianity in Taylor's moral theory as the premier or Ur-constitutive good for modernity.

Theory and history

As we have seen, Taylor sees his work as articulating both the different goods by which modern individuals live and the constitutive goods that lie behind these life goods. His claim that articulating constitutive goods can inspire greater love for and allegiance to them applies here reflexively, for Taylor hopes that his work will revitalize these obscured moral sources (1989a: 520).[41] As we have seen, for him the path to such articulation is necessarily historical (*ibid.*: 104),[42] and this is what links the first part of *Sources of the Self* to the following four. However, it is a curious feature of the following four parts that they do not, as a rule, outline these moral sources or constitutive goods in the theoretical language laid out in the first section. While this provides another justification for the division of Chapters 1 and 2 in this book, it does pose some important questions about the theoretical integrity of Taylor's approach to moral life when many of the formal, conceptual elements he lays out play little or no role in the historical discussions.

This disjunction becomes even stranger given Taylor's prefatory remarks pointing to the connections between these two facets of his moral philosophy:

> because my entire way of proceeding involves mapping connections between senses of the self and moral visions, between identity and the good, I didn't feel I could launch into this study without some preliminary discussion of these links.
>
> (1989a: x)

However, immediately after this he suggests that these two facets are quite separable, for he recommends that readers uninterested in arguments about modern moral philosophy should ignore Part I, while those uninterested in the history of ideas should read nothing else. There is a dilemma here. If the two facets of Taylor's approach to morality – the theoretical and the historical – are detachable from one another, this means that his initial analysis of the self in moral space is irrelevant to the history he then constructs about the changing and multiplying goods that command our allegiance. Yet this would undermine the universal and necessary status he claims for this analysis and would have important consequences for the credibility of many of the claims made in Part I about the moral life. Yet if the two parts are not detachable from one another, why would Taylor suggest otherwise? Moreover, if they are not detachable, why do Taylor's discussions in Parts II–V contain barely an echo of the language of his analysis in Part 1? This silence seems especially puzzling from a philosopher who contends that theoretical explanations of moral behaviour must at some level connect with the self-understandings of the individuals explained therein.

Chapter 2

Interpreting selfhood

Introduction

In *Sources of the Self*, Taylor contends that while people have always had some perception of themselves as individuated beings, their self-understandings have not always revolved around the concept of the self. In any society at any time, an individual can experience himself as the source of a particular experience or sensation. As an example he takes an individual's fear that a mammoth is charging toward him. The individual's terror passes into relief when he is spared but then regret that his friend was eaten. In this situation, the survivor clearly has a sense of himself as a being who is in some way delineated and separate from others (Taylor 1989a: 112–13, 118–19). None the less, the idea that one has a self, that we can talk about selfhood as some distinct phenomenon is, Taylor proposes, a modern development (*ibid.*: 28; cf. 1988c: 298–9; 1991c: 304, 307). The same applies to the notion of identity: "Talk about 'identity' in the modern sense would have been incomprehensible to our forebears of a couple of centuries ago". As this suggests, he thinks that the ways in which people understand themselves change, both over time and across cultures: "There are different ways of being a person, and these are linked with different understandings of what it is to be a person" (1985c: 276). A major portion of this chapter is, therefore, devoted to charting the changing understandings of what it is to be a person that Taylor identifies as pivotal in the history of western thought and in the creation of the modern identity.

But the self is not only change. As we saw in Chapter 1, Taylor believes the self to be an inherently moral entity; selves are always situated in moral space. He must therefore contend that there are some perennial features of the self, irrespective of changes in the ways in which these are expressed or understood. He gestures toward this sort of two-dimensional approach to the self when he writes that:

> I believe that what we are as human agents is profoundly interpretation-dependent, that human beings in different cultures can be radically diverse, in keeping with their fundamentally different self-understandings. But I think that a constant is to be found in the shape of the questions that all cultures must address. (1988c: 299; cf. 1998b: 111)

A useful way of understanding Taylor's approach to selfhood is to distinguish two different but complementary aspects: its historicist and its ontological dimensions. This chapter begins with an overview of the ontological dimensions of the self, those that do not change. Some of the ontological features of the self to be discussed are the centrality of self-interpretation, the fact that humans are animals with language and the dialogical nature of selfhood. The chapter then moves into a description of Taylor's historicist reading of the modern self, charting the changing conceptions of the western self that have emerged over the centuries.

Yet not all of Taylor's interpreters have appreciated his two-dimensional approach to the self. Olafson, for example, claims that Taylor:

> is really quite uncertain about how radically historical he is prepared to make this self . . . [I] find it extremely difficult to see what kind of balance Taylor thinks he has struck between a common and universal selfhood and the historically quite diverse versions of what selfhood involves that he discusses.
> (Olafson 1994: 192–3)

Rosa detects more than uncertainty in these twin aspects of selfhood, writing that "Taylor's attempt to have recourse to some [substantive] universal human constants . . . is incompatible with his view of man as a fundamentally open and self-interpreting animal" (Rosa 1995: 25). Flanagan finds it "extremely puzzling that such a historicist as Taylor is tempted to make such essential-ist claims at all" (Flanagan 1996: 154). As will emerge, I do not see uncertainty, contradiction or puzzlement in Taylor's depiction of these two dimensions of selfhood.

In presenting Taylor's theory of the self, I follow what I take to be his lead and use the terms self, person and subject, as well as selfhood, personhood and identity, interchangeably. Taylor does not share some philosophers' interest in differentiating these terms from one another, and according them precise meanings. For him, all these terms relate to the wider question of what it is to be human. As such, they touch on some of the same issues that used to be raised under the rubric of human nature or that now fall under investigations of philosophical anthropology. A good illus-tration of Taylor's relaxed attitude to these questions of definition appears in his approach to identity. For him:

> to have an identity is to know "where you're coming from" when it comes to questions of value, or issues of importance. Your identity defines the background against which you know where you stand on such matters.   (1991c: 305–6)

So while Taylor is keen to specify the things that make some-one a person or that inform identity, he is not concerned with expressing these arguments with precise and consistent terminol-ogy.[1] One exception to his general lack of concern with termino-logical exactitude in this discussion comes with the term "agent". This term is not synonymous with personhood or selfhood. For Taylor, being an agent is a necessary but not sufficient condition of being a person. One of the reasons for this is that being an agent is not unique to humans: animals also exercise agency in so far as they devise ways to realize their desires and to achieve their ends (1995c; Forthcoming b).[2] Taylor's ontological account of selfhood goes beyond this rather minimalist, agentic understand-ing to advocate a thicker description of what it means to be a person.

Charles Taylor

Ontological dimensions of selfhood

Self-interpretation

"Human beings are self-interpreting subject" (1985a: 4). This captures Taylor's belief that one of the things that makes a person what she is is the understanding she has of herself. For Taylor the fact and significance of self-interpretation are human universals and part of the species distinction. While human beings are natural entities, we are beings with self-understandings as well, and in order to understand and explain us, consideration has to be given to these understandings. Taylor claims that humans are partly constituted by our self-understandings: how a person views or interprets herself is not all there is to know about her, but it is a vital component of identity, one that cannot be overlooked. While this point might now seem uncontroversial to many, it initially emerged in Taylor's work in the context of his sustained critique of behaviouralism as an explanation of human action. Behavioural-ism strove to develop an account of human behaviour that did not make reference to subject-dependent properties like self-understandings. It aspired to an objective, scientific explanation of humans and society by focusing on those things that could be known by an outside observer. Structuralism and some versions of Marxism provide other examples of this attempt to generate an explanation of society along the model of the natural sciences, one that avoids all the subject-relative properties of humans. Rational choice theory, sociobiology and, more recently, evolutionary psychology represent more contemporary examples of this aim. Taylor even detects its application to the philosophy of language in the work of W. V. Quine and Donald Davidson (*ibid.*: 281–2). It is also apparent in the understanding of personhood propounded by Derek Parfit (1989).[3]

Taylor's reaction against the ambition to give an account of behaviour, action and subjectivity that does not refer to subject-dependent properties like self-understandings, and his concomi-tant attention to the contribution that self-definition makes to identity, are linked to his more general insistence on the need to differentiate human from natural sciences. One of the most impor-tant reasons why human behaviour and society are not wholly amenable to models of explanation derived from the natural sciences is the salience of self-interpretation. Whereas the objects of natural science do not interpret themselves, as far as we know, those of the human sciences necessarily do, and this means that scientific approaches to society have to be modified to take account of this, if they are to be employed at all in social explanation (Taylor 1985a: 106).[4]

So in order to understand the person, we need not just empirical information about his race, class, occupation, age, background and so on, but also some sense of how he sees himself. As Taylor says, "To ask what a person is, in abstraction from his or her self-interpretations, is to ask a fundamentally misguided question, one to which there couldn't in principle be an answer" (1989a: 34; cf. 1985a: 189–91). A series of caveats is necessary to explain what Taylor's claim that humans are self-interpreting subjects means. Firstly, my self-understanding is not something I forge all by myself: how I see myself is shaped by how I am seen by and relate to others (which is discussed more fully below). Secondly, just thinking about myself in a particular way does not necessarily or automatically make me that: I can have a deluded or exaggerated interpretation of my sporting prowess or of my intellectual acumen, for example. However, even when someone's self-interpretation is erroneous, the way in which that person under-stands himself is still a crucial feature of his identity. The self-understanding does not have to be valid in order to be significant. Nor is there any sense in which Taylor takes a person's self-understanding to be unitary. A person can have multiple and even conflicting ways of understanding herself. These can also change over time; no self-interpretation needs to be fixed and given in perpetuity. Some of a person's interpreted aspects of identity, such as their religious affiliations or sense of family belonging, might persist for many years, while others are amenable to change. For a variety of reasons and in a variety of ways, new understandings of the self can be acquired and old ones shed or marginalized.

"Our formulations about ourselves can alter what they are about" (1985a: 101; cf. 35–8, 191; 1985b: 26–7). As this claim suggests, for Taylor a change in my self-interpretation is at the same time a change in me: it is a change in the self that is both the interpreter and the interpreted. As a person acquires different vocabularies for talking about her experiences, emotions or aspira-tions, her understanding of those things and of herself changes. So changes in the vocabularies of self-understanding change the self that is thereby understood. Making this same point in slightly different language, Taylor declares that "man is a self-defining animal. With changes in his self-definition go changes in what man is, such that he has to be understood in different terms" (1985b: 55). Much of Taylor's inspiration for thinking about the self in this way comes from the hermeneutical tradition and its concern with the meaning and interpretation of texts (1985a: 3; 1985b: 15–57) A self resembles a text in that there is a meaning to be understood and in the way that new interpretations can supersede earlier ones. But when it comes to selfhood, the self is not just the text to be interpreted but also the interpreter of that text.

Feminism as a social and theoretical movement provides many illustrations of Taylor's point that changes in self-understanding change the self.[5] Feminism gives many women a new vocabulary for interpreting their experiences and emotions. I might, for example, feel embarrassed and self-conscious by the attention my male supervisor pays me at work. I infer that he must be romantically interested in me because of his repeated and highly personal remarks about my hair, clothes and figure. However, once I am familiar with the notion of sexual harassment, I am able to interpret his behaviour and my reaction in a different way: the language of power and domination supersedes that of romance in my interpretation of our interactions. This new understanding of the situation changes my sense of self and might also change my responses to him. Whereas once I blushed and stammered, now I receive his remarks in a different way, one that no longer constructs me as an object of romantic attention. Such examples can be multiplied in a host of social, political and psychological movements and theories. Along with feminism, traditions such as Marxism, queer theory and psychoanalysis all provide new vocabularies through which individuals can understand themselves. In understanding themselves in new and different ways, they change as people.

Taylor's belief that articulating something in a particular way transforms it is also connected to a view of language that he traces to the eighteenth-century German thinkers von Humboldt and Herder. In the earlier theories of language propounded by Hobbes, Locke and then Condillac, words had been seen as devices for conveying and organizing internal things. Rather than seeing language in this way, as simply a vehicle for communicating ideas that exist independently of their expression in language, the newer approach presented words as constitutive of thoughts and emotions (Taylor 1985a: 10). "Expressivism" is the term Taylor coins to capture some of the insights he draws and develops from Herder's thought.[6] As he reads it:

> the revolutionary idea of expressivism was that the development of new modes of expression enables us to have new feelings, more powerful or more refined, and certainly more self-aware. In being able to express our feelings, we give them a reflective dimension which transforms them.
>
> (1985a: 233; cf. 1995a: 92, 97–8)[7]

In this outlook, language is a more creative medium than it was taken to be by the older, instrumental one. In the older view, words were simply attached to things as labels; giving a thing a name did not change the thing thus named in any significant way. The newer view of language included a sense that describing something in a different way could change a person's perception of it. Taylor applies the insights of expressivism not just to language but also to selfhood. He writes, for example, that:

> Reading a good, powerful novel may give me the picture of an emotion which I had not previously been aware of. But we cannot draw a neat line between an increased ability to identify and an altered ability to feel emotions which this enables.
>
> (1985b: 26; cf. 1985b: 191; 1995a: 101–5)

Taylor further believes that for the individual undergoing a change in self-interpretation, the process is perceived as progress. When an individual adopts a new interpretation of some experience, event or emotion, he sees himself as selecting not simply a different interpretation but a better, truer or more perspicacious one. So the individual's self-interpretations are not simply arbitrary impositions or constructions of meaning; there is no sense that any reading of myself will do. Just as Taylor argues that the individual's moral life is typically construed in narrative terms, so he proposes that the succession of self-understandings that individuals adopt is seen by them to be part of a progressive story about the unfolding or enhancing of self-knowledge. His following remarks about strong evaluation are, therefore, more broadly applicable to the question of self-interpretation:

our descriptions of our motivations, and our attempts to formulate what we hold important, are not simple descriptions, in that their objects are not fully independent. And yet they are not . . . simply arbitrary either, such that anything goes. There are more or less adequate, more or less truthful, more self-clairvoyant, or self-deluding interpretations.

(1976a: 295–6)

Purposes

Although individuals can alter and amend the ways in which they interpret themselves, Taylor maintains, as we have seen, that these self-interpretations are not wholly arbitrary or capricious. Another way in which he argues against the possibility of their being arbitrary appears in his claim that a person's self-understanding will always make reference to their purposes (1985c: 259). He goes beyond the traditional association of personhood with self-consciousness and even with agency to claim that selves are beings with original or intrinsic purposes. This is another factor that he takes to be constitutive of selfhood: persons are beings with purposes that have special significance for them, playing an important part in their sense of who they are. Purposes are, of course, closely related to goals: to have a purpose means that one desires a particular outcome and strives or acts to achieve it (1964a: 5, 27). These are not purposes that can be assigned or imputed by others but are goals that the individual can claim as her own and that direct her action (1985a: 98–9).

From his standpoint that having purposes is an ontological feature of selfhood, Taylor is able to enter the debate about artificial intelligence. No matter how intelligent or capable a machine is, what distinguishes it from a person, and even from an animal, is that no machine is the original source of purpose; its goals must always be attributed to it by human beings. Indeed, humans create and use machines in order to fulfil their own purposes: the machine's *raison d'être* is necessarily derivative, always relative to its designer's or user's intentions (*ibid.*: 98–9, 194–8, 201). However, this need not presuppose some pure notion of human purposes, unsullied by the possibilities that different technologies offer at different points in time. Because of his historicist sensibility, Taylor would accept the claim that humans' purposes can be shaped by the technology available to them. The difference is that, no matter what historical influences shape them, humans are the originators of purposes for themselves in a way that machines are not.

This emphasis on humans and even animals as creatures with purposes dates from Taylor's first book, *The Explanation of Behaviour*. For him the presence of purposes that direct and shape action creates a qualitative distinction between humans and animals on the one hand and the rest of nature and inanimate objects on the other (1964a: 3, 8, 64, 67, 70, 268, 272). The fact that humans and animals possess and are to some degree directed by their purposes means that in so far as order can be observed in social life, this has to be partly explained by reference to the purposes or goals of the beings who constitute that society. Order or patterns of behaviour cannot simply be accounted for by reference to external forces or impersonal laws: the purposes of the agents have to be considered in explaining this outcome. The link between purposes and goals explains Taylor's claim that understanding the behaviour of humans and animals requires a teleological explanation. By this he means one that makes reference to the "the result for the sake of which the events concerned occur" (*ibid.*: 9; cf. 6, 26, 37, 196, 220). In arguing thus, Taylor is again responding to the behaviourist approach to social science in general and to psychology in particular. Indeed, the whole of *The Explanation of Behaviour* is an engagement with and critique of behaviourism. The behaviourist approach tries to emulate the natural sciences and thereby commits itself to the view that there are no significant differences between explaining the behaviour of animals and humans on the one hand and that of other natural phenomena like earthquakes or icebergs on the other. It must, therefore, discount the part that purposes play in motivating the behaviour of humans and animals. From this standpoint, the teleological approach is seen as unscientific; it is believed to introduce considerations that are non-empirical and even metaphysical in nature (*ibid.*: 3, 6, 26, 112, 114, 270). Teleological explanations of the natural world, which were associated with Aristotelian and medieval natural philosophy, and which posited final causes in nature and saw the cosmos as a meaningful, ordered whole, were roundly criticized during the scientific revolution of the seventeenth century. Teleological explanations have suffered the stigma of being un- or anti-scientific ever since.[8]

One of the ways in which Taylor challenges the behaviourist approach is to appeal to humans' ordinary understandings of ourselves and our action. He claims that we understand ourselves as creatures with purposes and goals and see our action as guided or informed by these things. He points to ordinary language to show how entrenched this way of thinking is, discussing common understandings of concepts like action, desire, intention and responsibility. All of these presuppose a belief in humans as purposeful beings. For example, when we think of someone acting in a certain way, we normally assume some intention to do so and to bring about some sort of outcome. If I inadvertently bump someone in my haste to leave a meeting, this is seen to be quite a different occurrence from my deliberately elbowing someone who has annoyed me or pushing into someone in the hope of provoking a fight. In the first case, the outcome was not part of the end-condition or result I was aiming at, and even though the person might be annoyed by my bumping him, when I apologise and explain that this was an accident, he should be mollified. However, if I said this to the bully I had been trying to provoke a fight with, the apology could be read as a sudden surge of rational cowardice on my part. Using this sort of argument, Taylor concludes that "the normal notion of an action is of a piece of behaviour which not only brings about a certain condition but is directed towards bringing about that condition as an end" (*ibid.*: 32). This explains his further point that action is typically linked with responsibility. If it is my purpose or goal to achieve a certain outcome, and I succeed in this, I can usually be held accountable for that outcome. If, on the contrary, I create or contribute to an outcome that was no part of my desires or purpose, my personal responsibility diminishes. In the example above, the person I inadvertently bumped could advise me to be more careful in future, which is imputing some responsibility to me for the outcome, but it is a mitigated responsibility (*ibid.*: 26–37, 40, 54, 61, 220).

Of course the scientist's retort to this line of argument could be that appealing to everyday notions of action and behaviour is useless; why privilege the knowledge of ordinary people? The findings of natural science are replete with counter-intuitive explanations of natural phenomena, and besides, most ordinary people probably think that the sun really does rise and set every day. So the fact that a line of argument meshes with everyday understanding provides no guarantee of its explanatory credibility, and should perhaps make us even more wary of it. Taylor's rejoinder to this objection would be similar to the phenomeno-logical point he makes about the role of moral theory in Chapter 1: that what is to be explained is the behaviour of ordinary people living their lives, and as such their understandings of what they are doing matter. Their understandings influence their behaviour and so must be taken into consideration.

Of course this particular defence of teleological explanations of behaviour applies to humans only. Although humans might, as Taylor does, use concepts like action, desire and purpose to inter-pret animal behaviour, we have to rely on observation and hypoth-eses about what animals are doing. No appeal can be made to their language of self-understanding as informed by notions of inten-tionality and purpose because, if animals do have such a language, it remains inaccessible (*ibid.*: 26–7). So while many of Taylor's arguments about the necessary role of goals and purposes in shaping and therefore explaining behaviour apply to both animals and humans, he is not eschewing all species distinctions. In order to understand a person, it is necessary to have a sense of the purposes that direct her action. Such purposes inform and perhaps even structure the individual's self-interpretations. This relation-ship between purposes and self-interpretation distinguishes humans from animals, for while animals are conscious beings with agency and purposiveness (1985c: 257), their sense of their own purposes plays no part in their self-understandings (*ibid.*: 263). This is, of course, directly connected to the fact that animals are not language users. In *The Explanation of Behaviour*, Taylor represents this difference between humans and other animals by talking about "self-avowal". He means that humans can declare our purposes to ourselves and to others by articulating them, either before, during or after the action or even in the event of a failure to execute the proposed action. This ability to present our purposes to ourselves in language, and to make them an object of reflection, alters the way in which humans have purposes from the way in which animals do. So while humans and animals are both natural creatures with needs, drives, desires and emotions, the fact that human beings articulate these aspects of ourselves cre-ates a qualitative difference from animal experience (1985a: 158). (This provides another variation on the expressivist theme that to articulate something is to transform it, which emerged in Chapter 1 in the context of articulation's function in moral theory and in the above discussion of the way in which finding a new vocabulary to describe some emotion or experience changes its meaning.) However, Taylor concludes that this qualitative difference does not override the more basic fact that both humans and animals have purposes that shape their behaviour, and that must be taken into account if that behaviour is to be explained (1964a: 65, 67–70).

This implies another ontological feature of selfhood: humans are language users. "Man is above all the language animal" (1985a: 216). The fact that humans interpret ourselves in language can be linked to another salient feature of self-interpretation: its relationship to strong evaluation (explored in Chapter 1). Taylor believes that any person's sense of identity will be structured by the goods in their lives that they that take to be higher or more worthy than the others (*ibid.*: 3; 1985c: 266, 278). Given Taylor's belief in the tight relationship between selfhood and morality it comes as no surprise that he takes strong evaluation to be a necessary feature of identity (1978a: 146), just as he takes it to be a permanent feature of moral life. He further maintains that it is only in and through language that the sort of discriminations involved in strong evaluation, such as those between higher and lower, noble and base, essential and dispensable, can be made. This means that only a being with language and access to the sorts of rank ordering it makes possible can be considered moral (or immoral) (1985a: 263; 1985c: 263, 271–2).

Just as the way in which an individual understands herself can change over time, so the cultural resources available for interpreting the self change historically too: as the above discussion of feminism as a language of self-interpretation illustrates, new possibilities become available and old ones fade. So while the fact of self-interpretation is a permanent or ontological aspect of human identity, the content of self-interpretation varies across cultures and historical epochs (1985a: 9). When all the features of an individual's self-interpretation are aggregated this might amount to something unique, but this interpretation always points beyond the individual to the wider society and culture to which she belongs. This is because the array of linguistic, intellectual, emotional and aesthetic resources available for interpreting oneself are furnished by one's culture. This claim is combined with the earlier point about the constitutive role played by self-interpretations in the following passage:

The individual possesses this culture, and hence his identity, by participating in this larger [community] life . . . our experience is what it is, is shaped in part, by the way we interpret it; and this has a lot to do with the terms which are available to us in our culture. (1978a: 138)[9]

This general point about the role of culture, and therefore the wider society to which one belongs, in shaping self-interpretations can be illustrated by reference to language. Taylor is at pains to point out that the language in which I understand myself is never something of my own creation; while I might tailor and customize linguistic resources to describe and understand myself, the language with which I do this is provided by my society or culture. Hence his insistence that "The language I speak . . . can never be just *my* language, it is always *our* language" (1995a: 99; cf. 1978a: 138; 1985c: 276).[10] However, this language is just one of the wider social forces that influences self-interpretations. Taylor also suggests that the resources for self-interpretation come from the whole gamut of symbolic forms that a culture contains, such as art, dance, music, literature, philosophy, religion, ritual and so on (1985a: 216). This explains his claim that "the self-interpretations which define him [the individual] are drawn from the interchange which the community carries on" (*ibid.*: 8; cf. 11, 209; 1989a: 38).[11]

Dialogical selves

Taylor's insistence that individuals' self-interpretations are shaped by the wider culture to which they belong brings us to another ontological feature of the self: its dialogical nature. He believes that at the very core of identity is the ongoing real or imagined exchange with others:

My discovering my own identity doesn't mean that I work it out in isolation, but that I negotiate it through dialogue, partly overt, partly internal, with others . . . My own identity crucially depends on my dialogical relations with others.
(1995a: 231; cf. 1985a: 209; 1989a: 36)

This image of the dialogical self is drawn from the work of the twentieth century Russian literary theorist Mikhail Bakhtin.[12] Taylor uses it to convey his belief that individuals are continuously formed through conversation; this is not just a feature of maturation from childhood to adulthood but an inevitable dynamic of identity (1989a: 38). It is helpful to think of the dialogical aspect of the self as embedded in the linguistic one, which in turn is part of the individual's wider cultural background. But just because these conversations with significant others occur against the wider linguistic and cultural backdrop, it does not mean that one's interlocutors must be members of the same culture. It is possible to conduct these formative conversations with people from other cultures, but in order for the conversation to take place, there must have been some "fusion of horizons", some point of contact uniting people from different cultures so that they can go on to understand one another and even to recognize the differences between them (1985a: 281).[13]

In his depiction of the dialogical self, Taylor's terminology is best understood as imagery rather than a more literal account of what is taking place. Dialogue must be understood to encompass a broad range of human interactions or encounters or even imaginings. This is because his dialogical perspective on the self includes not just actual conversations with one's fellow humans but also imagined or internalized conversations. For example, even as I approach 40, I might ask what my mother would think of the things I have just said to one of my friends or the reactions I have just had to a new acquaintance. These sorts of imagined conversations can occur with those who are dead and perhaps even with those not born; I might imagine what I will say to my grandson when telling him about my childhood. Similarly, reading a philosopher, novelist or poet can make such an impact on an individual that the writer becomes their imagined interlocutor, for a time or for a lifetime. For religious people, their god is such an interlocutor, and so on. What the idea of the dialogical self points to in general is a psychological blurring of boundaries between self and other. While humans might be physically individuated, as per the vignette that opens this chapter, Taylor contends that psychologically we are not. Our inner life is a series or polyphony (or cacophony) of conversations with other people or beings, so that who I am always points beyond me as an individual to my relationships with significant others, to my partners in the dialogues who help to constitute my identity (1989a: 36).

The dialogical dimension of selfhood has been eclipsed with the modern western accent on individual freedom, autonomy and independence. These ideals are, in turn, often associated with a picture of the self-responsible individual thinking for and by himself and overcoming dependence on others. Yet for Taylor this image of the autonomous, self-responsible individual is a myth, or rather it is something that can only be achieved in degrees and not in any absolute way. Taylor's emphasis on the self as informed by and continuously involved in dialogical relationships with others leads him to the opposite conclusion from ontological individualism: "One cannot be a self on one's own. I am a self only in relation to certain interlocutors ... A self only exists within what I call 'webs of interlocution'" (*ibid.*: 36; cf. 1985c: 276). Of course one can change the web of interlocutors with whom one engages in reality or empathetically and imaginatively, but Taylor believes that existing within a web of interlocution, being in some sort of conversation with some others, is an inescapable, ontological feature of selfhood (1991a: 33–5).[14] Yet this is not to say that he jettisons the traditional western ideals of autonomy and self-responsibility entirely. Just as in his political theory he is trying to synthesize some of the liberal tradition's values with a communitarian ontology (see Chapter 3), so in a parallel movement, he gestures toward the need for a post-interiorized notion of the self. This would preserve these ideals of autonomy, individuality and responsibility but take the necessarily dialogical nature of the self into account when thinking about what they mean and how they might be realized (1985c: 278).

"Man is above all the language animal." This statement can be seen as providing the overarching feature in Taylor's account of the things about the self that are perennial, those things that endure despite changes in self-understanding. Because humans are beings with language, we interpret ourselves. These self-interpretations form part of a person's identity, so that a change in self-interpretation is a change in the self that is both the interpreter and the interpreted. Because humans are beings with language, we can make the sorts of discriminations that Taylor takes to be constitutive of strong evaluation and indeed that make morality possible at all. And finally, because humans are beings with language, we must be understood dialogically. Language is never a private matter; it always reaches beyond the self to posit another in conversation. Of course all of this presupposes a particular view of language – the expressivist one described above – which sees language as not merely a medium for representing an independently existing reality but which is aware of the power of language to shape and perhaps transform those things that come into its domain.

So while Taylor shares the traditional view that selfhood includes the properties of consciousness and agency, for him these are necessary but not sufficient conditions of personhood. To be a person or a self one must also have the capacity for self-interpretation and be in possession of original purposes that inform both one's actions and one's self-interpretations. In the light of his approach to personhood, it is interesting to consider what he would say about the sorts of debates that rage within bioethics circles about whether the categories of human being and personhood are co-extensive.[15] What are we to say of those human beings who either from birth or through some accident are devoid of the characteristics Taylor ascribes to selves or persons? A profoundly disabled individual or someone on a life-support system might be neither a self-interpreting being nor the bearer of original purposes. At one point Taylor touches on this sort of question but only very briefly, and his conclusions seem quite unsatisfactory. He claims that in such cases, where human beings have been severely damaged, they are still seen as belonging to the human species. This species is defined as having the potential to exercise these sorts of capacities, and so they can also be seen as having this potential (1985a: 103). Yet to say that all humans belong to the species that has the potential for personhood simply begs the question of whether all humans should be considered as persons. Earlier on in this essay Taylor says that "a person must be the kind of being who is in principle capable of all this, however damaged these capacities may be in practice" (*ibid.*: 97). To say that because a person is a member of the human species, he is, by definition, in principle capable of self-interpretation, purposiveness and morality seems abstract in the extreme. What does it mean for something to exist in principle if in some particular cases the capacity can never be activated? While it is easy to understand Taylor's reluctance to classify some humans as non-persons, it would seem that the thick characterization of personhood he offers does effectively exclude some human beings from the category of persons.

However, to infer what sort of contribution Taylor's philosophy of selfhood might yield to these debates, it is necessary to go beyond questions about correctly defining persons. In this context,

Taylor would endorse the Nietzschean claim that "life is no argument" (Nietzsche 1974: #121): matters about membership in the moral community and the significance of a human existence cannot be resolved by definitions alone. Other considerations have to be introduced, such as the fact that humans are always socially situated. While a person on a life-support system might not meet the philosophical criteria of personhood, he still exists in a web of social relationships, and is someone's brother, father, nephew, husband, friend or neighbour. That Taylor takes it to be an onto-logical fact that an individual always points beyond itself demands that social relationships be considered in discussing matters of life and death. There is an obverse side to this intersubjective approach to identity and selfhood too; it means that those making decisions about the life and death of others must ask what it does to their personhood when they put themselves into this position. What sort of standpoint is a person arrogating to himself when he claims the entitlement to judge another's fate? Secondly, Taylor's point about lives being construed as narratives is salient here. While a person currently suffering from Alzheimer's disease might not satisfy the philosophical criteria of personhood, in order to understand him and his life it is necessary to view it as a whole, and not simply make decisions about that life based on only one segment of it. These sorts of wider considerations would have to be included were a Taylorean perspective on bioethics to be adduced.

This overview of the ontological properties of selfhood has focused on important but intangible aspects of selfhood such as ideas, values, beliefs and self-understandings. From this it should not be inferred that Taylor ignores the material aspects of personhood: rather, he posits embodiment as another ontological feature of selfhood. Of course the way humans interpret their embodiment varies with cultures, eras, classes and gender. But this just represents again Taylor's two-dimensional approach to the self; he wants to both acknowledge the features that are common to all humans while also allowing for the great variety of ways in which these same features are experienced. As the impor-tance of embodiment for subjectivity is discussed in more detail in Chapter 4, here it suffices to note Taylor's description of bodily style as a component and an expression of identity:

> By "bodily style", I mean what we refer to when we say of some-one that he habitually acts cool, or eager, or reserved, or stand-

offish, or with much sense of dignity, or like James Bond. The style consists in the way the person talks, walks, smokes, orders coffee, addresses strangers, speaks to women/men, etc. It is a matter of how we project ourselves, something we all do, although some do it in more obtrusive fashion than others.

(1979b: 80)

Historicist dimensions of selfhood

In presenting Taylor's historicist account of identity, I draw largely from *Sources of the Self*. This is because, as its title signals, it represents his *magnum opus* on this topic as well as being his largest single work so far.[16] It is the major work that he anticipates in the introduction to *Philosophical Papers 1* (1985a: 7–8), although the article 'Legitimation Crisis?' in Volume II of this collection contains an abbreviated version of the historicist argument in *Sources of the Self*. However, before presenting this account of identity, it is appropriate to consider what Taylor is doing in *Sources of the Self* and how he does it.

As I see it, Taylor's purpose in writing this book was fourfold. Firstly, his express ambition is a genealogical one: to "articulate and write a history of the modern identity" (1989a: ix). People might, by nature, be self-interpreting beings, but the materials and resources with which we interpret ourselves change. Some of these changes and developments are catalogued in *Sources of the Self*. As Taylor explains:

> The book is genealogical. I start from the present situation, from formative ideas, from our conflicting forms of self-understanding, and I try to unearth certain earlier forms from which they arise . . . it is not a complete historical reconstruction, it is a very selective step backwards to rediscover certain sources.
>
> (1998b: 110)

Secondly, his ambition to write a history of the modern self has the practical aim of contributing to self-knowledge. Taylor believes that telling the history of the modern self will illuminate "the modern identity as we live it today" (1989a: 319). Recounting or reconstructing the history of the modern self contributes to self-knowledge by shedding light on those aspects of the self that are historical rather than ontological, for it shows how certain parts of ourselves that are often taken for granted or seen as natural have come into being over time (1985b: 257). In this regard, *Sources of the Self* exemplifies Taylor's point that "one can indeed convert the proposition . . . that there is no self-understanding without historical understanding – and claim that there is no historical understanding without self-understanding" (1978b: 24; cf. 25).

Thirdly, an emancipatory intent can be discerned behind this sort of historical reconstruction of identity. Taylor hopes that uncovering the complexity of the modern self and its different strands will free people from the tendency to deny and stifle the plurality of goods that modern selves effectively, if not always knowingly, affirm (1989a: 112, 503, 511, 514, 520). He therefore hopes that this work will influence the way people interpret themselves. Another salutary effect that Taylor hopes will come from appreciating the modern western identity as something particular that has been created over time is that its adherents will be able to see their culture as one among many. When westerners can better understand their own culture, they will, Taylor hopes, be better placed to understand other cultures (1995a: xii; 1999b: 143–4). In connection with this, he suggests that by better understanding the history and specificity of their culture, westerners can come to identify the spiritual and moral dimensions woven into their own cultural beliefs. This will, he hopes, make them more open to the value of other cultures, and more receptive to the fact that the moral and spiritual values woven into them, although differing from the western ones, are not same strange aberration but an inherent aspect of human culture. So the fourth purpose of *Sources of the Self* seems to be to enhance the cultural self-knowledge of its western readers and thereby improve interpretations of other cultures and communication across cultures.

Methodology

Although *Sources of the Self* represents an immensely ambitious and potentially enormous undertaking, some parameters are established by Taylor's particular approach to the history of modern selfhood. In recounting or reconstructing a history of the modern self, his almost exclusive focus is the cultural realm. He pays little attention to the ways in which changes in modes of production, in science and technology, in systems of government and law, have shaped the modern identity (see Calhoun 1991: 239, 260). His purview is narrowed further by the fact that within the realm of culture itself, the accent tends to fall on canonical works of philosophy. Taylor examines well-known philosophers such as Plato, St Augustine, Montaigne, Locke, Descartes, Rousseau, Bentham and Nietzsche. Exceptions to this tendency to discuss writings that are seen by many to be milestones in western thought include his attention to relatively minor figures such as Shatftesbury, Hutcheson and Herder. When he turns his attention beyond philosophy to other cultural products, his interest tends to remain in written texts; he refers to writers such as Rilke, Wordsworth, Beaudelaire, Proust, Pound and Eliot. Some attention is paid to the ways in which other forms of cultural creativity, such as music and the visual arts, have contributed to the modern identity. For these reasons, some critics have seen his work as excessively idealist. Some also see it as excessively highbrow, for the cultural creations he discusses tend to be those of the middle and upper classes.[17]

Taylor anticipates the objection that his approach is unduly idealist and addresses and justifies his method in Chapter 12 of *Sources of the Self*, "A Digression on Historical Explanation". There he rejects the charge that his approach is idealist, if this implies that he is advancing these texts as the sole engines of social change. He acknowledges in principle the role that changing material and institutional factors, such as those in the economic, administrative, legal, military, technological and political realms, play in shaping identity (1989a: 199, 202, 306, 316; cf. 1978a: 150).[18] He further contends that these are related in complex and synergistic ways to changes in ideas or mentalities: there is no single causal arrow pointing in either direction. Thus new philosophical conceptions of the self can justify existing practices, prepare the ground for new ones or both. Philosophers and other makers of meaning can reflect, articulate, intensify and expedite the changes that occur in these other milieux (1989a: 173–4; cf. 199, 206, 285, 306–7; 1991d: 239–40).

So given his concession that multiple and interacting forces have forged the modern western identity (1989a: 199), the question arises as to why Taylor devotes almost all of his interpretative efforts to philosophical texts as the major turning points in tracking these developments. His answer is that his interest lies not so

much in identifying the myriad causes of social change as in determining what the drawing power of these changes were, why so
many people found and continue to find them so appealing. To
answer this question he believes it necessary to disinter the visions
of goodness that inspired and/or articulated these historical shifts.
His key question is "What gives these new self-understandings
their spiritual power?" (*ibid.*: 203). He means spiritual here not in
a strictly religious sense, but more in the sense that we use it when
we refer to the human spirit, of the things that people find compelling and worthy of affirmation.[19]

Yet this seems to be an aspect of his methodology that some of
his critics have missed. Both Quentin Skinner and Judith Shklar,
for example, chide Taylor for offering a relentlessly positive reading of the history of ideas and for ignoring both the losses incurred
along the way and the darker side of some of the influential
philosophies he discusses. As Shklar says, "Throughout his review
of virtually every phase of European literary culture, Taylor only
seems to dwell on the sunny side of the street . . . This is a very
upbeat book" (1991: 106; cf. Skinner 1991: 142–4).[20] Three points
can be made here. Firstly, a sense of loss with regard to the past is
acknowledged in *Sources of the Self*. The fact that this appears in a
footnote (Taylor 1989a: 576 n.6) could, however, add to, rather
than weaken, the force of Shklar and Skinner's objection. Secondly, Taylor observes that it is rare for older ways of life to evapo-
rate altogether: remnants of earlier ethics or self-understandings
can persist in the modern world. He points to the ancient warrior
ethic, the enduring importance of honour, the survival of monastic
lifestyles and practices and to the model of the active citizen to
illustrate this claim (*ibid.*: 117; 1994d: 225; 1995a: 226; 1997d).

Thirdly, and most importantly, accentuating the positive developments of modernity is a deliberate strategy on Taylor's part. It
comes from his belief that the best way to explain the power of an
ideal is to appreciate the idea or image of the good that it embodies
and affirms.[21] He does not, to be sure, defend this assumption
against assaults from the opposite point of view: that people are
drawn by the lure of evil or moved by the impulses of self-interest.
Rather, this premise about the compelling appeal of notions of
goodness provides the starting point of his approach to moral life
and the self. It is of course directly linked to the point in Chapter 1
about the place accorded to love in moral theory. When this element of Taylor's method is appreciated, it becomes incumbent

upon those who would criticize him for being too sunny or upbeat in his reconstruction of the history of ideas to do more than just observe that this narrative could have been told in a darker way. Rather, they should address and explore the assumption underlying his approach, which privileges the attractions of goodness over other forces.[22]

However persuasive one finds it, this accent on the power of goodness to draw adherents explains Taylor's positive focus. He believes that one place in which such inspiring visions of the good can be recovered is philosophical and other written texts (see Waldron 1990: 325). Whereas the wider changes in notions of the self manifest themselves in diffuse and uneven ways across a variety of social practices, philosophical texts provide a formulation and summary of the ideals involved in these changes. By its very nature, or perhaps because of its history in the western tradition from Socrates onward, those who practise philosophy strive to give a rational account and defence of particular positions or prescriptions. Other cultural products, such as music, literature and the visual and performing arts, might embody a vision of the good but do not present it in quite the same was as philosophical texts do (Taylor 1989a: 307). Taylor maintains, moreover, that philosophical texts typically attempt to express the constitutive good that underpins the changes in life goods. As discussed in Chapter 1, making contact with this foundational good is seen by him to be vital to the full appreciation of the power of the life goods to move people.

However, in order for these new ideas and ideals to take hold, they need to become embodied in practices; they cannot simply remain expressed in philosophical texts. The central role that practices have played in shaping the modern identity appears in Taylor's general claim that this identity "arose because changes in the self-understandings connected with a wide range of practices – religious, political, economic, familial, intellectual, artistic – converged and reinforced each other to produce it" (*ibid.*: 206; cf. 1985b: 287; 1988c: 310; 1991a: 58). A practice is a shared and relatively stable pattern of activity that is reproduced in the course of daily life. It represents an established way of doing things, one that embodies some understanding between the participants, even if this remains largely unarticulated. This is so whether what is done is the raising of children, the greeting of friends or strangers, or the conduct of economic transactions (1989a: 204; 1984a: 22–3).

With this suggestion that ideas and ideals become entrenched, reproduced and transmitted in an array of practices in daily life, Taylor is able to show how his analysis of canonical writings has a relevance beyond the academy. From this perspective too, the origin of a set of ideals is less significant than the fact that it has taken hold and become popularized. For example, Taylor concedes that many of the values and practices relating to family life, work and individualism of the modern west originated in the upper middle classes of England, the USA and France. From here they spread outward and downward, modifying their form in the process of dissemination. What resulted was a range of ethical outlooks and practices that shared a broad family resemblance rather than simply being carbon copies of their originals (1975a: 9; 1989a: 305, 334, 394).[23] Taylor implies that ultimately the relationship between notions of the good and the practices that become a vehicle for them is a symbiotic one: notions of the good can only really take hold when they become instantiated in practices and practices come to express and perpetuate notions of the good (1978a: 139, 153).

In some of the writings after *Sources of the Self*,[24] Taylor has returned to these questions of method in his analysis of modernity. Although his focus is the problem of understanding how different societies make the transition to modernity rather than defending his own methodology, many of the points made there contribute to the comprehension of the project of *Sources of the Self*. Taylor distinguishes two theories of modernity, although what he really seems to be describing are two broad approaches: the first is cultural, the second acultural. The cultural approach to explaining modernity begins with an appreciation of existing, pre-modern cultures and sees modernization primarily as ushering in cultural change. By a culture, Taylor is referring to a broad set of beliefs and understandings about personhood, nature, society and morality, or the good. As per the observation in Chapter 1 that strong evaluations often belong to the tacit background of a person's awareness, these beliefs about personhood and so on do not have to be fully present to the consciousness of all members of the culture.

Acultural theories of modernity provide a mirror-image of cultural ones. They do not begin with the extant pre-modern culture and do not focus on cultural change. No attention is paid to understandings of selfhood, nature or the good because of the belief that modernization is primarily about institutions, structures and processes. In this approach, modernization is conceived of as a series of culturally neutral processes that any society could, and all probably will, undergo. These changes include secularization, urbanization, industrialization, the disenchantment of the world, increased emphasis on instrumental rationality, the rise of science and a concomitant belief in the separation of fact and value. The point of origin is irrelevant in this acultural approach, and the destination is projected as similar, if not identical, for all cultures undergoing these transitions. What distinguishes these two approaches to modernity is not their evaluation of its effects: theorists from either approach can interpret this change as positive or negative, as a gain in clear-sightedness and rationality or as a loss of meaning, horizons, order, community, heroism, morality and so on.

Although most theories of modernization have been of the acultural variety, Taylor prefers the cultural approach and, as *Sources of the Self* illustrates, this is what he practises. For him, a crucial ingredient in explaining modernization is the new view of the self, nature and the good that it brought into being. And because Taylor thinks that understanding the "starting point" of modernization is essential to understanding its consequences, he contends that the western versions of modernity differ from the way modernity will unfold in non-western societies. This explains his insistence that modernization should not be thought of as a single, neutral process that all societies are bound to undergo in a similar way and with similar results. What is needed is the recognition of alternative modernities. As different cultures undergo modernization, parallel processes might be involved but salient differences will also occur in the ways in which they incorporate the elements associated with modernity. This is because culture plays a crucial role in this process of incorporation.

So Taylor sees modernization as involving a massive cultural shift: as he puts it:

> one constellation of implicit understandings of our relation to God, the cosmos, other humans, and time was replaced by another in a multifaceted mutation. Seeing things this way not only gives us a better handle on what happened but also allows us to understand ourselves better.   (1999c: 171)

His emphasis on western culture's self-understanding is evident again here, and his point about its dialectical relationship with the interpretation of other cultures also appears in this article. As he says, "As long as we leave Western notions of identity unexamined, we will fail to see how other cultures differ and how this difference crucially conditions the way in which they integrate the truly universal features of modernity" (*ibid.*: 161).

Because the approaches to modernity that have been influential so far have neglected the vital and differentiating role of culture in influencing how a society modernizes, the drawing power of modern ideals has also been neglected. Taylor maintains that in so far as these ideals of disengaged freedom, instrumental rationality and universal equality have been acknowledged, it has been either as by-products of institutional forces or in terms of the strategic possibilities these ideas offer by allowing us to control nature better or do what we want without interference. He is more than suspicious of the relegation of these ideals to either derivative or instrumental status; indeed, it is, as we have seen, just their "inherent power" (*ibid.*: 158) that he is trying to capture in *Sources of the Self.*[25] His determination to explore modernization in this way, to show it as the replacement of one set of views about the self, nature and the good with another, no doubt compounds the impression, discussed above, that he is too sanguine about modernity. However, while he is keen to show that modernity does not just involve the loss and attrition of meaning and while he does believe that there is much to affirm in modern morality (1989a: 106–7), he is not, as noted above, wholly oblivious to the losses or diminutions that have been incurred in this change.

A distinctly modern self

What, according to Taylor, are the distinctive aspects of the modern western self or identity? One is the particular notion of freedom that the modern self aspires to: for it, freedom is defined as radical disengagement (*ibid.*: ix). A second is its sense of inwardness: the modern self sees itself as an entity with inner depths (*ibid.*: 158) A third is the self's sense of its own individuality or uniqueness, which Taylor takes to be a legacy of the Romantic movement (*ibid.*: ix, 28). This combines with the universalist and egalitarian aspects of modern identity, for all selves are seen as equally unique, or at least as having the potential for this (*ibid.*: 12; 1991a: 50). This gives rise to the huge emphasis on authenticity in modern culture; people feel a sort of ethical imperative to be true to their particular selves. And although authenticity is now a universal value in the sense that it that can be claimed by all, being true to myself cannot be construed in wholly universal terms. Others would doubt my authenticity if I simply lived according to readily available, "off the rack" models rather than investing these with my own personal style. The modern self is also informed by a cultural movement that Taylor calls the affirmation of ordinary life. Related to, but not the same as this movement, is the widespread ethic of benevolence, for according to Taylor one of the distinctive features of the modern moral sensibility is its ambition to diminish avoidable suffering (1989a: 12–13). This is in turn linked with another universal aspect of modern selfhood, for there is a sense in which all individuals should be entitled to a life with minimal unnecessary pain (*ibid.*: 394–5). This is linked with a deeper imputation of dignity and respect to all persons, simply by virtue of their being human.

Before embarking on a description of each of these elements of the modern self, the fact that Taylor is trading in ideals must be underscored. Of course these ideals, if they are to have the shaping power he attributes to them, must be instantiated in practices, but there can be and often are incomplete or imperfect realizations of these ideals. To say, for example, that in the modern world many people do suffer avoidable pain and deprivation is not necessarily to gainsay the ideal of universal benevolence (*ibid.*: 13). This amounts rather to saying that this an incomplete project. To gainsay the ideal's contribution to modern selfhood, one would have to prove that it is not acted upon, or not widely acted upon and/or that most people are insensitive or indifferent to its importunings. One further caveat: Taylor makes it clear in response to one of his critics that this bundle of ideals that makes up the modern identity is something towards which more and more people in more and more societies are converging. This movement happens at different times, at different speeds and in different ways in various parts of the world. He does not claim to be describing "where everyone now is" (1991d: 247), but rather a collection of ways of understanding the self that would be alien and probably even incomprehensible to those in pre-modern cultures.

Disengaged freedom

One of the distinctive features of the modern western outlook is that humans no longer see ourselves as ensconced in, and in important ways defined by, some larger cosmic order. People no longer see ourselves as being part of a world of forms, nor situated in the hierarchy of God's creation above the animals but just below the angels, nor as belonging to a great chain of being. Because the modern world is considered a disenchanted one, without any intrinsic moral meaning, the modern self is freed of the need to find preordained meaning or order in the world (1985b: 256–60; 1989a: 18, 160, 395; 1994f: 18–19). This erosion of belief in an inherently meaningful cosmos, one which contained prescriptions for human life, makes possible the meaninglessness, loss of horizons and nihilism that Nietzsche expressed so vividly (1989a: 16–18). While Taylor acknowledges this consequence of the erosion of belief in a meaningful order, he also considers this development from the other side, finding freedom as well as loss, and pointing to the positive possibilities that this notion of the disengaged self provides. Rather than perceiving itself as connected to some wider cosmic-cum-moral order, the modern self makes of its world an object, and stands toward it as a subject whose task it is to understand and control this world (1975a: 7, 539; 1989a: 188).[26] This view of the self clearly influenced and was influenced by the scientific revolution of the seventeenth century and Taylor identifies René Descartes, Francis Bacon and John Locke as being among its major exponents (1985b: 258).

Another way in which Taylor describes this distinctively modern approach to selfhood is by reference to the self-defining nature of the modern self. Many traditional doctrines saw human beings as realizing themselves fully only when they were in touch with, or rightly situated *vis-à-vis,* the wider cosmic order. The idea that a human could understand himself correctly without reference to this wider order was inconceivable. What is new in the modern sense of the self is the faith that I can properly understand and define myself in the absence of any attachment to this wider and more ultimate reality that surrounds me. Hence the image of the modern self as disengaged (1975a: 6–7).

Of course Taylor is not claiming that no denizens of modern western society believe in God or any other transcendent moral source any more. This would be a curious claim for a Catholic like him to make and would require a studied ignorance of the social and political movements in western countries that are predicated on and appeal to belief in God. Rather Taylor's point about the modern disengaged self is that while individuals might go on believing that there is a meaningful cosmic order, this belief no longer underpins any shared, public, overarching framework of meaning. No system of belief or understanding can be taken for granted, and each is faced with challenges from contending frameworks of meaning (1989a: 312, 381, 401, 491; 1997d).[27]

This modern ideal of the free, disengaged individual continues the emphasis on rationality that has characterized so much of western philosophy from Socrates onwards, but construes this in a new way. Being rational now comes to mean taking some distance from ordinary, embodied human existence and striving to acquire mastery over the self and the world. The disengagement that this involves is mental or intellectual; the mind tries to prescind from its involvement in ordinary existence and aspires to a more detached, disinterested perspective on the world (1989a: 149). In a related shift, the emphasis within correct knowing comes to be on its process or method; there is a belief that if knowledge is pursued in the proper way, its outcomes will be reliable. The goal of this process is not, however, just the generation of true knowledge, for this knowledge in turn affords a way of controlling and organizing the world. Descartes's work provides the *locus classicus* of this outlook but Taylor sees its influence as spreading far more widely across several branches of western culture.

It is important to understand why what seems to be basically an epistemological doctrine counts for Taylor as an approach to selfhood. Firstly there is the obvious point that this doctrine constructs the self in a particular way, as detachable from the surrounding world and standing over against it as a subject *vis-à-vis* an object where the boundaries of each can be clearly demarcated. Secondly, this stance of disengagement is also taken toward the self (*ibid.*: 161). The possibility of rational control and reorganization of the material world includes the self: some parts of the self are perceived as if they were an object that the other rational, disengaged part of the self, the mind, can reorder (1988c: 303–4, 308–9). Taylor describes this posture of radical disengagement from and toward the self as "a new, unprecedentedly radical form of self-objectification" (1989a: 171). He finds its fullest articulation in the work of Locke, describing it thus:

The disengagement both from the activities of thought and from our unreflecting desires and tastes allows us to see ourselves as objects of far-reaching reformation. Rational control can extend to the re-creation of our habits, and hence of ourselves ... The subject who can take this kind of radical stance of disengagement to himself or herself with a view to remaking, is what I want to call the "punctual" self. To take this stance is to identify oneself with the power to objectify and remake, and by this act to distance oneself from all the particular features which are objects of potential change. What we are essentially is none of the latter, but what finds itself capable of fixing them and working on them.   (*ibid.*: 171)[28]

But perhaps the most salient feature of this epistemological doctrine that earns it such importance in Taylor's narrative of changing conceptions of the self relates to the earlier points about the self as necessarily situated in moral space and the power of ideals of goodness to inspire adherence. On Taylor's reading, this modern aspiration to disengagement represents a moral ideal as well as an epistemological doctrine. It encapsulates ideas about how humans should live, or what he calls strong evaluations. It posits one way of being as superior or more admirable than others. Underpinning its claims about correct knowledge of the self and the world are ideals about freedom from nature and determinism, a belief in the dignity that comes from human reason and the pursuit of truth, and the appeal of the power and instrumental control it promises. It is these deeper moral sources of the doctrine that must be understood if its power and influence are to be fully appreciated (1975a: 9; 1985a: 112–13; 1988c: 312; 1989a: 152, 163, 168, 174–5, 177; 1991a: 103–5; 1994f 17–20).

One way of expressing Taylor's argument that there is something distinctive about the modern notion of the self is to say that while all societies have a notion of reflexivity, in that there are some things and experiences that pertain to myself, not all have the sense of what he calls "radical reflexivity". This term refers to a focus on the self *qua* self, the turning of attention toward what sort of self it is that has experiences of knowing, feeling and so on. In this process, the inquiry's concern moves from the objects of experience to the subject of experience. Taylor contrasts general reflexivity and radical reflexivity in the following way:

> If I attend to my wounded hand, or begin (belatedly) to think
> about the state of my soul instead of about worldly success, I
> am indeed concerned with myself, but not yet radically. I am
> not focussing on myself as the agent of experience and making
> this my object . . . Radical reflexivity brings to the fore a kind of
> presence to oneself which is inseparable from one's being the
> agent of experience.
>
> $\hspace{4cm}$ (Taylor 1989a: 130–31; cf. 176; 1985b: 266–7;
> $\hspace{6cm}$ 1988c: 310–12; 1991c: 304–5).

He claims that the emergence of a radically reflexive stance,
which he traces to St Augustine, is a precondition of the disengaged subject of modern epistemology. This is connected with the
ambition of modern science to know the world "in itself" rather
than as it is "for us"; to find a way of knowing purged of the properties of the knowing subject. In order to attain this sort of knowledge, it is imperative to identify what the knowing subject brings
or contributes to the process of knowing (1985a: 112; 1989a: 174–5,
232).[29]

However, Taylor points out that this stance of radical reflexivity
developed in another way as well; it provided the underpinnings of
an idea of the person as a being with inner depths that, while
mysterious, could be explored (1989a: 173, 178, 183). Despite their
common source in the idea of radical reflexivity, these two
approaches to the self soon diverged. That associated with Cartesian disengagement urged individuals to abstract themselves from
their ordinary experience and idiosyncrasies, whereas that associated with recognition of inner depths encouraged a deeper exploration of the self immersed in its everyday particularity (*ibid.*: 175,
182).

Inner depths

The modern sense that the self is disconnected from any larger
cosmic order of meaning is also associated with this aspect of the
modern self: inwardness. Taylor contends that the inside/outside
distinction is not as salient in other cultures' approaches to the
person as it is in the modern western one. Nor is the modern
emphasis on turning inward to find meaning universal (*ibid.*: 111,
114, 121). There is, of course, a direct connection between the in-

ward orientation and the attrition of cosmic orders of meaning. As Taylor explains:

> For the pre-modern . . . I am an element in a larger order . . . The order in which I am placed is an external horizon which is essential to answering the question, who am I? . . . for the modern, the horizon of identity is to be found within, while for the pre-modern it is without. (Taylor 1985b: 258)

Yet as his depiction of St Augustine's thought is designed to show, this link between finding oneself in a disenchanted world and turning inward is contingent rather than necessary. Taylor traces the modern emphasis on inwardness to St Augustine (1988c: 313–15; 1989a: 128–9, 140, 177), yet shows how its emphasis has changed since St Augustine's time. In St Augustine's thought, turning inward was a prelude to moving upward to God (1989a: 132, 134, 136, 390; 1991a: 26). In the modern, post-Augustinian outlook however, the individual turning inward finds himself as a being whose richness and complexity call for self-exploration. This approach to the self can be characterized as post-Augustinian because it draws on but goes beyond the inward turn pioneered by St Augustine.

Another way in which modern variations on the theme of inwardness carry over St Augustine's idea that turning inward was a path toward God and his goodness, is via the belief that when one turns inward one finds not just a self to be explored but also a moral source. Taylor identifies Jean-Jacques Rousseau as one of the major exponents of this idea of the self having inner depths, and of this attitude toward selfhood having a moral dimension. In order to ascertain the right thing to do, be or feel, the self should turn inward, not outward to the opinions of others (Taylor 1985b: 272, 1991a: 27–9). By turning inward one can hearken to the voice of nature, which guides one to goodness. So in Rousseau's variation on the theme of inwardness, there is actually a close connection between inside and outside. Just as contact with the natural world is a source of moral renewal, so turning attention to this spontaneous flow of life that also runs through the self, attending to the voice of nature within, is a source of moral guidance and of happiness (Taylor 1975a: 25, 1989a: 357, 359, 362, 461). In proposing that nature is a moral source, Rousseau is reacting against the disenchantment of the world referred to above, just as he is sceptical of many of the benefits typically associated with the rise of science. In fact Rousseau is troubled by the whole bundle of goods bequeathed by the scientific revolution of the seventeenth century, and fears that the hegemony of instrumental reason has had deleterious consequences, partly because it obscures humans' natural feelings, which are typically benevolent. For all these reasons, Rousseau's thought was a great source of inspiration to the whole Romantic movement and its reaction against the Enlightenment (1989a: 368–9, 429, 456–7, 461).

Expressions of authenticity

The injunction to be true to one's self in one's individuality captures what Taylor takes to be another very important and distinctive aspect of the modern western approach to selfhood. It is connected to the previous point about the self becoming a being with inner depths, and with this acquiring a moral dimension. Behind this injunction to be true to oneself is a belief that being a self is ultimately an individual project or undertaking in that each individual must decide for himself or herself what being authentic means. Each person is seen as having his or her own mode of being human and is encouraged to realize this rather than conform to a pre-existing model or a pattern imposed from outside. Each has to discover an original way of being, has to recognize it as a true or faithful expression of who they are, and has to adopt and take responsibility for it.

Taylor argues that the late eighteenth century represents a watershed with regard to the moral significance of individual differences. While the existence of such differences in taste, temperament, preferences, values, abilities, inclinations and so on has always been recognized, they have not always been invested with the sort of ethical salience they now enjoy. As he says:

> nowhere before the modern era was the notion entertained that what was essential to us might be found in our particular being. But this is the assumption underlying the identity question.   (1988c: 316; 1989a: 375; 1991a: 28).

However, while pointing to the late eighteenth century as the important turning point here, he does acknowledge that traces of this ideal can be found in the seventeenth century in the work of Michel de Montaigne. The French thinker exemplified a turn toward the self as a mystery to be unravelled. As Taylor describes it, Montaigne's position is that:

> We seek self-knowledge, but this can no longer mean just impersonal lore about human nature, as it could for Plato. Each of us has to discover his or her own form. We are not looking for the universal nature; we each look for our own being. Montaigne therefore inaugurates a new kind of reflection which is intensely individual . . . it is entirely a first-person study.   (Taylor 1989a: 181; cf. 1985b: 272; 1988c: 315–16)

Notwithstanding Montaigne's early embodiment of this ideal, and the way it draws on the notion of inwardness and the idea of nature as source, Taylor sees this injunction to discover and live in accordance with our own particular originality as reaching its fullest formulation in the eighteenth-century doctrines he calls expressivism. In striving to be true to myself, I turn inward to discover or get in touch with who I am. No one else can know exactly who I am called to be: I need to express what I find in this introspective process in my own way. In expressing what I find within, I both give voice to and shape my identity. It is not as if the truth of my identity could pre-exist my own particular formulation of it, so that it was potentially retrievable by someone else. As Taylor says, "the idea which a man realizes is not wholly determinate beforehand; it is only made fully determinate in being fulfilled" (1975a: 16) In this process of interpreting and expressing individuality, the involvement and uniqueness of the interpreter is as crucial as the findings or the content.

Despite its accent on the unique facets of the self, the ethic of authenticity is not necessarily at odds with Taylor's dialogical approach to the self. The ethic of authenticity need not preclude the features of myself that I share with others nor the features of myself that I work out and understand via my relationships with others. There is no proscription against the aspects that I see as central to myself including shared ones, such as gender, race, ethnicity, religion, or class and so on. In invoking or accentuating these parts of myself, I am identifying with certain other people, but these shared features can figure in modern identity in so far as they are claimed by me as part of who I am rather than imposed on, or ascribed to, me by others.

In *The Malaise of Modernity* (also published as *The Ethics of Authenticity*), Taylor argues that while the contemporary ideal of living according to one's own style or inclinations, of "doing one's own thing", of prizing self-fulfilment above all else, might generate behaviour that seems selfish and unmindful of the needs of others, it is actually powered by a moral ideal (1991a: 15–17). As we have just seen, the ideal of authenticity exhorts all individuals to find their own way of being and its injunctions can be cast in a moral vocabulary, using terms such as freedom, questing, responsibility and dignity. Indeed, authenticity itself is a powerfully evaluative term: how many people want to be told that any aspect of their life is inauthentic, fake or artificial?

Taylor underlines the immense importance to the modern identity of expressing authenticity when he writes that "Expressive individuation has become one of the cornerstones of modern culture. So much so that we barely notice it, and we find it hard to accept that it is such a recent idea in human history and would have been incomprehensible in earlier times" (1989a: 376). To illustrate just how historically novel this now-familiar attitude towards identity is, he takes the case of the Protestant reformer, Martin Luther. There is a sense in which the process of rejecting Catholicism plunged Luther into an identity crisis. If we consider one of the ontological aspects of identity discussed above, if we see identity as that which orients us in moral space, then Luther's doubts about Catholicism disoriented him; they shook his identity. None the less, Taylor contends that Luther did not and could not have understood this experience in the terms of expressive authenticity that modern western selves find ready to hand. Luther could not have looked upon the ultimate horizon of meaning as a personal one. His identity crisis, and its resolution, did not revolve around the issue of defining himself authentically as an individual, but of defining the condition of every human being as depraved by sin and redeemed by grace. By Taylor's reading, it would be anachronistic to see Luther's identity crisis in exactly the same terms as we would interpret such a crisis for someone today:

> Before such a crisis and such spiritual struggles could be described in terms of identity, it was necessary to conceive the ultimate horizon of each individual as being in some sense personal. (1997d; cf. 1989a: 28)

While the figure of Martin Luther provides a good foil to the dimension of modern selfhood that I have called expressive authenticity, his position changes when it comes to the affirmation of ordinary life. Luther stands at the threshold of this distinctive aspect of modern identity.

Ordinary life

The phrase "the affirmation of ordinary life" refers to an aspect of the modern identity that Taylor portrays as a legacy of Protestantism but which now manifests itself in a wholly secular way. What it means to affirm ordinary or everyday life is to believe that a significant part of one's identity is expressed in the realms of work and family life, and that what happens in these domains makes a substantial contribution to one's sense of the value or meaning of life (1985a: 155, 255; 1991a: 45, 49–50). Taylor contrasts this with the outlook of classical Greece, where these sorts of activities were associated with the production and reproduction of mere life, and were contrasted with the pursuit of the good life, which involved political activity and philosophical contemplation. These latter activities were seen as inherently worthier or nobler than those associated with quotidian life. Indeed, the domestic arenas of production and reproduction were seen as largely instrumental to these higher activities. A life devoted exclusively to labour, reproduction and bodily needs was seen as a less than fully human one, for in pursuing these activities humans were not seen as really doing anything to distinguish them from animals (1985b: 155–6; 1989a: 13–14, 211, 314; 1994f: 31).

Protestantism rejected the belief that some sorts of activities are qualitatively superior than others and proposed instead that all activities are potentially worthy; what matters is how they are conducted. The accent shifted from what one does to how one does it. What mattered was that one carry out one's deeds worshipfully, to the glory of God. From this perspective, even the most menial activity could become sanctified, if practised with the appropriate attitude (1989a: 13–14, 218, 221–224). One way of expressing this transition is to say that the object of strong evaluation changed. Previously activities themselves had been deemed noble or base, whereas now it was one's way of participating in them that became admirable or degenerate. This explains Taylor's emphasis on adverbs in expounding this doctrine, for the way in which one behaves becomes crucial for judging that behaviour. To put this change colloquially, "it ain't what you do, it's the way that you do it".

This Protestant outlook challenged not just the traditionally aristocratic ethos but also the traditionally Catholic one. Catholicism had been premised on the belief that certain activities were inherently worthier than others. The activity of the priest, for example, was seen to be nobler than that of ordinary people engaged in working and raising families. This privilege was challenged during the Reformation, when it was argued that it was not what the believer did but the commitment with which she or he did it that determined the spiritual quality of an action. The Protestant reformers, especially the Calvinists, also attacked the traditional Catholic separation of the sacred from the profane (1975a: 9). So there is a levelling movement inherent in the affirmation of ordinary life: what determines individuals' worth is not status or activity but how they conduct themselves. In the place of a hierarchy of status, rank or activity it puts a hierarchy of attitudes or dispositions (1989a: 214–17).

The consequence of this change in religious outlook was that the worlds of production and reproduction acquired a new significance. Working with dedication and diligence became more important than the sort of work one did. Marriage and family life could be devoted to God (*ibid.*: 226–7, 292). As this indicates, these things were not originally seen as sources of personal fulfilment in their own right; they were valorized because they could lead humans to God and could demonstrate their piety and devotion to him. But over time the religious justification for their importance became obscured, and by the late twentieth century ordinary life is seen to be an inherently important part of a person's identity and arena of self-realization and fulfilment (*ibid.*: 289).[30] Taylor is not, of course, saying that prior to the spread of the doctrine affirming ordinary life people did not love their children or spouses nor that they gained no satisfaction from their work. What changes is not the existence of these things but the ethical importance with which they are imbued. With the affirmation of everyday life, family relationships and work come to occupy a central place in people's sense of what makes life worth living and this, according to Taylor, is unprecedented (*ibid.*: 292–3; cf. 1985b: 254–5).

Illustrating his wider claim that ideals alone do not cause the sort of immense social change involved in something like the affirmation of ordinary life, Taylor points to a series of other social developments that consolidated the importance of the domestic and work worlds originally valorized by Protestantism. These include industrialization and its systematic separation of the workplace from the home, urbanization and the rise of the nuclear family. However, along with these changes in the material conditions of life came the doctrine of Marxism, which Taylor sees as furthering the affirmation of ordinary life (1985b: 215) Of course Marxism does this in a formally secular way; it focuses on production as pivotal to human identity, and is centrally concerned with the quality of human work and the fulfilment derived therefrom. The key adverbs for assessing the significance of human work in the Marxist outlook are not "rationally" or "worshipfully", but "freely", "creatively" and "expressively". For Marx the way in which human beings reproduce our material lives can, potentially at least, distinguish us markedly from the animals. What Taylor fails to note is that while Marx accords immense importance to work in human life, he is less voluble on the topic of family life, the importance of domestic work and the reproduction of the species. So in Marxism we see a force that furthered one side of the affirmation of ordinary life, that of work and production, largely to the neglect of family life and love relationships. These issues have, however, been taken up by many feminist scholars.[31]

Practical benevolence

The final distinctive aspect of the modern self is its commitment to practical universal benevolence. This refers to a belief that society should do as much as it can to minimize unnecessary human suffering. This development complemented the affirmation of ordinary life and the two have been mutually reinforcing, which explains Taylor's tendency to discuss them in tandem (1985b: 156; 1989a: 14, 258, 394–5; 1991a: 104, 1995a: 56; 1999b: 140). Taylor claims that no ancient ethical view gave the place to universal benevolence that modern morality does, and that no civilization has been as concerned with the reduction of suffering as the modern western world is (1989a: 12, 314, 316; 1999b: 143). Of course, the Stoics promoted universal moral duties,[32] and versions of Christianity have always advocated, in principle at least, the ideal of universal benevolence, of loving one's fellow human beings because they are God's creatures (1989a: 13). As this signals, Taylor is not proposing that pre-modern cultures were unconcerned with or indifferent to pain and suffering. Rather than suggesting that the urge to minimize unnecessary suffering emerged *ex nihilo* in the modern west, he claims that with the rise of the ethic of practical benevolence, an existing concern with suffering took on greater proportions compared to other ethical considerations (1995a: 49–50).

Yet notwithstanding its ethical antecedents, one of the distinctive things about the modern morality of benevolence is its practical bent, its emphasis not just on one's duty to love others or to give them equal consideration along with one's neighbours and familiars, but to act to relieve their suffering where possible. Taylor traces the origins of this outlook to the scientific revolution of the seventeenth century and its belief that one of the benefits of understanding the natural world more accurately would be an increased ability to control it. One of the things that drove this quest for power over nature was the ambition to improve the condition of everyday life, to relieve suffering and to improve man's natural estate, to paraphrase one of the first philosophers of modern science, Francis Bacon (Taylor 1989a: 230; 1991a: 104). This impulse was given further backing by the Enlightenment and its dedication to improving living conditions (1989a: 318, 331, 394). According to Taylor's reading, Enlightenment thinkers were effectively forwarding what was originally the Christian project of universal benevolence, notwithstanding the fact that a common target of their criticism was the cruelty they detected in religion and the church. Taylor summarizes the immense impact that the imperative to reduce unnecessary or avoidable suffering has had on western culture thus:

> We are heirs of Bacon, in that today, for instance, we mount great international campaigns for famine relief or to help the victims of floods. We have come to accept a universal solidarity today, at least in theory, however imperfect our practice, and we accept this under the premiss of an active interventionism in nature. We don't accept that people should continue to be the potential victims of hurricanes or famines. We think of these as in principle curable or preventable evils.
>
> (1991a: 104)

However, it is not just thinkers impressed by the potential of science and the power of reason to improve society that drove this doctrine of universal benevolence. This outlook was complemented by a quite different one; the theory of moral sentiments that Taylor discerns in the eighteenth century. Its key proponents were the Earl of Shaftesbury and then Francis Hutcheson (Taylor 1989a: 248). Influenced by neo-Platonist thinkers, this doctrine depicted the world as a harmonious whole, which is ordered for the best and whose parts are complementary. Anyone who correctly understood the world would grow to appreciate its goodness and to love its whole and each of its components (*ibid.*: 253–4). A Christian conception of God plays a key role in this teaching, for he is the one who made the world so good in the first place, and the love owed to him should also be conferred upon his creation (*ibid.*: 264, 315). Benevolence toward oneself and to others also emerges as a key good in this worldview: indeed, such self-love and fellow feeling emerge spontaneously in those who are rightly disposed toward the world (*ibid.*: 264).

In many ways this doctrine prefigures Romanticism. It shares, for example, the idea that feelings or emotions have moral value and that hearkening to them can inspire people to act properly (*ibid.*: 282, 284). Closely related to this is the belief that by turning inward it is possible to make contact with moral sources, so this movement also develops the turn inward that Taylor sees as pioneered by St Augustine (*ibid.*: 264). Moreover, for this outlook, as for Romanticism, there is no strong separation between inner and outer; there is a sense that nature is a source of goodness, and that there is a close bond between self and world. As Taylor puts it, "Our moral sentiments are an integral part of the whole providential order" (*ibid.*: 282). As the image of nature as a source of goodness and moral guidance rather than a disenchanted, mechanistic realm suggests, the theory of moral sentiments must also be understood as a reaction against the scientific outlook deriving from the seventeenth century, with its emphasis on disengaging from the world, rendering it an object and exercising instrumental control over it (*ibid.*: 254, 265). It is perhaps no surprise then that Rousseau echoed this doctrine's emphasis on benevolence or a feeling of sympathy towards one's fellow beings (*ibid.*: 411).

Charles Taylor

Plural selves

The peculiarly modern western self that Taylor traces or reconstructs through his historical narrative is clearly a multifaceted one. As he says, "our identities . . . are complex and many-tiered" (*ibid.*: 28–9) He shares Nietzsche's powerful awareness of the multiplicity and complexity of the modern self. However, it seems that for Taylor, the template for thinking about humans as inherently plural is theistic. He claims that "human diversity is part of the way in which we are made in the image of God", and links this to the Trinitarian view of God as three persons in one (1999a: 14–15).

When it comes to distinctively modern diversity, we find that not only does the modern self comprise several different strands, but these can be related to one another in varying ways. In some cases, theoretically distinct aspects of the self are mutually reinforcing. Consider the hybrid pedigree of practical, universal benevolence. This ethic has been fuelled by outlooks as disparate as the scientific revolution, the affirmation of ordinary life, the theory of moral sentiments and Romanticism. These different, and in some cases seemingly rival, traditions converge to affirm the same good. Other analytically discrete aspects of the modern self conspire to compromise or converge too. The idea of the self as an entity with inner depths to be plumbed is, for example, closely linked to the doctrine of expressivism. As Taylor explains:

> only with the expressivist idea of articulating our inner nature do we see the grounds for construing this inner domain as having *depth*, that is, a domain which reaches farther than we can ever articulate, which still stretches beyond our furthest point of clear expression. (1989a: 389; cf. 390, 548 n.1)

This is also the case with the image of the free, disengaged self and the affirmation of ordinary life (*ibid.*: 234). The ethic affirming ordinary life also complements the ideal of authentic individualism, as domestic life and the family become the site of self-discovery and emotional fulfilment for many. The increasing physical privacy of family life contributes further to this symbiosis. Describing this relationship, Taylor writes of:

a society in which (in principle) everyone has adequate private space for a full family life. This is central to the fulfilment of the man and wife, as companions and lovers, and also as parents. And it is also the locus in which the next generation is nurtured, so that the children in turn will be able to discover and seek their own kind of fulfilment, including the formation of marriages based on their own affinities. The contemporary family ideally has not only the space to live an unmediated existence unhampered, but also the means to foster the development and self-discovery of its children.

(1985b: 262; cf. 272)

So while the modern self is a complex, plural and over-determined creation, there are times when its different strands unite in the same ethical recommendation.

In other ways, however, aspects of the modern self stand in a more tense and ambivalent relationship. While the affirmation of ordinary life and ideal of authenticity and self-fulfilment can be complementary, they can also drive in opposite directions. For some individuals, realizing the injunction to be oneself and to pursue their own course can lead them to loosen the bonds and obligations of family life. As Taylor says, "If my development, or even my discovery of myself, should be incompatible with a long-standing association, then this will come to be felt as a prison, rather than a locus of identity. So marriage is under great strain" (*ibid.*: 283; cf. 285).[33] A further example of the tension among various strands of the modern self appears in Taylor's interpretation of the Romantic, expressivist parts of the self as a reaction against the disengaged free self, which is capable of scientific knowledge and which also affirms ordinary life (1975a: 22–3, 540; 1979a: 2–3; 1985b: 270–71; 1989a: 390, 495). Yet the Romantic self is at the same time building on the individualism of the disengaged self (1991a: 25).

From even this brief sketch of some of the complexities, ambiguities and tensions in the modern notion of selfhood, we witness Taylor's pluralism forcefully (1985b: 273, 276–7, 287), and can appreciate anew his claim that becoming aware of the multifariousness of the modern self should caution us against reductionist or unitary theories of morality. But in the face of this plurality, is there any way in which we can summarize or organize the various facets of the modern identity? In his books on Hegel, Taylor presents and partly defuses these tensions by suggesting that different facets of the self have been effectively relegated to different spheres of life. The Romantic, expressivist self in pursuit of personal fulfilment has been largely confined to the private realm, while the public self is shaped by utilitarian notions of the individual bequeathed from the Enlightenment. Here the individual is subordinated to larger collective structures, which have the goal of maximizing efficiency and which run according to a conception of instrumental rationality. This is clear in the economy and in the bureaucratization of politics. This is not to suggest that everyone has been complacent about this division of labour: there have been periodic outbursts against the technical nature of social organization and ideals of Romantic expressivism have been applied to the public realm (1975a: 541–3; 1979a: 70–71). But this claim about the self's division tends to drop out of Taylor's later work, and we are presented with a less binary depiction of plurality.

In *Sources of the Self* a different way of mapping this pluralism is proffered. From the eighteenth century onwards, three broad horizons of identity or moral exploration can be discerned. The first centres around the individual while the second points to the larger order beyond. The third is the traditional theistic one. Allowing for some mutations, Taylor believes that identifying these three broad frontiers helps us to make sense of the changing notions of modern selfhood from the scientific revolution to the present day (1989a: 390, 495, 498). The first moral horizon or frontier focuses on the self and its powers. It includes the individual's aspirations to disengagement and to rational ordering and instrumental control of both the natural world and the non-rational parts of the self. As such it covers the ideas discussed above under the heading of disengaged freedom. However, this individualist frontier also encompasses the expressive powers of the self and its quest to articulate and live in accordance with its own authenticity. As we have seen, this latter aspect of modern selfhood evolved partly as a reaction to the ideal of disengaged freedom. But what unites them from this perspective is that they centre on the individual.

The second new moral horizon or frontier refers to nature as the wider whole of which the individual is a part. The idea is, as discussed above in connection with the theory of moral sentiments, that the world is an entity whose components conduce to each other's benefit and preservation. This wider vista is also present in the Romantic idea that nature is a source of the good. However, there is also a place for the individual within this wider vista, as evidenced by the beliefs that human emotions and sentiments are important constituents of this larger harmonious whole, and that in order to make contact with nature I can turn inward as well as outward (*ibid.*: 314–15). This inward turn brings to the second frontier a focus on the individual and her powers. However, this outlook sees no strong separation between the individual and the outside world; rather the emphasis is on a proper appreciation of the connection between the two. Turning inward can connect or reconnect the individual to the wider whole of which he or she is a part (1991a: 91). The possibility of this helps to explain Taylor's claim that the individualism of modern culture need not express itself only in unbridled selfishness and lack of concern for others or for nature (1991a: 35, 40–41).

This close connection between inside and outside that is posited in the second frontier, the link between the individual and the wider world, also informs Taylor's analysis of post-Romantic art. He calls this sort of art epiphanic, and considers such works of art as moral sources, talking about "the search for moral sources *outside* the subject through languages which resonate *within* him or her" (1989a: 510, original emphasis; cf. 420, 479). In this new understanding of art there is a clear sense that the artist is articulating a personal vision, rather than giving expression to some readily available public framework of meaning. So this sort of art is obviously downstream from the scientific revolution and the disenchantment of the world described above. However, the artist's vision is not exclusively personal; there is a sense that he or she is giving personal expression to a reality that can be made available to others through the work of art. The work of art gives expression to something that is of the highest moral or spiritual significance, yet this reality and its availability are not separable from the individual artist's expression of it. In Taylor's terms, this sort of moral vision, which has transpersonal resonance, is indexed to the artist's personal vision (*ibid.*: 420, 427–9, 491–2, 510). To explain this development he distinguishes between a subjectivization of manner and of matter in post-Romantic, epiphanic art. The manner of expression is subjective in that the artist gives a powerfully personal expression of his or her vision. But the matter is not wholly subjective; the artist is connecting his or her audience with a wider reality, connecting them with a moral source (*ibid.*: 425;

1991a: 84–9). Taylor's remarks about poetry apply to this sort of art in general:

> In the post-Enlightenment world, the epiphanic power of words cannot be treated as a fact about the order of things which holds unmediated by the works of the creative imagination . . . To be moved by the poem is also to be drawn into the personal sensibility which holds all these together. The deeper, more general truth emerges only through this.
>
> (1989a: 481; cf. 492)

Just as both of these two new moral frontiers with their focus on the individual and his or her powers on the one hand, and the wider world on the other, intersect with one another, so they both overlap with the third, older moral frontier, which is the theistic one. As noted earlier, Taylor argues that the emphasis on the disengaged, punctual self that grew out of the scientific revolution was religious in its origins. It placed great emphasis on reason, on the possibility of rational control over nature and the non-rational parts of the self. "The awesome powers of human reason and will are God-made and part of God's plan; more, they are what constitutes the image of God in us" (*ibid.*: 315). So in exercising reason, the disengaged individual was deploying a capacity conferred by God, one that distinguished humans from the rest of creation. This explains why the capacity for and exercise of reason were so closely bound up with a sense of human dignity. The same applies to the second new moral frontier; it too had Christian origins. Nature was originally seen as good, by the deists and then by Rousseau, because it was God's creation, an expression of his goodness and love.

However, in a move that parallels the career of the affirmation of ordinary life, over time both these moral horizons lost touch with their theistic foundations and developed a life and rationale of their own. Their goods came to be seen as goods in their own right, no longer needing reference to a Christian god to validate them. Indeed, in some cases they even seemed hostile to Christianity, or at least to organized religion. Taylor expresses this change when he writes that:

> something important and irreversible did happen in the latter part of the nineteenth century with the rise of unbelief in

Anglo-Saxon countries. It was then that they moved from a horizon in which belief in God in some form was virtually unchallengeable to our present predicament in which theism is one option among others, in which moral sources are ontologically diverse.   (*ibid.*: 401; cf. 408)

It is at this point that Taylor's historicist approach to the self dovetails with his more formal argument about constitutive goods in moral theory, for he claims that recovering the original foundations of a moral outlook can inspire or re-inspire adherence to it.[34]

Taylor's powerful sense of the multiplicity of the modern identity explains his claim that the modern self always exceeds its articulations of itself. As naturally self-interpreting animals, humans are led to try to understand and define ourselves, but what the modern era has shown, and intensified, is that this ambition can never be fully realized, that this project of self-interpretation will always necessarily remain incomplete.

Politics and selfhood

Reviewing *Sources of the Self*, Shklar observes that politics "is not a significant component of the self-interpreting self that Taylor traces here" (1991: 105). While it is true that the discussion of politics does not occupy a major place in *Sources of the Self*, it is not wholly absent either. Taylor points, for example, to the idea of individuals being rights bearers as a distinctively modern one and to the fact that some form of democracy is seen as the only legitimate form of rule in modern western societies. This is partly connected with the levelling tendencies associated with the affirmation of everyday life (Taylor 1989a: 395). Modern individuals are, in principle at least, one another's equals in the civil and political spheres (1999b: 139). The emphasis on individual authenticity has its counterpart at the cultural and political level and has given rise to a positive view of nationalism as expressing the specific characteristics of different cultures. Taylor nominates Herder as pivotal in the articulation of both the personal and the political strands of the ethic of authenticity (1975a: 20; 1989a: 376, 414–15). The rise of nationalism is itself connected with the collapse of traditional hierarchies and the levelling tendencies previously mentioned, for nationalism provides a new, horizontal way of integrating people into a political community. The attrition of fixed, traditional social hierarchies that made the presumption of equality imaginable creates the need for new approaches to identity and recognition in the political sphere (1985b: 274–6).

None the less, Shklar is correct to note that politics does not play a major role in fashioning selfhood in *Sources of the Self*. However, it should not be inferred that Taylor sees politics and selfhood as being largely disconnected from one another. The ideal of the free, disengaged self that Taylor traces to the scientific revolution is, for example, also free of social embedding (Taylor 1991c: 307), and it is just this atomistic view of the self that he criticizes in many of his writings on politics. As we have seen, one of the ways in which he rejects ontological individualism is to posit the dialogical self. The way in which this aspect of the self can take on political significance is explored in his analysis of the politics of recognition. Such connections between politics and selfhood are examined in the discussion in Chapter 3 of Taylor's political theory.

Chapter 3

Theorizing politics

This chapter examines Taylor's contributions to political theory. It begins with the communitarian elements of his thought. These are, following Taylor's own advice, broken down into two types: ontological and advocacy. His long-standing critiques of negative freedom and of atomism feature prominently in the account of his communitarianism. There is a discussion of the role of shared goods in politics and of his attempt to raise awareness about the significance of the republican or civic humanist tradition in western politics. The second part of the chapter explores Taylor's complicated relationship with liberalism. It covers his defence of rights, the value he accords civil society and his critique of the idea of state neutrality. The challenges posed to traditional conceptions of liberalism by the politics of recognition are also considered. Taylor's interest in the social and political manifestations and consequences of pluralism also wends its way through this chapter.

Taylor and the communitarian tradition

When it comes to political theory, Taylor is typically characterized as a communitarian. Communitarianism is a broad philosophical approach to questions of politics, law, society and identity. When numbered among communitarians, Taylor joins a group of Anglo-American political philosophers whose better known members include Alasdair MacIntyre, Michael Sandel, Michael Walzer, Jean Bethke Elshtain and Amitai Etzioni.[1] Philosophers as politically different as Aristotle, David Hume, Edmund Burke and Karl Marx can be considered, retrospectively at least, as contributing to the communitarian tradition.

As its name suggests, communitarianism's general concern is with the bonds of community – their importance, creation, maintenance and reproduction. Some communitarians associate the community with the nation-state, and argue that the state should be active in promoting the conditions that allow communities to flourish. Others point to the myriad ways in which people participate in communities that are both given and chosen, from the household to neighbourhoods, clubs and associations, schools and parishes.[2] It is even possible to belong to a virtual community by feeling a sense of shared belonging to and involvement in a group that is not confined to a particular place and whose members might never see one another's faces. Some users of the Internet fall into this category,[3] but so do members of Amnesty International and the Rotary Club.

A deeper understanding of communitarianism can be obtained via Taylor's identification of the two levels of thinking within this tradition. He calls these the ontological and advocacy aspects of communitarianism (Taylor 1995a: 181–203). At the ontological level, communitarian thinkers insist on the importance of communal or collective forces in explaining such things as social life and individual identity. Instead of seeing society as an aggregate of cooperating and competing individuals, or as a sort of tacit contract among individual citizens in the way liberalism traditionally has, communitarians point to the shared elements that make social life possible, that cannot be reduced to individual choices, desires, intentions or possessions.

Communitarians point, for example, to the social preconditions of individual rights. In order for individuals to bear and exercise their rights, there must also be a community of people carrying out their social responsibilities or duties (1994b: 130). In western societies, individuals have long been entitled to claim the right to trial by a jury of their peers, but this right can only be realized if their fellow citizens fulfil their jury duty. In some countries university students claim a right to publicly funded or subsidized education, but this is only possible if their fellow citizens pay taxes, and they eventually reciprocate in this responsibility, and so on.

At a deeper level, however, even the language of individualism is shown to be available only within a certain culture, and culture, like language, is not an accretion of individual choices but a shared, collective heritage. Communitarians draw attention to the fact that it is only within this broader social and cultural context that certain possibilities and self-conceptions for individuals become conceivable. For example, it is not possible for an individual to value autonomy or to see himself or herself as a bearer of rights and freedoms unless these goods are available in the wider culture. Hence Taylor's claim that even "the free individual or autonomous agent", so heavily inscribed in the common sense of liberal cultures, "can only achieve and maintain his identity in a certain type of culture". Such an individual "is only what he is by virtue of the whole society and civilisation which brought him to be and which nourishes him" (1985b: 205–6; cf. 207, 209).[4] So at the ontological level, communitarianism is an explanatory approach to certain issues, drawing attention to the centrality of social rather than purely individual forces in creating, reproducing and recreating society and culture.

The other level of communitarianism identified by Taylor deals with what he calls advocacy issues. These encompass the things that a political theorist or tradition values and valorizes. At this level communitarians affirm and promote shared goods, things that cannot be enjoyed by individuals alone or that call for collective action. For many communitarians, invigorating a sense of solidarity is as difficult as it is urgent in a world where social and economic forces like the movements of global capital, privatization, multiculturalism and the changed nature of work threaten any immediate sense of community. Both levels of communitarian thinking – the ontological and the advocacy – operate in Taylor's political thought. Turning first to the ontological level, two enduring features of his political thought stand out. The first is his attack on atomism, which can be found from his first book onwards (1964: 10–17) and the second is his critique of negative freedom.

Atomism

Taylor's insistence that the self is always socially situated and always points beyond itself to its social relationships, which is discussed in Chapter 2, is the basis for his attack on atomism. In the context of political philosophy he associates atomism directly with the rise of social contract thought from the seventeenth century onwards, and in particular the work of English philosophers Thomas Hobbes and John Locke. For Taylor's purposes, one of the distinctive features of this tradition is the ontological priority it accords the individual. (1989a: 193–4)[5] Notwithstanding the salient differences between Hobbes and Locke, both, as social contract thinkers, conjure an image of life in the state of nature, and conjecture about what existence would be like without political structures (1995a: 213–14). They try to explain why individuals would freely and rationally choose to create a government for themselves; why they would consent to give up some of their individual power and freedom to the state. Not only is the fact of politics something to be explained from this perspective, but it is explained in terms of individual choices, interests or motivations. According to Hobbes, for example, individuals in the state of nature agree to establish a government with extensive power over them in return for security and stability. The author of the *Leviathan* believes that without this security and stability, a range of basic material and cultural goods would be impossible. When individuals transfer power to government through the mechanism of the social contract, they are not only protecting their existence but also improving the quality and comfort of their lives; they are making "commodious living" possible. The rationale for government is that it can generate the conditions that allow individuals to achieve their desires and improve the quality of their lives.

According individuals ontological primacy in this way is, in Taylor's belief, theoretically untenable. From his point of view social contract theorists are wrong to assume that individuals who exist outside political society are capable of reason and speech, let alone the mechanisms for attaining agreement among themselves. Following Aristotle, Hume and Rousseau, he contends that these distinctively human capacities can only be realized in a social and political context. Taylor distinguishes his approach from the atomist one by saying that he adheres to:

> a social view of man . . . which holds that an essential constitutive condition of seeking the human good is bound up with being in society . . . man cannot even be a moral subject . . . [nor] a candidate for realisation of the human good, outside of

a community of language and mutual discourse about the good
and bad, just and unjust . . . what man derives from society is
not some aid in realising his good, but the very possibility of
being an agent seeking that good.   (1985b: 292)

As this suggests, part of what makes Taylor a communitarian
thinker at the ontological level is his claim that certain possibilities for, choices of and goods valued by individuals can only appear
against a wider cultural background.

In this context then, Taylor replaces the primacy of the individual with the primacy of community. This is not to suggest that
individuals do not matter in his outlook nor that identifying the
power of social forces that shape them is tantamount to claiming
that all individuals are wholly determined by society. Rather, the
liberal ideal of the individual taking a critical distance from her
society's values, customs and traditions is, from the communitarian point of view, a position made possible by a wider culture
that values and promotes critical reasoning and independent
thinking.[6] Taylor's concern here is to draw attention to a fundamental aspect of individual identity, which comes from the fact of
belonging to a community. Community membership is important
in a couple of ways. Firstly, because certain goods and even conceptions of the self are only available to individuals by virtue of the
culture to which they belong, the fact of belonging to a community
or society takes pride of place in explaining political norms, values
and practices. By Taylor's analysis, any affirmation of individual
freedom or rights effectively points beyond itself to affirm the
conditions of possibility of this good; that is, the wider community
and culture (*ibid.*: 275–6). From the fact that certain goods are only
available by virtue of the community to which one belongs, Taylor
infers an obligation to the community. The logic of his claim is that:

if I affirm A (individual freedom) and
if B (my membership in the community) is a necessary
    condition of A
therefore, in affirming A I should affirm B.

This explains his conclusion that "the free individual who affirms
himself as such *already* has an obligation to complete, restore, or
sustain the society within which this identity is possible" (*ibid.*: 209,
original emphasis).[7] According to this logic, affirming something as

good for myself as an individual entails an obligation to others in my society, for without the wider society, my "individual" good would be unavailable.

The powerful impact of Hegel on Taylor's thought is discernible here, for this argument that affirming goods entails the affirmation of the conditions of their possibility is very close to the Hegelian notion of *Sittlichkeit*. As Taylor explains it, this notion refers to the obligations which members of a society have to sustain and develop it: "what Hegel calls *Sittlichkeit* . . . refers to the moral obligations I have to an ongoing community of which I am part" (1979a: 83). In Hegel's doctrine, what makes a society worthy of affirmation and reproduction is that it is founded on the "Idea". Taylor jettisons this aspect of Hegel's thought but retains the idea that the individual has an obligation to affirm and perpetuate the goods he enjoys and affirms that are made possible by his membership in society. What Taylor takes to be "the crucial characteristic of *Sittlichkeit* is that it enjoins us to bring about what already is" (*ibid.*: 83; cf. 85, 89, 125, 129; 1975a: 376; 1978a: 137; 1991e: 71). He is not proposing that individuals are obliged to perpetuate their society no matter what its character, nor even every aspect of their society. No bonds of identification and loyalty to societies that are corrupt or exploitative are being recommended by him. Rather the idea is that in so far as a person values, affirms and identifies with the goods of his or her society, then he or she is obliged to contribute to their maintenance and reproduction (see Friedman 1994: 303; Flanagan 1996: 165).

Hegel is, in fact, an important influence on Taylor's rejection of atomism in general because of the importance he imputes to locating the individual within his or her wider community (Taylor 1979a: 86–7). Taylor's immersion in Hegel's thought helped him to identify the ubiquity of atomist assumptions in western culture generally and within the social sciences more particularly. So tight is the hold of atomism on the modern western social and political imagination that it comes to be taken for granted as the "natural" or default position. Taylor's diagnosis is that

> Atomist views always seem nearer to common sense, more immediately available . . . It's as though without a special effort of reflection on this issue, we tend to fall back into an atomist/instrumental way of seeing. This seems to dominate our unreflecting experience of society. (1989a: 196; cf. 1991a: 58).

One thing that arises from this account of Taylor's criticism of atomism is how closely connected the ontological and advocacy levels of a theoretical position can be. His critique begins with the charge of analytical inadequacy and concludes with a claim about the wider cultural conditions and goods that should be acknowledged and promoted by individuals who value their freedom. He believes that this sort of criticism of the atomism of western political thinking is not of historical interest only, for he finds that many aspects of the individualism of social contract thought remain entrenched in western politics today (1989a: 195).[8] More specifically, some of the ideas and assumptions from early social contract theory continue to ramify through liberal political thought; he points to the work of influential American thinkers such as Robert Nozick, John Rawls and Bruce Ackerman. This individualism is also firmly embedded in the Public Choice school of thought, which applies categories from economics such as preferences, utility maximization, self-interest, rent-seeking, collective action problems and so forth to the explanation of political behaviour.[9]

Taylor's strong challenge to political theories that accord ontological primacy to the individual clearly gives him some common cause with communitarians. Another enduring feature of his political philosophy has been his analysis of negative freedom.[10] This culminates in his endorsement of positive freedom, which gives his thought a communitarian cast at the advocacy level too.

Freedom

The distinction between positive and negative freedom was given its influential twentieth-century formulation by Isaiah Berlin. He offered this as a way of summarizing two distinct conceptions of freedom in the western tradition of political thought (Berlin 1969: 118–72; Taylor 1975a: 560). The phrase "negative freedom" applies to approaches that focus on the individual and associate freedom with the absence of interference from outside sources, whether this external force is the state or society in general. The classical statement of this sort of freedom is usually seen as appearing in Chapter 1 of John Stuart Mill's essay *On Liberty*, where the harm principle is also formulated (Mill, 1980). According to this, an individual should be free from interference or constraint in so far as his or her actions do no harm to others. However, the negative view of freedom is older and wider than Mill's account: an earlier negative approach to freedom appears in Hobbes's work when he defines freedom as the absence of impediments to motion (Hobbes 1974: 204). Some of the other thinkers who are seen to espouse a negative conception of freedom include John Locke, Thomas Paine, Jeremy Bentham, Benjamin Constant and Thomas Jefferson. Those who advocate a range of freedoms for individuals, such as the freedoms of speech, worship, assembly, publication, occupation, marriage, travel and so forth are also championing a negative view of freedom.

It is important to understand that the labels negative and positive are not being used here in an evaluative way. Calling one of these conceptions of freedom "negative" is not intended to signify any criticism of it. On the contrary, many liberals have been very positive (in the evaluative and colloquial sense) about negative liberty. They have, conversely, been negative about positive liberty, in the sense of being sceptical or critical about this conception of freedom. So rather than understanding these labels in the usual colloquial way, it is important to appreciate they that are being used here in a technical sense. Negative freedom exists when things are *not* done to the individual against his or her will. The positive approach to freedom focuses not on leaving individuals a sphere of free space in which they can do as they please without interference from others but on enabling or empowering them to do certain things, to achieve outcomes or to realize particular purposes. The accent here is on the individual achieving some control over his or her own life, some measure of self-mastery or self-direction. In some areas, the self-mastery promoted by positive freedom might not be attainable by acting, or being left, alone. If, for example, achieving some control over one's life or exercising some self-direction requires self-government or some level of participation in democratic decision making, then cooperation with others is necessary for realizing positive freedom. From this standpoint, a whole people or society can only be considered free if they rule themselves. Even if individuals within the subjugated population are left alone and uninterfered with, they still cannot be thought of as free according to the positive notion. A benevolent despot might allow his or her subjects all sorts of negative freedoms, but this would not make them free because they are not self-governing.

Taylor is a champion of this sort of positive freedom in the political realm (he is positive about positive liberty!) and part of his political philosophy involves applying this approach to politics. As one sympathetic to the tradition of positive freedom, Taylor could complain that Berlin's depiction of this approach is caricatured and unfair. Berlin could be accused of moving too quickly from associating positive freedom with the requirement that the government create conditions for individuals to realize their potential to linking it with the excesses and unfreedom of totalitarian regimes.[11] So part of Taylor's response to Berlin's influential essay involves a reappraisal of positive freedom, a recognition of its more appealing aspects. However, Taylor's critique of negative freedom is not based simply on a normative preference for positive freedom nor his interest in participation in politics; rather he thinks that there are certain aspects of the negative approach to freedom that are problematic and even incoherent.

Taylor begins his critique of negative freedom by questioning the line of demarcation that supposedly separates positive and negative freedom. He contrasts an "exercise concept of freedom" with an "opportunity concept of freedom" (1985b: 213). Some forms of negative freedom can be understood wholly in terms of an opportunity concept, while others require an exercise concept of freedom. In this they resemble all positive notions of freedom. Taylor is, in effect, deconstructing the putative opposition between positive and negative freedom by showing that there is a salient characteristic that is shared by all notions of positive freedom and some notions of negative freedom. This characteristic is the exercise concept of freedom.

Exercise concepts associate freedom with activating some capacity; for self-rule, self-mastery or self-direction, for example. The strict version of negative freedom, by contrast, presupposes an opportunity concept of freedom, because it is enough that individuals are left alone to do as they please: there is no requirement that anything be done or realized for an individual to be free. All that is necessary is that individuals have the chance to act or not act as they choose. In the most basic negative approach to freedom, what matters is the opportunity or possibility to act in a certain way, not whether this possibility is taken advantage of. As long as one is free from outside interference, one is free, irrespective of what one does within that space of freedom as non-intervention. As Berlin puts it, "The wider the area of non-interference the wider my freedom" (1969: 123).[12]

Not all versions of negative freedom adhere to this opportunity concept of freedom, however. Taylor distinguishes between the crude versions of negative freedom, such as those outlined by Hobbes and Bentham, and others that veer towards an exercise concept of freedom. For these other types of negative freedom, the absence of external interference is simply a pre-condition for the individual to determine his or her own direction or to realize certain possibilities, such as autonomy. For this line of thinking, absence of interference is a necessary but not sufficient condition of freedom. Freedom requires something more than the mere absence of intervention from others. Mill's emphasis on autonomy and self-development seems to illustrate this; having a sphere of negative freedom is important because it allows individuals to develop in their own peculiar ways, according to their own values, rather than being pressured to conform by society at large.[13]

From revealing this salient difference among the advocates of negative freedom, Taylor goes on to argue that those who promote the crude version are advocating an indefensible view of freedom. In making this move he goes beyond deconstructing the boundary between positive and negative types of freedom to challenging the very bases of the strict notion of negative freedom. He argues that for a notion of freedom to be coherent, it must presuppose discriminations among types of action and, conversely, among limitations on freedom. Strict versions of negative freedom fail or refuse to make these sorts of qualitative judgements, and therein lies their appeal to many people. Instead, they tend to depict freedom in quantitative terms. By refusing to uphold some forms of action, some human capacities or some individual choices as superior to others, they adopt a non-judgemental stance that derives from a respect for human equality and individual freedom. But Taylor insists that this undifferentiated approach to freedom is implausible: understanding freedom demands that qualitative discriminations be drawn among an individual's motivations, desires and capacities. If the idea of freedom is to be compelling, it must be recognized that some choices, interests, motivations and purposes are higher, more important, worthier or more deserving of respect than others.

To illustrate this point, consider the Hobbesian notion of freedom. Defining freedom as the absence of impediments to motion, this negative approach works with an opportunity concept of freedom. This definition covers an array of quite different possibilities for free action and, conversely, freedom can be impinged on or violated in a variety of ways (Taylor 1985b: 218). I can, for example, complain that my freedom of motion is impeded when roadworks require me to take an unwelcome detour on my way home from work. This is, after all, an impediment to motion. However, I can also complain that on my way home from a political rally the police have unlawfully detained me. Once again, my freedom of movement has been violated. Under the strict definition of freedom, both are equally violations. Yet most people would agree that by comparison with the second, the first is relatively trivial and barely qualifies as an intrusion on freedom. This is not just because the first is a minor inconvenience, but because it makes little dent in my capacity to live my life in the way that I see fit. No integral part of an individual's personality is damaged when he or she is required to take a detour to work. The second violation of freedom, my unlawful detention, is, by contrast, a major inconvenience and, more importantly, could be a source of great injustice. It might infringe my rights as a citizen and seriously interfere with the conduct of my life. For Taylor, to consider these two sorts of violations of freedom as comparable, as the crude, negative notion of freedom does, robs the idea of freedom of its critical leverage and its most important connotations.

For Taylor then, in order for a concept of freedom to be meaningful it necessarily involves, even if only implicitly, the recognition of qualitative differences in desires or purposes. Being free in a meaningful sense requires more than just being able to do what one wants. There must be some rank-ordering of the individual's wants or desires: the desire to get home as quickly as possible is not of the same order as the desire to be free to criticize the government without the threat of incarceration. A meaningful concept of freedom must include, therefore, the possibility of discriminating among individual wants or desires and realizing that some are higher, more significant or less negotiable than others. Taylor's insistence on the rank-ordering of goods contains echoes of his argument about strong evaluation in moral life (*ibid.*: 220–26).[14] Freedom requires that the individual live in accordance with his or her higher goals or at least strive to realize them. We would not really classify someone as free just because they could ride directly home every night if their life did not also involve the realization of some other, more important, purpose or goal.

The obvious question to arise from this is which capacities, purposes or desires are more important than others. Taylor's response is that the process of working out which are more or less significant draws on background understandings of what is important in human life. These background understandings are heavily inscribed in the wider culture, and they vary across cultures. In western culture, being free from arbitrary arrest has long been a central good for all sorts of reasons, many of which are bound up with the idea of being a free citizen rather than simply a pawn of the state. It could be that on some far away planet, arriving home punctually *is* more important than not being detained unlawfully by the police. But this would be a very distant planet and it would be a stretch of our semantics to call this society free if their freedom resided solely in the absence of roadblocks.

Yet this language of higher goals, or more and less significant desires, which Taylor believes is essential to the correct understanding of freedom, deters many people, including Berlin, from this approach. It sounds metaphysical and/or elitist to talk of higher purposes. Similar scepticism is directed at the idea of the divided self, which seems to be presupposed by the positive approach to liberty. In order to talk about self-mastery for an individual, there must be some part of the self that is mastered, and another that masters. The idea that the self can be divided into parts, with the higher, better or truer part striving to control the lower, weaker or inauthentic self sounds Platonic and anachronistic to critics of positive liberty.

Undeterred by such reservations, Taylor defends the positive conception of freedom by insisting that such discriminations must be made if freedom is to be fully understood. He further contends that sometimes the individual is not the best judge of his or her own real interests and higher motivations, nor of whether he or she is in the process of realizing or acting upon them. To advocates of strict negative freedom who believe that freedom inheres in non-interference from others, this concession that someone else might be a better judge of an individual's progress towards a significant goal or purpose in his or her life opens the door to totalitarianism or domination of some form. For them the concession that the individual is not always the best judge of the direction of his or her life stands at the start of a slippery (and steep, short) slope to the concession that society, the party or the government can decide for others.

However, for Taylor it seems logical that once we have conceded that freedom involves some sense of self-direction, and that some motivations and desires are more integral to an individual's identity than others, we can also agree that the individual's motivations are not always perspicuous to him or her. An individual might not always be directed by the things that are most important to him or her; there can be internal barriers to acting in accordance with one's higher motivations, purposes, interests or goals. These barriers need not betoken some abnormal psychological condition; rather, they are familiar to us from everyday life. In some circumstances an individual might be confused about what really matters in his or her life and contemplate a move that would jeopardize core interests or goals. In others he or she might be deceiving himself or herself about these things. At others he or she might lack the confidence to attempt certain tasks that would help him or her to achieve the things that really matter. Once these admissions of the human, all too human, have been made, it can be agreed that individuals, even rational, adult ones, are not always the best judges of their interests, goals and motivations. From this standpoint, the error of equating freedom simply with being able to do what one wants, free from outside intervention, becomes manifest. As Taylor says, in those cases where:

> we are quite self-deceived, or utterly fail to discriminate properly the ends we seek, or have lost self-control, we can quite easily be doing what we want in the sense of what we can identify as our wants, without being free; indeed, we can be further entrenching our unfreedom.
>
> (1985b: 215; cf. 222, 227)

Just how far Taylor's account of positive liberty is from Berlin's depiction of the party or state having privileged knowledge of the individuals' higher, truer or deeper selves and forcing them to be free by acting in conformity with this knowledge also becomes apparent. The basic point Taylor is trying to drive home is that the proper understanding of freedom requires making qualitative discriminations among an individual's desires and goals. The limits that any society puts on individual freedom must also be considered in this way; do the constraints impair some of its citizens' central aspirations? The problem with the blanket Hobbesian claim that liberty lies in the silence of the laws (Hobbes 1974: ch. 21), along with the contemporary view that deregulation will necessarily increase freedom, is that both outlooks are too general to tell us anything useful about freedom. Not all laws, restrictions or regulations are equally constraining, and all the aspects of our lives constrained by them are not equally significant. In order to promote freedom, Taylor believes that it is essential to distinguish those laws that restrict or hamper significant human capacities from those that do not. These, in turn, need to be distinguished from those rules and laws that might promote significant human capacities – such as the requirement that all children undergo compulsory education for a certain number of years. This general belief that the law can sometimes protect and promote liberty is one of the aspects of the republican tradition that informs Taylor's approach to politics.[15] It is, moreover, through his admiration for this tradition that we can see most clearly the implications that his positive conception of freedom has for politics.

Republicanism

Taylor's critique of the negative notion of freedom is not motivated solely by his perceptions of its errors and inadequacies. He is a champion of the positive notion of freedom and this extends into his normative political thinking as well. At one point he suggests that when it comes to political theory, negative freedom can be called liberal freedom and, by implication, positive freedom is "civic freedom" (1999a: 94). The positive conception sees freedom as involving self-mastery and self-direction and for Taylor an important aspect of such self-direction is participation in democratic politics. He believes that the person who lives in a democracy without making any attempt to influence the decisions that affect his or her life is in a sense unfree (1985b: 275; 1995a: 192–3, 199–200). More broadly, he perpetuates Aristotle's belief that participation in democratic politics is a component of the good life, and that the individual who avoids, or is disbarred from, involvement in politics is failing to realize the distinctive human capacity for debate and deliberation about issues of shared concern (1985b: 208, 1994d: 252; 1994f: 33; 1995a: 192).[16] As this illustrates, Taylor's political theory cannot be wholly divorced from his views about personhood and ethics, from what it means to be a human being and what it is good to be and to do.

In this regard, Taylor's political thought is very different from the dominant tradition within liberalism, which has tended to view politics with suspicion. Many liberals fear the coercive power of the state and seek to minimize its size and scope. As the earlier reference to the social contract tradition indicates, liberals have also tended to see politics primarily in instrumental terms, asking what functions the state can fulfil that cannot be fulfilled in other ways (1995a: 220). Because this negative view of politics has been so influential in western societies, part of Taylor's political philosophy is dedicated to retrieving and endorsing some of the elements of the civic humanist or republican approach to politics.[17] He believes that while this tradition has also been influential in modern western democracies, it has not always been recognized or articulated as such. He is therefore trying to give more formal expression to elements that exist tacitly in, which form part of the background of, the political culture of these societies (1985b: 132, 275, 313; 1984a: 26–7; 1989a: 197; 1994d: 225; 1998c: 151).[18] As he writes:

> Modern western societies are all citizen republics, or strive to be. Their conception of the good is partly shaped by the tradition of civic humanism. The citizen republic is to be valued not just as a guarantee of general utility, or as a bulwark of rights. It might even endanger these in certain circumstances. We value it also because we generally hold that the form of life in which men govern themselves, and decide their own fate through common deliberation, is higher than one in which they live as subjects of even an enlightened despotism.
>
> (1985b: 245; cf. 275)

As this suggests, the civic humanist tradition emphasizes citizen self-rule, and takes patriotism, solidarity, a sense of allegiance to one's political community, collective action and participation in government to be crucial components of this (1989a: 196–7; 1995a: 141, 192; 1999d).[19]

Hegel is an important source for Taylor's thinking about the civic humanist tradition and its association of freedom with citizen self-rule (1991e). Yet some liberals have endorsed the values of civic freedom too. John Stuart Mill is a clear example of a liberal who promotes citizen participation in politics, not just in order to keep a watch on officers of the state but because such involvement is valuable in itself and contributes to personal development. Montesquieu and De Tocqueville are other figures in the liberal tradition who see participation in politics as intrinsically valuable (indeed, the latter was an important influence on Mill's thought). In invoking these liberals as champions of political participation, Taylor is not only challenging any absolute separation of liberal and civic freedom but he is also mounting an immanent critique of liberalism. He believes that the way liberalism has been interpreted has privileged negative freedom to the neglect of civic freedom, and he is trying to challenge that reading from within the liberal tradition itself, by countering one interpretation of liberalism with another (1995a: 221). (This point about duelling liberalisms is discussed further below.)

More generally, Taylor believes that while these two types of freedom, liberal or negative on the one hand and civic on the other, can push in contrary directions, both are necessary for democracy to flourish. In contemporary democracies, for example, it would be hard to imagine what it would mean to value citizen participation in politics yet refuse people the negative liberty of free speech (1990a: 94–5, 98). So here again we witness his tendency to challenge what seem to be binary separations and to question just how antagonistic seeming antitheses really are.

Patriotism

Taylor contends that not only has participation in politics been devalued by the liberal tradition, but so has the significance of individuals seeing themselves as part of a political community and identifying with that community (1999a: 98–9). In this he is echoing one of the general communitarian criticisms of liberalism; that it neglects the value and importance of political community (Kymlicka 1993: 366). Making a general communitarian point, he contends that individuals' sense of belonging to a political community is an important layer of their identity. In modern western societies, this sense of being part of a community has typically manifested itself in nationalism, in feeling some special attachment to the country in which one was born or to which one has migrated (or both) (Taylor 1997b: 40; 1998c: 150). Although Taylor acknowledges that the twentieth century is replete with virulent, damaging manifestations of nationalism (1995a: 196, 199), he sees the sense of belonging to a political community as a necessary feature of political life. Seeing all appeals to nationalism as necessarily myopic, xenophobic and destructive is symptomatic of the reductionist temper of much modern thought and simply hampers attempts to understand this phenomenon. Characteristically, he seeks to complicate matters, pointing out that nationalism can take many different forms. Of those who see all nationalisms as essentially the same, albeit with milder and stronger manifestations, he asks:

> Is there a single phenomenon? Maybe we're making things even harder for ourselves by assuming that there is something called "nationalism" that is the same wherever people make demands in the name of ethnic/cultural self-determination, so that Bosnian Serbs and Québécois are placed in the same category.　　　　　　(1997b: 31; cf. 52; 1990a: 97–8)

While the sort of nationalism that grew up in modern, western societies does have something in common with other damaging forms of nationalism, Taylor argues that its civic character also distinguishes it from them. As he explains, "National pride and identification seems to be an indispensable feature of any modern society, but it is a matter of considerable moment that in many liberal democracies the national identity is defined partly in terms of the institutions of political freedom" (1990a: 98).[20] To further illustrate his claim that not all nationalism is aggressively xenophobic, he points to Herder's early idea of nationalism as something that expresses distinct and valuable collective identities, and that can be practised by different societies in a peaceful and mutually respectful way. Because it militated against the imposition of uniformity, this was a potentially liberating doctrine, and one compatible with democratic ideas (1999d).

The fact that modern patriotism typically takes the form of nationalism should not, therefore, blind us to some of the benefits of patriotism. Defining patriotism in a very general sense as "strong citizen identification around a sense of common good" (1995a: 194), Taylor points to some of its more positive and productive aspects. At the practical level, he believes that the rather anorexic liberal view of politics is incapable of generating the necessary sense of attachment to the state. When politics is portrayed as a necessary evil, as simply providing a framework of rules and laws that allows everyone to pursue the more important things in life, or when the state is seen simply as a mechanism for the provision of public goods that would not be generated by individuals acting alone, it becomes difficult to wrest from citizens the sacrifices that membership of a polity can demand. When politics is seen simply in this atomist and instrumental way, it becomes difficult, if not impossible, to explain how that sort of polity sustains and reproduces itself: what would motivate any individual to make sacrifices for this society and to work to ensure its continuation (1989a: 413–14; 1990a: 95; 1991a: 9–10, 112–13)?[21] Such burdens and sacrifices range from taxation for redistributive purposes, through participation in democratic institutions, to risking one's life in war. Of course these can be extracted forcibly from citizens, but in democracies coercion cannot be the dominant force in achieving compliance. Many people make these sacrifices in a seemingly voluntary manner because of some sense of attachment and obligation to their political community, however unreflective and habitual this sense might be (1978a: 146; 1995a: 187, 193; 1996a: 119–21; 1997b: 39; 1998a: 43). So Taylor would argue that the pure liberal doctrine of politics is unrealistic and unrealizable, and that the functioning of liberal polities has typically depended on other views of politics that impute it, and allegiance to the political community, more than purely instrumental significance (1985: 110; cf. 1994d: 225). He illustrates this with reference to the USA, which many see as the purest model of procedural liberalism. Taylor proposes that in order to make sense of the public response to climactic political events like Watergate and Contragate, it is necessary to appreciate the power of political values and ideals from the republican tradition (1990a: 96; 108–9; 1991e: 73; 1995a: 194–7).

Shared goods

Taylor's criticism of the liberal approach to politics derives not just from the fact that he thinks it is unrealistic and unworkable, although in the study of political theory these are important grounds for critique. He also believes that the atomism of the liberal approach to politics occludes awareness of what he calls "irreducibly social goods".[22] This is another concern that unites Taylor with communitarians (cf. Kymlicka 1993: 367). What the phrase "irreducibly social goods" captures is a category of goods that cannot be disaggregated or decomposed into individual goods but that must be shared by two or more individuals – hence their description as irreducibly social. These shared goods are, at one level, goods for individuals, things that they experience and enjoy. However, Taylor argues that it is a category error to think of them as only individual goods. They are both goods for individuals and goods that can only be generated in common with others. He uses the example of friendship to illustrate this rather abstract claim. When two people are friends, their friendship becomes a good that is shared between them. It is a mistake to understand it as something that could, in theory, be broken down into the sum of two individual goods. The general point he is trying to drive home here is that some things can only be appreciated when they are understood as shared; some goods can only be realized in concert with others. While the existence of the shared good does not depend on the parties' acknowledgment of it as such, it is, however, strengthened by their shared understanding that it is good. To continue the example, it is usually important to the quality of a friendship that the friends value their relationship; even though they might never talk about their relationship as such, it is essential that both parties know in some way that the bond is mutually valued. Without this shared understanding of its value, the relationship is likely to fall into crisis or disintegration, because each party will expect different things of the other.[23]

As this example indicates, the sort of shared goods most people experience exist in that area of life that is typically designated as private in western societies; that is, through friendship, love and other relationships involving such close affective ties. As Taylor says, "our understanding of the good things in life can be transformed by our enjoying them in common with people we love; . . . some goods become accessible to us only through such common enjoyment" (1992a: 33). However, he is adamant that these shared goods play an important role in politics too (1985b: 101).[24] He points again to the civic republican tradition which places great value on public things (*res publica*) such as the laws, public space and the political community's shared history. These things can only be generated, reproduced or commemorated by the citizens acting in common, and they are the joint property of all citizens of that community, including those of the past and future. This sense of attachment to the public things is intimately connected to the ethos of self-government mentioned above; individuals feel a special attachment to the laws and practices of their polity partly because they, and/or their ancestors, have played a role in shaping and maintaining these things. And this sense of attachment provides further motivation for ongoing participation, establishing a virtuous circle between these aspects of politics: participation promotes attachment, which promotes further participation, which strengthens attachment (1995a: 285).[25]

The existence of such goods in politics and elsewhere has, however, been largely neglected by the liberal tradition with its atomist temperament and its unwillingness to see politics as a valuable arena of human action for anything other than instrumental purposes (*ibid.*: 188, 194). Of course Taylor is not suggesting that all political goods are irreducibly social or shared. To do so would simply perpetuate the exclusivist error of the atomist approach: either all goods are individual or they are all social. Instead, he distinguishes shared goods from convergent ones, or subjective goods from inter-subjective ones. Convergent goods are more individual; there is no sense that the goods so valued belong inescapably to a "we". In any society there can be a greater or lesser consensus about convergent goods; they can be values that individuals happen to share, but just as easily might not. As Taylor says, these beliefs and values "could be the property of a single person, or many or all" whereas shared goods or meanings "could not be the property of a single person" (1985b: 37; cf. 1990a: 109). In this he offers political theory a counterpart of his pluralist ontology in moral theory (see Chapter 1).

Taylor's aim in drawing attention to this type of shared good is to shed light on an important feature of politics that has been eclipsed by liberal analyses. More generally, he hopes to redress one of the major weaknesses of mainstream social science, for its atomist ontology lacks any "notion of meaning as not simply for an individual subject; of a subject who can be a 'we' as well as an 'I'" (1985b: 40). But in so doing he is making more than a theoretical point, for his argument has practical consequences. Identifying the existence of shared goods will allow people to acknowledge the distinctive sort of goods they enjoy when they experience things that derive their full meaning from being held in common. Without this recognition, Taylor believes that the power of these goods will be limited. Shared goods like collective action become more vigorous in public life when they are explicitly acknowledged (*ibid.*: 101; 1990a: 99). This points, in turn, to the important role that articulation plays in politics. A necessary, but not sufficient condition of political community is that its members see themselves as belonging to such a community; they must constitute a community for themselves, must understand themselves as a group (1995a: 276). Speech can play an important, but not exclusive, role in building this sense of community; talking about community can strengthen it. Conversely, the failure to talk about shared interests, concerns and identity can atrophy them. Such failure might not destroy the shared interests and concerns, but it does mean that they will not be recognized or acted upon.

Public space

Another important role that language plays in Taylor's analysis of politics emerges from his thesis about language creating public or common space. Language brings things into public space because when something is said it exists in the imagined space between the interlocutors. It is there for them to acknowledge together.[26] Bringing something into public space might not change what is known, but it changes how it is known and how we can talk about it. Something like a political leader's penchant for extra-marital affairs might have been an "open secret" among many, but once it is placed in public space and brought into public knowledge the way it is known changes. It is now something we can remark on freely and openly; we know that others know about or have access to this information. Of course, language alone does not create physical public spaces such as parks or civic centres; rather Taylor is using this term metaphorically. The reason why the metaphor is apt is that in both cases the idea of public space describes something that is shared by those who create, maintain or use it.

In the conventional forum of politics, what is said in parliament, in the media, at political conventions, protest rallies and so on brings things into public space. Ideas, criticism, facts, information and interpretations of history thereby become matters of shared concern and are publicly available for all to remark upon and contest (1985a: 259–60; 1985c: 273–4). However, if language brings something into public space or opens such a space between speakers, not all that is said in this way is political in the usual sense of the term. A conversation between intimates, for example, brings something into common space, but would not be considered political in the traditional sense of the term. So there are different common spaces opened up by language, and the public space of formal politics is one of these.

The idea that there is a public space in which debate and deliberation can take place about matters of shared concern has been central to the democratic tradition in western politics. In the ancient world, collective, formal debate and deliberation about politics occurred in a particular place and brought the participants into face-to-face contact. While the modern process of forming public opinion continued this emphasis on debate and discussion, the ability to communicate through printed material widened the circle of possible interlocutors and obviated the need for assembly in a single place. Participants in the debate resembled what today are called "virtual communities"; groups of people who feel themselves united by a common cause or concern but who need never meet physically. This explains Taylor's description of the public sphere as a "metatopical common space" (1995a: 263): although it brought people together in debate and discussion, it was not confined to a single physical location: it went beyond (*meta*) any particular place (*topos*). Today, of course, changes in technology mean that debate in the public sphere is conducted in a host of ways; newspapers, radio, television and the Internet. Moreover, the discussions conducted in these various media intersect with one another, so that an issue raised in the newspaper will be discussed on talkback radio and/or on television and on the Internet. So notwithstanding their physical separation and the multiple lines of communication, participants in the public sphere have a sense of themselves as involved in the same discussion and as focusing on a common object or issue. So the public space of western politics is now a virtual rather than a physical realm; in principle it unites and is available to all the citizens in the democracy. These participants might never meet or even see one another in a face-to-face way, but they interact about and debate matters of shared concern and behave as if the opinions of others in this space matter (1999c: 169).

While the progress of democracy over the centuries from ancient times to now can be seen as a process of increasing inclusion and widening franchise, Taylor also identifies a dynamic of exclusion in the logic of democracy (1998c; 1999d). His argument runs like this: In order for the democratic principle of popular sovereignty to be realized or even conceptualized, an entity, a people, that can rule itself is required. This body must be capable of common deliberation and the formation of a shared will. This need not demand unanimity, but it does entail the idea that there is a will or opinion held by the majority of people that guides decision making. In the modern world, this idea of the people, of the self-ruling collective entity, has typically been conceived of as the citizenry of a state, and the state has typically been construed as a nation-state. With the rise of nationalism, the state has been seen as providing not only the forum for self-government but as an important source of a common cultural identity. To describe this as the dominant idea is not to deny the reality of multicultural societies nor of nationalist and secessionist movements. However, secessionist drives serve to confirm this understanding of popular sovereignty by proposing that "we" belong to a different people from "you", our rulers, and that as a separate people we are entitled to rule ourselves.

As this point about secessionist impulses signals, democracy's conception of popular sovereignty requires a high degree of cohesion and mutual trust. Those who belong to the collective democratic entity must identify with it to some degree and so must identify with one another to some extent. They must be willing to listen to, and believe themselves to be heard by, their fellows.[27] Yet according to Taylor, it is just this need for a cohesive common identity that generates exclusion in democratic societies. For example, an ethnic minority might see itself and/or be seen by others as not being part of the group. Immigrants might be compelled to assimilate to the dominant culture before they can be accepted as full participants in political society. Women or gay or disabled people might be seen as not really fitting into politics at the highest levels, and so on. Yet this dynamic of exclusion runs counter to the democratic ethos with its emphasis on equality, participation and rule by the people. Taylor summarizes the situation thus:

> Democracies are in a standing dilemma. They need strong cohesion around a political identity, and precisely this provides a strong temptation to exclude those who can't or won't fit easily into the identity which the majority feels comfortable with, or believes can hold them together. And yet exclusion, besides being profoundly morally objectionable, also goes against the legitimacy idea of popular sovereignty, which is to realize the government of *all* the people. The need to form a people as a collective agent runs against the demand for inclusion of all who have a legitimate claim on citizenship.
>
> (Taylor 1999d: 156, original emphasis)

Democracy's logic of exclusion is not, however, insuperable, and in western societies many groups are challenging the demand that they conform in order to belong. Taylor predicts that democracies will face the ongoing challenge of reinventing themselves, and finding new ways of including minority groups. The understandable temptation in this context is simply to advocate the liberal ideals of individual rights, a neutral state and the priority of the right over the good (1998c: 151) (these latter terms are explained below). But for Taylor more of the same is too limited a response to accommodating increasing expressions of diversity. He believes that new understandings of democratic belonging and less rigid conceptions of citizenship will need to be forged (*ibid.*: 150–51). Inspired by the work of Wilhelm von Humboldt, he adumbrates an alternative model of democratic inclusion, one that celebrates the differences among groups and encourages citizens not simply to tolerate but to learn about and engage with one another in the understanding that their differences enrich one another and the polity as a whole (*ibid.*: 153–4). Taylor presents the ideal underlying this as the Christian one that the fullness of humanity cannot be achieved by any individual alone but only through interaction with others who realize different aspects of human potential (*ibid.*: 153). Here we see another way in which Taylor's awareness of and respect for diversity is informed by the Christian tradition (see Chapter 1).[28] This gesture in a Humboldtian direction might seem like a rather loose response to the problem, but Taylor is suspicious of generalizable remedies to such problems and aware of the limited contribution that philosophy can make. How any particular democratic polity reconciles belonging with diversity will depend on its own culture and complexion and cannot be decided from without (*ibid.*: 151).

Communitarianism qualified

Thus far it appears that as a political philosopher Taylor is a communitarian at both the ontological and the advocacy levels. His thought is communitarian ontologically because it continually points to the wider social forces that are needed to explain politics. It is communitarian at the advocacy level because he thinks that acknowledging and affirming some of the goods identified at the ontological level is important.[29] Yet notwithstanding his obvious affinities with the communitarian tradition, Taylor has expressed some reservations about the communitarian epithet being applied to his work (1994d: 250; 1995a: 182–3; 1996c). One reason is that the adjective "communitarian" groups together thinkers who are actually separated by some important differences. It can, therefore, be misleading; it can impute too much similarity to these different thinkers and conceal significant points of disagreement. However, the more important reason why Taylor recoils from the label "communitarian" seems to be the common perception about its relationship to the liberal tradition of political thought. It is not unusual to find communitarianism and liberalism depicted as rival approaches to social and political life. As Alan Ryan says, "hostility to liberalism is . . . the main defining feature of communitarianism" (Ryan 1993: 292). Likewise, Philip Pettit observes that, "In contemporary political theory, liberalism and communitarianism are often presented as the main alternative approaches" (Pettit 1997: 120).

In attacking the atomism of the social contract tradition and criticizing the strict version of negative freedom, Taylor is indeed challenging some of the fundamental tenets of mainstream liberalism. However, Taylor is unwilling to reject liberalism *tout court* (cf. Mulhall & Swift 1997: 102, 164). He prefers to see his project as one of retrieval; rather than repudiate liberalism altogether, he is more interested in recognizing the richness of the liberal tradition and using certain strands of it to challenge some of the more limited, mainstream approaches to liberalism. He thus draws attention to the need to consider liberalism broadly, to reinvigorate some of its strands in order to criticize others and thereby develop a theory of complex liberalism (Taylor 1996c; 1998c: 154).[30]

Taylor's sense of the richness of the liberal tradition stands in marked contrast to what he sees as the dominant urge within contemporary Anglo-American political thought, which strives for "a single principle liberalism". The ambition here is reductionist; to find a simple and straightforward principle or set of related principles that will guide liberals in the organization of society and the resolution of disputes. For example, many liberals adhere to a belief in the priority of the right over the good as the basic principle of political life (this is explained below). Sharing Berlin's awareness of the pluralism of goods, observing the increasing diversity of society, and being generally suspicious of reductionism in any aspect of the human sciences, Taylor rejects any such abstract principles as being necessary or sufficient in all cases. As he says:

Berlin has tirelessly pointed out the irreconcilable conflict that
we frequently face between different goods which we cannot
help subscribing to. The modern vogue of ethical thinking,
which tends to try to derive all our obligations from some
single principle, has tended to hide and muffle these conflicts.
(1994d: 213; cf. 248).

In a move that parallels his critique of formalism in moral theory,
Taylor asserts that "no single-consideration procedure, be it that of
utilitarianism, or a theory of justice based on an ideal contract, can
do justice to the diversity of goods we have to weigh together in
normative political thinking" (1985b: 245; cf. 1994e: 177).

Taylor's pluralism therefore informs his view of politics as much
as it does his moral theory and approach to selfhood. For him,
politics will always involve complexity and conflicts and it is a
dangerous fantasy to believe that any single principle or formula
will be adequate in resolving these. The sort of decision making
involved in politics demands something closer to Aristotle's notion
of practical wisdom than the appeal to any basic principle that can
be invoked to resolve all disputes.[31] As he says:

There are always a plurality of goods, vying for our allegiance,
and one of the most difficult issues is how to combine them,
how to adjudicate at the places where they come into conflict,
or mutually restrict each other. I have no difficulty with the
idea that offering the greatest scope for different modes of life
and conceptions of the good is *an* important goal. I cavil at the
idea that it can be *the* goal; that is, that it doesn't have at
certain points to compose with other ends, which will require
its limitation. (Taylor 1994d: 250, original emphasis)

Such resistance to reducing complex questions of politics to single
principles also informs Taylor's reluctance to be counted as a
communitarian. In so far as communitarians see themselves, or
are seen by others, as wanting to make community the fundamental good in political life, then for Taylor they are simply substitut-
ing the liberal individual with the community and mimicking the
reductionism and simplification of social life evident in much
contemporary liberalism.[32]

Rights

Because liberalism and communitarianism have been seen as alternative approaches to politics, theorists typically believe that assuming a communitarian stance at the ontological level necessarily commits one to a communitarian stance at the advocacy level and *vice versa*. This would mean that because the defence of individual rights has traditionally been couched in atomist terms, it would be unacceptable for a communitarian analysis of politics to be combined with the advocacy of something like individual rights.[33] Taylor, however, sees the debate between liberals and communitarians as actually being much more complex and multi-layered than even many of its participants seem to realize. For him the supposed antagonism between liberalism and communitarianism is false; it is possible to combine some features of the liberal tradition with communitarianism at the ontological and advocacy levels. Liberalism and communitarianism need not be mutually exclusive approaches to politics. So rather than see them as two hostile camps, Taylor wants, in his characteristic manner, to mediate between them, to take some of the analytical and advocacy aspects from both traditions and produce a complex liberalism.

This insistence on the richness and internal diversity of the liberal tradition,[34] and use of some strands of liberalism to criticize and counteract others, is not of purely theoretical interest. Taylor is also concerned to widen the criteria used in considering whether a society should be called liberal. This attempt is no doubt partly inspired by the argument that the province of Quebec cannot be called a liberal society because certain rights are limited there.[35] Notwithstanding its pejorative connotations for some members of the American right, the kudos accompanying the adjective "liberal" is growing internationally, so the questions of which societies can legitimately lay claim to this title, and what it means to call a society liberal, are significant political questions. Taylor's position is that just as there is great variety in the philosophies of liberalism, so there are many types of politics that deserve the appellation liberal.[36]Associating liberalism only with the form of liberalism that prevails in the USA is too narrow and parochial an approach to politics (1995a: 203, 242–8, 287; 1995c: 104).

Taylor's synthetic approach to political theory is illustrated by his accommodation, and even advocacy in some circumstances, of the typically liberal belief in individual rights. Taylor accepts that the enjoyment of certain basic civil and political rights, such as those of speech, press, assembly, *habeas corpus* and the right to a fair trial are central to western political culture. This is an historical legacy that he takes to be worthy of defence and preservation. As he says, some rights "are so fundamental that we can more or less commit ourselves in advance to upholding them in all possible contexts. The right to life, to personal liberty, to freedom of opinion, etc. are in this group" (1986a: 55). Although he does not offer unqualified support for the spread of rights culture, he depicts it as one of the greatest achievements of modern politics. What he finds most remarkable and admirable about this culture is its ambition "to call political power to book against a yardstick of fundamental human requirements, universally applied" (1999a: 18; cf. 30, 107, 116–17). But Taylor's understanding of rights differs from that of most liberals. Rights are typically seen as the properties of individuals, and understood in a monological, atomistic way. In analysing the rights that individuals exercise, Taylor's focus turns from the individual to the wider culture that makes this possible. As he says, one of the aims of his political philosophy is "to purge our key normative notions – freedom, justice, rights – of their atomist distortions" (1985a: 9).

It must be noted here, though, that it is not Taylor's acknowledgement of the importance of certain core individual rights and freedoms that separates him from communitarians. Some communitarians in liberal democracies, sometimes known as the new communitarians, share this belief that some basic rights and freedoms are inalienable and therefore not negotiable. They believe, like liberals, that the right to due process, free speech, *habeas corpus*, freedom of religion and of association must be respected (1995a: 247; 1998d: 63). However, like Taylor, these communitarians do not assume that individual rights are the ultimate good in every case; they reject the idea that "rights are trumps". Depending on the circumstances, the appeal to rights might need to be tempered by a concern with the common welfare. For example, liberalism has traditionally prized freedom of mobility and freedom of occupation for individuals and so would argue that doctors should be free to work where they choose. However, from a communitarian standpoint, this freedom might need to be balanced against the need remote communities have for medical services. From this point of view it might be legitimate to require newly graduated doctors to work in rural areas for a period. This would violate their freedom as individuals, but this violation could be seen as less important than the need of rural citizens for basic medical services.

Taylor offers a brief history of how rights came to be seen in atomist terms. He claims that:

> we inherit from this [the seventeenth] century our theories of rights, the modern tendency to frame the immunities accorded people by law in terms of subjective rights ... This ... is a conception which puts the autonomous individual at the centre of our system of law. (1989a: 195)

He contends that throughout the medieval period the idea that people were entitled to certain immunities and protections was expressed through the idea of natural law. This outlook held that it was wrong to treat people in certain ways – such as torturing them or punishing the innocent – but these moral values were not conceived of as entitlements or immunities that inhered within individuals. With the advent of rights discourse in the seventeenth century, they came to be seen as innate properties of individuals rather than values that were protected by an overarching law. They also came to be understood as legal claims that people could make against the state and against one another (1996b: 16–17; 1999b: 127–8). The disenchantment of the world that Taylor associates with the scientific revolution of the seventeenth century is part of the wider background to the emergence of individual rights (1999b: 135–6).[37] What was also revolutionary about the approach to rights in the seventeenth century was that they were seen to inhere in all humans equally, at least in principle (1989a: 11; 1999a: 117–18). Prior to this time, different strata of society had enjoyed particular rights and duties, but the Lockean idea that all humans were equally entitled to the fundamental rights of life, liberty and property ushered in a changed understanding of politics, society and selfhood that is still working itself out today.

As Taylor sees it, the language of rights provides a shorthand for the sorts of moral discriminations a culture makes (1985b: 291; 1986a: 53, 57): it is a shorthand for "strong evaluations" to use the language of his moral theory (see Chapter 1). To assert that humans have a right to something is, in effect, to make a statement of the worth or value of that thing. This may be an assertion of the value of the activity involved, such as free expression of dissenting political ideas, but at a deeper level it also expresses the value of the human capacity involved in acting in this way; in this case the value of free thought. When the language of rights begins to be unpacked, what seems to be a political theory about the properties and prerogatives of individuals is actually underpinned by a series of commitments about what it means to be a fully human person and to enjoy the dignity associated with this and about what human capacities deserve to be fostered. This sort of analysis of rights is incompatible with the "thin conception of the good" that liberals like Rawls advocate. What emerges when rights are analysed in this way is their embeddedness in a set of background understandings about personhood, human capacities and potential and the things that contribute to a good life. As discussed in Chapter 4, background understandings might remain tacit, but they are crucial for the full appreciation of the more overt claims made about rights.

When the vocabulary of rights is seen to be underpinned and made meaningful by a deeper moral language, it becomes apparent that some way of balancing competing needs, interests and capacities is required. The assertion of rights cannot put an end to all debate and judgement about competing goods. Those who believe that it can adhere to what Taylor calls "single principle liberalism"; the belief that somehow if we accept that rights are of paramount importance we will be able to resolve political and social disputes fairly and efficiently. His refrain in response to such a position is that:

> We don't have any formula to render these [conflicting] demands harmonious. We can only make difficult judgements in which these demands are balanced against each other, at some sacrifice to one or both. (1994d: 214)

While Taylor believes that rights have become a necessary part of modern western politics and that they provide protection for an important range of individual freedoms, he also maintains that they do not provide a sufficient way of dealing with all, or even with some of the most important, social conflicts and problems (1985b: 301–2).

Another reason why Taylor is unwilling to see the appeal to rights as a panacea for all political and social demands and disputes, is the juridical approach to politics they entail. It is no coincidence that the idea of individual rights that can be claimed against the state or against others and enforced by the state, grew up with the imagery of the social contract. Rights retrieval typically occurs through the mechanism of the courts and involves an élite of professionals using specialist language to decide outcomes. This legalistic model of politics does not promote the sort of popular debate and discussion that Taylor holds as vital to the conduct of democratic politics. He sees this as a serious shortcoming for several reasons, all of which stem from his preferred conception of politics as an arena of difference, dialogue, negotiation and compromise (1998c: 155). One of these reasons is that the legalistic model of politics does not foster participation and the sense of collective involvement in, and responsibility for political decisions that accompanies this. Without this sense of participation there is, as indicated above, likely to be an attrition of the democratic sentiment. Another problem is that the diversity of opinions and interests in modern western societies is more likely to emerge through the debate and discussion of deliberative politics. This might make accommodation of these different and perhaps competing perspectives more difficult, but Taylor believes that the process of arriving at consensus and compromise through the exchange of different outlooks is invaluable (1991a: 114).

However, while he perpetuates Berlin's awareness of the plurality of political values,[38] Taylor does not share his predecessor's *a priori* assumption that these different values are necessarily incompatible. Taylor's position is that it is only through exchange, debate, discussion and common deliberation that we can discover how compatible or incommensurable the plural values of modern western politics are. As he observes when outlining his departure from Berlin on this, "We have made some such advances [towards reconciling seemingly contradictory goods] in history. For a long time, our ancestors couldn't conceive how to reconcile popular rule and public order. Now the most law-abiding societies are democratic" (1994d: 214). A final shortcoming of rights discourse Taylor points to is that claims and counter-claims tend to be expressed in zero-sum terms and this militates against the possibility of compromise. Rights language "lends itself to extravagance and intransigence" (1986a: 57). Consider here claims to free speech. Once this is claimed as an inalienable right, it becomes difficult to justify its limitation. As Taylor puts it, "The very concept of a right seems to call for integral satisfaction, if it's a right at all; and if not, then nothing" (1995a: 284; cf. 1991a: 116; 1999d: 62–3).[39] The winner-take-all mentality of rights discourse can intensify social divisions by leaving the losing parties resentful, alienated and feeling that their cause has been deemed illegitimate by being declared unconstitutional (1998c: 155).

Four major points emerge from this discussion of Taylor's attitudes towards rights. Firstly, the appeal to rights does not have to be underwritten by an atomist analysis of politics. Secondly, he thinks that the language of rights is a valuable legacy of western politics and wants to defend it. However, he does not see the appeal to rights as good in an unambiguous or unproblematic way; other important elements of politics have been eclipsed by the dominance of rights discourse. From this he concludes that while rights retrieval has an important part to play in modern western politics, other modes of politics, especially the deliberative one, need to be promoted alongside this.

Of course, rights discourse is no longer confined to western cultures but is spreading across the globe (1989a: 11; 1994d: 247; 1995a: 257, 287). In some of his recent writings, Taylor has addressed its dissemination and asked what it would take for an international consensus on human rights to evolve.[40] He proposes that such a development would be the international equivalent of what Rawls calls an "overlapping consensus" (Rawls 1993). Different groups, cultures or countries would reach an agreement about certain norms of human treatment but would arrive at this common destination by quite different routes. Underlying this agreement would be diverse and potentially rival approaches to metaphysics, theology and personhood, but despite these fundamentally different philosophical foundations, there could still be a common adoption of norms of conduct.

What would make such a consensus possible, despite the diverging worldviews underlying it, is that similar core values can be detected in different cultures. These revolve around the idea of respecting life, condemning murder and torture and not punishing innocent people. In western cultures from the seventeenth century onwards, these basic values have been realized through the mechanism of individual rights, and a whole understanding of politics, society and the self has grown up around and supported this appeal to rights. Taylor asks whether the appeal to rights is compatible with other understandings of politics, society and selfhood, and suggests that it is. One objection to this view that is, by Taylor's own admission, optimistic, is that any agreement on outcomes will be fragile if not underpinned by agreement on, or even understanding of, more fundamental worldviews. Taylor acknowledges this and, because of his pluralist outlook, focuses on the possibility of mutual understanding among different world-views rather than on one view becoming shared by all parties. He argues that, in some cases at least, the agreement on outcomes can be the beginning of a fusion of horizons, whereby those from differ-ent backgrounds come to appreciate the points of convergence and difference between them.[41] This need not involve a conversion of all to the same worldview, but would simply enhance the parties' mutual comprehension. In other cases however, mutual under-standing would be a prerequisite of the consensus on outcomes. So, with his signature style, Taylor concludes that there can be no single formula for arriving at a global consensus on human rights. Instead he sketches out different possible paths, and what each would involve. From this point onwards, it is up to the participants themselves to discuss and debate the issues and problems. While this could be seen as "copping out", Taylor would no doubt reply that only this sort of open-ended, deliberative approach could produce anything like an unforced international consensus on human rights.

Civil society

When Taylor turns his attention to the analysis of civil society, the idea of deliberation continues to play an important role. Civil society, as he uses the phrase, represents an important arena of freedom in liberal polities; indeed, he declares that "No society can be called free in which these voluntary associations are not able to function" (1995a: 258). Yet this sort of freedom cannot adequately be classified as either positive or negative. Taylor uses the term civil society to refer to areas of social life that enjoy "relative autonomy"[42] from the state, and in this sense they can be associ-ated with negative freedom, for these activities should be maximally free from government interference. Although the state is sovereign, and provides the basic rules and laws that underpin all social activities, the arena of civil society is not controlled by it (1991b: 117). The market economy is one important component of civil society, and liberal thinkers have tended to focus on it to the exclusion of others. However, the public sphere, or the realm where public opinion is formed and disseminated, is another aspect of civil society that Taylor draws attention to (*ibid.*: 127–8). In this regard, civil society can also be associated with some of the features of positive liberty, for it enables individuals to come together and try to shape the direction of their society in collaboration with others.

Although many forces have contributed to its development, the roots of civil society lie, according to Taylor, in the church's independence from the state. While liberals tend to focus on the state's independence from the church, and link this to the doctrine of state neutrality, Taylor considers the relationship from the other direction. During the medieval period, the church developed as an authority independent from the state and this established the expectation that the state should not be omnipotent; there were legitimate boundaries to its jurisdiction (*ibid.*: 122–3). The idea of civil society also evolved out of a Lockean, rather than Hobbesian, image of life in the state of nature. Whereas Hobbes insisted that without "a common power to over-awe us all" there would be no social life to speak of; life would be "solitary, poor, nasty, brutish and short" (Hobbes 1974: 143), Locke maintained that a quite extensive degree of social cooperation could develop without the state. The underlying belief here is that society has an existence independent of the state; as Taylor puts it, society is "an extra-political reality" (1995a: 215).

The possibility that sources of authority that were largely independent of the state could exist has expanded over the centuries, so that civil society now includes a host of diverse organizations with diverse purposes. While some of these have a religious basis, most are secular but their common feature is that none are controlled by the state. They are private in the sense of being non-governmental, but not in the sense of necessarily being confined to or concerned with the domestic sphere. As this suggests, some of the associations of civil society contribute to political debate; they are non-governmental but not, therefore, non-political. As the aim of some to influence the government's decisions indicates, while the organizations of civil society exist relatively independently of the state, there is also an expectation that politicians will respond to the demands, ideas and criticisms that emanate from civil society. The state must be responsive to this arena, and in this context Taylor discusses the development of the public sphere and the idea of public opinion.

Taylor's aims in analysing civil society are, characteristically, manifold. One of his purposes is to further his examination of the meaning of freedom, and to suggest that the positive/negative binary is unable to capture some of the important aspects of freedom in the western political tradition. He also wants to show that the ethos and practice of debate and deliberation has been a central force in the development of western liberalism, even though it seems to have slipped from the view of many contemporary liberals. This feeds into his wider ambition of articulating a complex liberalism and therefore provides further ammunition in his campaign against narrowing, reductionist approaches to liberalism. As usual though, his theoretical reflections point beyond philosophical debates to the world of practical politics. Taylor seems to hope that a better understanding the evolution of western politics will inform policies and approaches to the spread of some of its values and institutions into the non-western world (*ibid.*: 287).

The politics of recognition

Another way in which Taylor's sense of the complexity of contemporary politics manifests itself is in his depiction of the politics of recognition or the politics of equal recognition, as he sometimes calls it (*ibid.*: 232–3). His essay, "The Politics of Recognition" is a good illustration of the breadth of his thinking, encapsulating as it does many of the features of his political thought as a whole. Although it primarily addresses the challenge of multiculturalism for liberal democratic societies, the analysis draws freely on the history of western thought. Taylor also uses material from Canada to illustrate certain points; indeed, the ongoing question of Quebec's place in Canada was one of the spurs to his interest in this question.[43] There is an encounter with contemporary liberalism in this essay, and a consideration of its ability to grapple with these questions in a satisfactory way. Part of the essay also contributes to the debate about the "curriculum wars"; that is, questions about what sort of material should be taught in western universities today and why. In this essay, Taylor is also continuing his dialogue with Berlin, despite the fact that his name appears nowhere in the article.[44] On the question of recognition, however, Taylor and his former teacher find more to agree on than on the meaning of freedom. The following three paragraphs summarize

Berlin's views on recognition so that their affinities with Taylor's position can be elicited.

One of Berlin's major aims in identifying the negative and positive approaches to liberty is to show that freedom is not a univocal concept.[45] However, another aim of his essay, which appears somewhat at odds with this insistence on the polyvocality of liberty, is to demarcate freedom from other political goals and values. Although freedom can mean different and even conflicting things, its specificity should be appreciated: liberty should not be confused with justice, equality or solidarity (Berlin 1969: 125): "Everything is what it is: liberty is liberty, not equality or fairness or justice or culture, or human happiness or a quiet conscience" (*ibid.*: 125). In pursuit of this argument, Berlin devotes a section of his essay to "the search for status", where he talks about the profound human need for recognition. He insists that while this might be akin to the desire for liberty, it should not be confused with liberty in either its positive or negative variants. From this perspective, "The lack of freedom about which men or groups complain amounts, as often as not, to the lack of proper recognition"(*ibid.*: 155; cf. 158–9). As this suggests, he accepts that the quest for recognition can occur at the level of individuals or of groups:

> I may feel unfree in the sense of not being recognised as a self-governing individual human being; but I may feel it also as a member of an unrecognised or insufficiently respected group: then I wish for the emancipation of my entire class, or community, or nation, or race or profession. (*ibid.*: 157)

Berlin's analysis of this need for status or recognition proceeds from a basic communitarian point about the nature of identity. Who I am, and who I see myself as being, are closely connected with how I am perceived by those around me. As he says, "some, perhaps all, of my ideas about myself, in particular my sense of my own moral and social identity, are intelligible only in terms of the social network in which I am . . . an element" (*ibid.*: 155; cf. 157). Should an individual or group feel dissatisfied with their standing, with the way they are seen by others, they may embark on the quest for recognition. This typically involves the assertion of one's dignity and equality through the demand to be seen as an independent being, with one's own will and purposes, rather than being treated as a subaltern (*ibid.*: 156, 159).

Although Berlin characterizes recognition as something "profoundly needed and passionately fought for by human beings" (*ibid.*: 158), the immediate political events that formed the backdrop to his reflections seem to be the campaigns for national independence in regions that were, or recently had been, European colonies (*ibid.*: 159). This is why he so readily associates the drive for recognition with solidarity, fraternity, equality and the desire for self-rule (*ibid.*: 158). It also helps to explain why he differentiates this goal from freedom, at least in the negative sense. A group of people who have liberated themselves from rule by an external power and have attained independence as a nation might experience considerable infringements on their freedom in the new order; indeed, the population might have enjoyed greater freedom from interference under colonial rule. It would not be correct, therefore, from Berlin's vantage point, to characterize this change as an increase in freedom. Underscoring his point about freedom's distinction, he insists that the goods gained here – collective dignity, recognition and independence – are something other than freedom.[46]

When Taylor takes up these themes, it is in response to the rise of multiculturalism within liberal democratic societies rather than nationalism and decolonization, although the enduring campaign by some in the province of Quebec for secession from Canada does inform his interest in and approach to the politics of recognition. He explains that "the very understandable grievances of French Canadians were made more acute and complex by the perception they were not acknowledged by the English speaking world" (Taylor 1998b: 107; cf. 1995a: xi). Reflecting on the challenges for liberal democratic practices, values and institutions posed by the multicultural composition of many societies, Taylor notes that increasingly groups within these societies make claims for the public acknowledgment of their particularity. Ethnic origin is one major spur to demands for recognition, but they also can be made on the basis of sexuality, gender and religion. What these movements reflect is the emergence into the public realm of issues associated with identity, or what is often referred to as "the politics of identity" or "identity politics". Members of these groups are concerned with the collective aspect of individual identity; with who I am as a woman, or a gay man, or a Muslim, or a US citizen of Hispanic origin. This offers a good illustration of the general communitarian point that many of the forces shaping individual identity are collective ones.

These collective forces that shape identity change from social forces to political ones when the connection between identity and its recognition by others is acknowledged. In this part of his analysis Taylor assumes a parallel between identity formation at the intimate level and its operation at the broader public level. In both cases, recognition requires having who one is acknowledged by others. The individual seeks recognition from others not just as a courtesy owed to him or her, nor by appealing to the interests others have in a correct understanding of the individual (1995a: 226). Rather, there is a sense in which the failure to have one's identity accurately recognized by others actually distorts or damages the individual's sense of who he or she is. This is because part of what makes someone the person they are in a full, robust and free way is being recognized as this by other people. An extra assumption that seems to be implicit in Taylor's discussion is that others will acknowledge the individual's identity in a positive form (*ibid.*: 225). Recognition of racial identity from racists or of gender identity from sexists is hardly a gain. So the point Taylor is trying to make is that individuals can suffer real harm if who they are is not acknowledged in a positive way by others, be this in the personal, social or public arena. A person's sense of self is not independent of how others see him or her. In fact, if an individual or group is seen by others as in some way inferior, this feeling of inferiority can become internalized, shaping the person or group's self-perception. In making this point, Taylor is picking up on an earlier point from his critique of negative freedom, that there can be internal barriers to free action. He is also echoing Berlin's claim that when an individual is not recognized as an autonomous being by others, this can damage his or her sense of self: "if I am not so recognised, then I may fail to recognise, I may doubt, my own claim to be a fully independent human being" (Berlin 1969: 157).

It is clear that for Taylor, as for Berlin, the sense of identity is not something that the individual can achieve alone: it is an inter-subjective phenomenon, and because it depends on the participation of others for its realization, it can go wrong. A person might present herself in a certain way to others, but they might withhold recognition of her and insist on seeing her in another light. Or they might acknowledge who the person is at a superficial level, but deep down persist in thinking of her in their own way. For example, an aspiring businesswoman might present herself as cool, capable, enterprising and diligent so that she can join in the struggle in the workplace with male colleagues. However, if they only see her as an object of sexual desire or a supermodel *manquée* or someone marking time until she gets married, their misrecognition will be damaging to her sense of who she is.

Taylor portrays this need for recognition of identity, either at the individual level or as part of a wider social group, part of the larger aspect of identity that he calls the dialogical self (Taylor 1995a: 229–30; see Chapter 2). However, although he believes that the self is always dialogical, not all cultures have always presented the need for recognition in the way western ones do now. It was different in the history of western societies and it is different in non-western cultures (1991a: 48–9). Given this, Taylor tries to explain how the need for recognition has become such an important force in western politics and culture, and to achieve this he embarks on a genealogy of the politics of recognition. Some commentators point to the Hegelian roots of Taylor's concept of recognition (Oksenberg Rorty 1994: 161–2; Beiner 1997: 163),[47] and as Taylor himself acknowledges (1991e; 72; 1995a: 232 n.15), his thinking is shaped here by the master–slave dialectic in Hegel's *Phenomenology of Spirit* (Taylor 1975a: 153–7).

In the pre-modern era, society was more rigidly stratified than it now is (officially at least); it was unabashedly hierarchical, and social status was largely inherited. A certain type of recognition of identity from others was then part and parcel of one's social role, as lady, priest or peasant. In the modern era, by contrast, we would tend to think of someone as distressingly one-dimensional if they derived an exhaustive or even overriding sense of their identity from their social position as parent, teacher or resident of a certain country or even county. There is a strong perception that the social roles we fulfil or enact represent but part of our identity, and we readily sympathize with people who feel a gap or tension between who they really are and the role they are called upon to play. Consider the teacher who does not really feel comfortable in his position of power; he is required to exercise his authority in certain situations, but might feel that he is in some way betraying himself in so doing.

With the collapse of inherited social hierarchy and the spread of the idea of equality, the form of recognition attending the pre-modern social structure collapsed also. We see part of this struggle to disassemble the traditional idea of social hierarchy in Locke's campaign against Robert Filmer and his justification of patriarchal power. Filmer, a seventeenth-century English political philosopher, argued that the prerogative of exercising power over others went along with being a father. At the level of society as a whole, it was part of what it meant to be a monarch, who was likened to a father of his people. Filmer claimed that ultimately this power emanated from God, the first father, who transferred it to Adam, the father of all humans. Filmer thus attempts to provide a biblical grounding for the absolute power of the monarch, taking patriarchal power in its literal sense of the power of the father, as his basic model for power relations (Laslett 1949).

Working from an alternative set of Christian premises, Locke challenged this view that anyone has an instant or natural right to exercise power over others. He replaced it with the idea of individuals who are freely and equally born and who, therefore, must consent to the exercise of power over them before that power can be considered legitimate. This line of argument problematized the whole question of political authority in a radical way (Taylor 1989a: 195), and the ramifications of the idea that individuals are born free and equal rather than being born into relations of domination and subjection are still being worked out by political theorists and activists today. However, recognition no longer comes instantly, or rather everyone is entitled to a new sort of flat, egalitarian recognition as an equal individual (1995a: 226–7; 1991a: 46–7). Taylor summarizes this shift as the move from honour to dignity (1995a: 233). As he observes, honour is not honour if distributed in an egalitarian manner (*ibid.*: 226; 1985b: 311; 1997b: 45), whereas the dignity of being a person is inherently universal: it can in principle be extended to and demanded by all humans equally.

Over time, this demand for recognition as a free, equal individual has transmuted into demands for recognition by certain social groups who feel that they do not enjoy the status of free and equal beings. They demand that their identity as women or Aboriginals or Americans of Italian origin be recognized. In this process, the logic of treating people as free and equal individuals must extend into a recognition of their salient differences and particularities. Thus, as an extension of the ideals of universal freedom and equality, the recognition of one's own or others' dignity can now involve acknowledgement of difference. This is related to the rise of the ethic of authenticity (as discussed in Chapter 2), for there is now a sense that recognizing individuals as free and equal also means acknowledging what might be unique to them. Taylor formulates the fusion of these ideas and the paradox it represents thus:

> With the politics of equal dignity, what is established is meant to be universally the same, an identical basket of rights and immunities; with the politics of difference, what we are asked to recognise is the unique identity of this individual or group, its distinctness from everybody else. (1995a: 233–4).

In one sense, then, the politics of difference is an outgrowth of liberalism's traditional promise of universal freedom and equality and its respect for the dignity of the individual (Blum 1994: 182; Abbey 1999: 710–14; cf. Seglow 1998). Yet at the same time it challenges some of liberalism's other fundamental tenets, such as the belief in state neutrality, its idea of justice as requiring blindness to individual particularities and its notion of tolerance (Taylor 1995a: 234–7).

In his exploration of the politics of recognition Taylor also participates in the debate about what texts and topics should be taught in western universities. In this context he argues that extending equal recognition to different cultures makes no sense as an *a priori* principle. To operate on this basis would be to patronize, rather than respect and honour, the achievements of other cultures. Comparative investigations of cultures should begin with the presumption that all cultures might have something interesting or valuable to offer those outside them, but should not assert this as a conclusion before the comparison has begun. It is only by exploring what various cultures have created that westerners can decide on their relative value in comparison with other cultural products. Correctly understood, this process requires a fusion of horizons wherein the person comparing the cultures changes in the process because of his or her absorption of another culture (*ibid.*: 252–5).[48] However, as Susan Wolf notes in her commentary on Taylor's essay, when it comes to the culture wars, Taylor introduces a new criterion for determining what should be recognized and respected. The issue now becomes not the recognition of identity and the damage done by its absence but the universalist one of whether other cultures have something to say to all human beings (Wolf 1994: 79; cf. Blum 1994: 185–6).

State neutrality

Some aspects of the politics of recognition pose a direct challenge to the traditional liberal conception of the state. Essentially, the ideal of state neutrality refers to the belief that the government should treat all individuals and groups equally and indifferently; it should only discriminate among them in so far as they break the law. According to the principle of state neutrality, it is inappropriate for the government to foster one or some way(s) of life or ideologies over others. Decisions about how to live properly reside with individuals, and all the government should do is set up enabling conditions that allow individuals to pursue their choices and desires, in so far as these do not harm others. Many contemporary liberal values inform this ideal of state neutrality – the idea of limiting the power of government, the idea of respecting individuals' autonomy and equality and the idea of tolerating diversity (Taylor 1991a: 17–18, 51; 1994b: 258; 1996c: 9; 1998c: 152).[49]

The call by some groups for recognition of their difference and specificity has often be accompanied by calls for differential treatment: affirmative action programmes for example, or funding to accommodate special needs, such as language classes for the children of a particular ethnic group. When this occurs, the idea of state neutrality is threatened. If, for example, under a policy of multiculturalism, the state gives money to some groups to foster their cultural heritage, this obviously involves them being treated differently from other groups, either from those who are perceived as forming part of the mainstream culture or other less vocal or less visible ethnic minorities. Similarly, if the government rewards certain firms for meeting affirmative action targets or punishes others who fail in this regard, it could be accused of partiality and even discrimination. It could be seen as rewarding companies that share, confirm and/or promote its ideological position rather than remaining impartial among companies.[50]

Locke's *Letter Concerning Toleration* (1990) is an early formulation of the ideal of state neutrality. He argues that the church and state should have powers that are different in kind. Writing in the context of a society whose members have quite different religious convictions, and against the background of religious wars in Europe, he contends that it is inappropriate for the government to promote any particular religious beliefs or to reward or punish individuals on the basis of their beliefs. If the pursuit of a religion does not harm others, if it involves only actions that are legal and if it does not demand loyalty to the head of another state, then the government should permit this.

Taylor supports the liberal idea of a secular state because it is associated with the tolerance of diversity in religion and other ways of life (Taylor 1994d: 250).[51] It is especially valuable in multicultural democracies, for it means that, in principle at least, the public culture of that society will not privilege any religion over another. This should make it easier for people from different religious backgrounds to identify with the state (1998a: 46, 53). While many different ways of life benefit from the spaces opened up when no single religious view is officially promulgated by the state, he singles out the way in which the separation of church and state has been good for Christianity. Unhooking the message of the gospel from the coercive power of the state is beneficial because it creates "the freedom to come to God on one's own or . . . moved only by the Holy Spirit, whose barely audible voice will often be heard better when the loudspeakers of armed authority are silent" (1999a: 19; cf. 16, 26, 37).[52] So Taylor welcomes a certain version of the secular state, one which is maximally hospitable to diversity and which promotes an overlapping consensus among its members, allowing them to agree on certain values or outcomes on the basis of quite different starting points (1998a).

However, the secular state and the neutral state should not be seen as synonymous. Taylor dismisses the broader notion of state neutrality as unrealistic. This is not one of the aspects of the liberal tradition he is concerned to preserve because he finds it such an unhelpful way of thinking about politics. Even without multi-culturalism and the politics of recognition, it is hard to maintain the idea that the government could be neutral with respect to different ways of life once we go beyond the minimal state. As soon as governments formulate and implement public policy, and engage in the public spending that accompanies it, some notion of the good is being acted on, no matter how implicit. Even something as seemingly dry and pallid as a country's tax regime actually embeds a host of judgements about what is desirable behaviour. Providing tax relief in some areas is a way of tacitly encouraging some activities, such as having one parent stay at home to look after children or, conversely, allowing childcare outside the home to be a tax deduction. It is not hard to multiply the examples that illustrate the fact that through legislation and regulations, governments frequently promote some forms of behaviour and discourage others, notwithstanding the fact that this can sometimes be inadvertent and the consequence of unforeseen outcomes.[53] Hence Taylor's conclusion that "There's no way to be neutral. Neutral liberalism is an angelic view, unconnected to the real world in which democracies function" (1996c: 4–5; cf. 1998c: 153).

Another way in which the ideal of state neutrality can be actualized is for all individuals to be treated in an equal, undifferentiated way by the state, with no special advantages or disadvantages for any group. There are, however, a number of problems with this. One involves the accusation that can be levelled against neutrality in any context; that doing nothing or treating all parties indifferently actually amounts to favouring the strong and powerful. Neutrality is thus a form of disguised conservatism, for it effectively reinforces the status quo. This is particularly significant in societies where individuals and groups are unequal. To treat unequals equally is not to act impartially. For example, in countries like Canada and Australia, the government often pays special educational allowances to students from the indigenous population. This is defended on the grounds that many of them originate from a position of structural disadvantage and that it would be good for this to be overcome, or at least minimized. It is seen as desirable because, apart from the benefits that particular individuals might enjoy as a consequence, it serves to promote equality of opportunity and meritocracy. These goods have traditionally been central to the liberal outlook, especially in connection with its attack on aristocracy and inherited privilege in general. However, awarding indigenous students special benefits in this way is a decidedly non-neutral policy, for it is treating individuals differently in an *a priori* way. Defenders of this sort of discrimination can take recourse to one of Aristotle's points about justice; that it is only just to treat people equally in so far as they are equals. In areas where people are unequal, it is not just to treat them equally (Aristotle 1981: 3, ix; cf. Taylor 1985b: 289–317; 1994f: 37).[54] From this standpoint, the liberal ideal of neutrality actually militates against other liberal goods such as equality, meritocracy, respect for individuality and the fostering of conditions that maximize autonomy. In this contest Taylor would side with the latter cluster of liberal goods and jettison neutrality not only because it is unrealistic but also because it can be counterproductive when it comes to the liberal idea of respect for the person.

Another pivotal feature of the liberal tradition that is closely related to the ideal of state neutrality, and that can be challenged by the demand for equal recognition, is the liberal adherence to what is called "the priority of the right over the good" (Taylor 1996c: 8). This can also be characterized as the dominance of procedural over substantive goods, and explains why Taylor sometimes calls this approach "procedural liberalism" (1995a: 186–7, 194–5, 245, 285). What these phrases refer to is the idea that it is wrong for the government to promote any way of life, worldview or substantive goods over others. The role of government is not to advocate any particular morality (the good) but to provide and enforce a framework of laws and procedures (the right) that allows individuals to determine autonomously the direction of their own lives and to live in accordance with their own conceptions of the good. The purpose of the political community is not to promote collective goods, but simply to provide the conditions necessary for individuals or groups to pursue their own conceptions of the good. These preconditions include peace, order, stability, security of persons and possessions and equality before the law.

Within the overarching framework of the law, all individuals should be treated as equals and their life choices, so long as they do not infringe the basic rights of other citizens or violate the rules, should be a matter of indifference to the government and to their fellow citizens. Promotion of any particular way of life or enforcement of any particular moral code would violate the equality, freedom and dignity of those citizens who did not adhere to these beliefs. From this standpoint, living together in a society requires no particular consensus about the good life nor any shared substantive goods, but only a willingness to play by the same rules as everyone else, to respect the procedures according to which society operates. As this suggests, these two tenets of classical liberalism, the ideal of state neutrality and the priority of the right over the good, are mutually reinforcing. As Taylor describes this position, "A liberal society must remain neutral on the good life and restrict itself to ensuring that, however they see things, citizens deal fairly with one another and the state deals equally with all" (*ibid.*: 246).

Because these tenets are mutually reinforcing, it is unsurprising that one of the early expressions of the priority of the right, over the good also comes from Locke. He argues that political power should be concerned only with physical security, the protection of property and the guarantee of rights and freedoms. The state's jurisdiction does not extend to concern with the soul or the eternal well being of its citizens (Locke 1990: 19). As he puts it, "all the power of civil government relates only to men's civil interests, is confined to the care of the things of this world, and hath nothing to do with the world to come" (*ibid.*: 22; cf. 35). The laws must be made with a view to the interests of individuals living freely and peaceably together; their role is not to moralize or proselytize. Locke's claim that the government has no place meddling in people's religious beliefs has mutated over the centuries into the claim that it has no place interfering in people's conceptions of substantive goods, their beliefs about what is important in life and what makes life worth living, whether these beliefs comprise religious or purely secular goods.

One of the assumptions underlying the distinction between the right and the good is that the general principles and procedures embodied in the framework of rules and laws by which all members of society must abide are themselves untouched by particular notions of the good. Taylor, however, challenges this position is by insisting that the right and the good are not so easily separated and that liberalism's notion of "the right" is itself infused with values and ideas about what is the good way to live and with notions of personhood (see Mulhall & Swift 1997: 124).[55] From this standpoint the general framework within which individuals pursue their particular conceptions of the good is not itself outside the moral realm but rather instantiates a particular vision of the good life. As he says, "the good is what, in its articulation, gives the point of the rules which define the right"(Taylor 1989a: 89).

Traditionally liberal notions of justice and tolerance have required that social institutions be blind to individuals' particularities and treat them *prima facie* as undifferentiated equals (*ibid.*: 234). Individuals are all seen as bearers of rights and sometimes duties, as worthy of equal respect, as owed a certain dignity simply by virtue of being human, etc. This sort of recognition reposes on the similarities among individuals, the things that make them alike. However, Taylor and other critics of liberalism point out that the whole liberal ethos of politics, the belief in state neutrality and the priority of the right over the good, presupposes persons who can unproblematically divorce their private from their public persona, or their sense of the good from their duty to the right or their religious convictions from their political conduct. The complaint is that assimilating all individuals into a single model of public personhood amounts to an active denial of their equality and individuality. The idea behind this is that we can't all be equal if we have to conform to a single model of public personhood, because this model privileges, even if only tacitly, some forms of identity or ways of being over others. Liberalism is thus exposed as effectively privileging a certain approach to politics and to personal identity, and the relationship between them (1995a: 236–7, 249).

While it is probably impossible to find a political doctrine that does not privilege some way of life or conception of the person, the complaint here is that liberalism's pretensions to neutrality and its claim not to promote a view of the good are false. These pretensions conceal the privileging of one group or way of life or approach to politics over others. Because denizens of western societies are often blind to the particularity of their own values and practices, which are so familiar and seem natural, they often cannot appreciate that what is neutral to them is actually value-laden from another perspective. To illustrate this Taylor refers to the controversy in France over Muslim girls wearing headscarves to school. Students who wear crosses around their necks as a form of decoration are not seen to be making comparable declarations of religious identity, but it is not hard to see why tolerating this while banning headscarves can seem discriminatory rather than neutral (1998c: 147; cf. 1999d).

Liberalism's distinction between the right and the good is not one that can mediate neutrally among all cultures and outlooks but rather "is internal to *one* historical view" (1994d: 247 original emphasis). What Taylor opposes are not the liberal values of tolerance and the accommodation of diversity but rather liberalism's self-understanding; its failure to acknowledge that it actually does promote a range of substantive goods and is not wholly neutral among various conceptions of the good life. Hence his conclusion that "Liberalism is the political expression of one range of cultures, and quite incompatible with other ranges . . . liberalism can't and shouldn't claim complete cultural neutrality. Liberalism is also a fighting creed" (1995a: 249; cf. 236–7). Once again, Taylor contends that liberalism's notions of neutrality and equal treatment are blind to their own particularity and partiality, and he calls for liberalism to become more pellucid and articulate about its own ethical bases. In effect, then, although the politics of recognition began as a call for the acknowledgement of cultural, ethnic and gender differences among groups, it has resulted in the exposure of the particularisms masquerading as universalism within liberal thought.

Conclusion

As the political theorist Jean Hampton has observed, attacking liberalism's idea of the neutral state is not tantamount to a critique of liberalism *per se* (Hampton 1997: 212 n.36). Taylor's political thought should be seen as involving the attempt to defend some aspects of the liberal tradition while criticizing others. The aspects of liberalism he rejects are its atomism, its emphasis on the negative conception of freedom, its pretensions to neutrality and its attempt to prescind from the endorsement of any substantive goods. He remains unpersuaded by liberalism's instrumental view of politics. He also challenges any version of liberalism that aspires to formalism, for this underestimates the complexity of society and the multiplicity of goods that its members adhere to in the public, as well as the private, realm.

On the other hand, Taylor endorses the liberal concern with rights and autonomy, and joins liberals in reflecting on the meaning of freedom and the social and political conditions propitious to its attainment. His work on the politics of recognition can be seen as continuing the traditional liberal concern with how a society can peacefully accommodate significant and enduring differences among its population with minimal recourse to coercion. There are also those aspects of the liberal tradition that he feels have been neglected and seeks to revivify. These include a concern with openness, participation and deliberation, the need to balance diversity and universalism and the awareness of complex identities.

So there are many features of the liberal tradition that Taylor is willing to endorse or advocate. His analyses of these goods are, however, typically conducted from a communitarian standpoint. Consider here his repeated emphasis on the way social forces shape the self-understanding of groups and individuals and his identification of shared goods. However, it would be too simple to conclude that Taylor is a liberal at the advocacy level and a communitarian at the ontological level. This would ignore the liberal goods that he rejects, as listed above, as well as the communitarian goods that he endorses. These include his affirmation of shared goods in politics, particularly those associated with the civic republican tradition in politics.[56]

Chapter 4

Understanding knowledge

If it seems irregular to conclude an overview of Taylor's thought with an account of his ideas about epistemology, rather than beginning with this, it is probably related to the primacy of what Taylor calls the epistemological model.[1] The details of this model will be described later in the chapter, but one of its major features is foundationalism: the belief that understanding the nature of knowledge is primary in the philosophical enterprise. Taylor thinks that there is "a terrible and fateful illusion" in this approach to knowledge. As he says in the Preface to *Philosophical Arguments*:

> These are the assumptions Descartes gave articulation to; central is the view that we can somehow come to grips with the problem of knowledge, and then later proceed to determine what we can legitimately say about other things: about God, or the world, or human life. From Descartes's standpoint, this seems not only a *possible* way to proceed, but the only *defensible* way. Because, after all, whatever we say about God or the world represents a knowledge claim. So we first ought to be clear about the nature of knowledge, and about what it is to make a defensible claim.
>
> (1995a: vii, original emphasis; cf. 34)

But leaving the discussion of epistemology to the end is not intended to suggest that this is the least important aspect of Taylor's thinking either. As we shall see, he does accord primacy to ontology, but also repeatedly reminds us that epistemological concerns are bound up with issues of personhood, morality and so forth. So although this chapter focuses on his claims about knowledge, they are not wholly separable from his other philosophical interests and arguments.

This chapter begins by drawing attention to Taylor's ongoing insistence on a distinction between the natural and the human sciences. It brings out his admiration for and application of Gadamer's concept of the fusion of horizons and then moves into his conception of practical reason, which is also informed by the hermeneutical tradition. It explains why he sees these arguments as necessary by describing his view of the scientific revolution of the seventeenth century and its enduring legacy. Taylor believes that its legacy extends beyond epistemology in particular and philosophy in general to touch the whole of modern western culture. The chapter then outlines Taylor's contribution to debates about how to overcome this epistemological legacy, discussing his theory of embodied agency and his emphasis on the tacit background or pre-understanding of ordinary life. It concludes with a discussion of some of the aspects of his view of language not covered in previous chapters.

Natural versus human sciences

Taylor is well known for his insistence on distinguishing the approaches, methods and assumptions of the natural sciences from those appropriate to the social or human sciences. This has been one of his career-long preoccupations, beginning with *The Explanation of Behaviour* and echoing throughout his most recent writings. As Taylor wrote in his first book:

> Many students of the sciences of human behaviour [say] that there is no difference in principle between the behaviour of animate organisms and any other processes in nature, that the former can be accounted for in the same way as the latter, by laws relating physical events. (1964a: 3)

He uses the term "naturalism" to denote the belief that because humans are part of nature, the ways of knowing used in the natural science can and should be transported into the human sciences (1985a: 2; 1995b: 137, 141). The behaviouralism he took aim at in *The Explanation of Behaviour* was one expression of this. Socio-biology or evolutionary psychology are other expressions of naturalism. In general, the naturalist's logic runs that:

1. Everything in nature is to be explained in terms of post-Galilean science;
2. Humans and their life forms are part of nature; therefore
3. Humans, etc. are to be explained in post-Galilean terms.

(2000a: 246)[2]

In rejecting the logic of naturalism and insisting, contrariwise, on the development of different ways of understanding the social world from those deployed for the natural world, Taylor is following Aristotle's point about the need to adapt one's expectations to the object or area of study. In the *Nicomachean Ethics*, Aristotle advises that:

> Our discussion will be adequate if it has as much clearness as the subject-matter admits of, for precision is not to be sought for alike in all discussions, any more than in all the products of the crafts . . . It is the mark of an educated man to look for precision in each class of things just so far as the nature of the subject admits; it is evidently equally foolish to accept probable reasoning from a mathematician and to demand from a rhetorician scientific proofs. (1980: bk 1, ch. 3, 2–3)[3]

When this general point about the need to temper methods of inquiry according to the subject matter is applied to the debate about the natural and the human sciences, and in particular the question of how applicable the methods of the natural sciences are for understanding society and human action, a number of conclusions appear. Beginning with his 1971 essay "Interpretation and the Sciences of Man",[4] Taylor has argued that there is a double hermeneutic at work in the human sciences compared to the natural sciences. This is due directly to one of the ontological features he ascribes to persons. As outlined in Chapter 2, he believes that humans are self-interpreting beings and any attempt to explain their behaviour must take this into account. This is necessary for two reasons. Firstly, how humans understand themselves and their world is an essential or primary property of their existence, not one that can be bracketed out in the quest to explain them. Secondly, because humans' self-interpretations influence their actions and behaviour, any account that excludes this variable can not be adequate. So appreciating how the persons under study view their situation is an essential component of understanding them. As Taylor puts it, the demand "that we confront our language of explanation with the self-understanding of our subjects, is nothing else but the thesis of hermeneutical theory" (1988a: 228). The objects of the natural sciences do not share this ontological property, they are not self-interpreting beings, so what the planets might think about their movements is irrelevant to the astrophysicist.[5] This difference in the objects under study necessitates different methods and modes of understanding and, as per Aristotle, different expectations of exactitude in one's explanations.

Taylor is not claiming that social scientists must accept the self-interpretations of the people they study as the final word or ultimate truth; he concedes that such interpretations can be limited, mistaken or distorted (*ibid.*: 228). His claim is the more modest one that the social scientist must take these interpretations into account when trying to explain people and their behaviour. In his characteristic way, he is articulating a third, middle way between the extremes of bypassing the agent's viewpoint altogether, as naturalism does, and simply accepting the agent's point of view. He describes this latter position as based on "the incorrigibility thesis", for it suggests that the interpreter cannot criticize or correct the agent's self-understanding (1985b: 118, 123–4). In contrast to the idea that the interpreter must simply accept the agent's self-understanding as something that cannot be gainsaid, Taylor claims that sometimes the social scientist can come up with a more lucid and compelling account of the group or society's situation or actions. If this occurs, the social scientist's explanation might, in turn, feed back into the subjects' self-awareness and become part of the vocabulary of their self-definition. Freudian psychology is an example of this. Freud strove to explain his patients' behaviour in terms that were unfamiliar to them but that some of them could eventually come to adopt as valid interpretations of their behaviour. Irrespective of how accurate or useful one thinks Freudian psychology is, it cannot be denied that what began as an explanation of behaviour has become part of the language of self-interpretation for many in western societies. Even those who have not read Freud might describe themselves as repressing their drives or making a Freudian slip. The same can be said of Marxism: what began as a theory of society has come to shape the way some people interpret themselves. People talk freely about social class, false consciousness, ideology and so on even though they do not always do so with the strict definitions Marx formulated.

As the general point about the possibility of change in self-interpretations intimates, Taylor contends that humans can never be fully or finally understood; as self-interpretations change, so theories of human behaviour must alter to accommodate this (*ibid.*: 3). He also accepts as the corollary that the human sciences are necessarily open-ended hermeneutical endeavours and that the sort of knowledge they yield is inevitably more uncertain and labile than the knowledge aspired to in the natural sciences. Yet this does not lead him to conclude that because there are only competing interpretations within the human sciences that any interpretation is as good as any other. Taylor believes that we can identify better and worse explanations of social life, but the value of existing interpretations can only be challenged relatively, by better interpretations, not by some ultimate body of truth. So measuring the success or value of theories in the social sciences requires a different set of criteria from those in the natural sciences. At one point he writes that "for any hermeneutic explanation, interpretive plausibility is the ultimate criterion" (*ibid.*: 7). This of course raises the question of what makes one explanation more plausible than another. The criterion of comprehensiveness features in two ways in Taylor's response. Firstly, the better interpretation should encompass and explain more of the features of the phenomenon under study than the one do the alternatives. Comprehensiveness matters in another way when Taylor claims that theories can be rated according to their ability to give an account of rival theories, both of the rivals' insights and flaws. A better theory should be able to say why it can accommodate, build on or surpass its rivals' strengths while avoiding their weaknesses.

However, Taylor freely admits that there is something circular about establishing the superiority of one social science theory over another. An interpretation of some aspect of social life is plausible if it makes sense of the behaviour under discussion, and it is better than the alternatives if it makes better sense of the behaviour or society. "Making sense" here does not have to mean giving it a rational explanation: irrational behaviour can be made sense of without being re-described as rational if some explanation is advanced as to why it was engaged in. As he puts it, to make sense of something need not entail showing that it made sense (*ibid.*: 24, 117, 124). However, even when it is conceded that irrational, inconsistent, confused or self-defeating behaviour can be made sense of, what counts as making sense of something typically varies within and among the humanities disciplines. Taylor accepts that if there is no consensus among theorists about what it means to make sense of an action, then it might not be possible to persuade one's rivals that one's interpretation is better than theirs (*ibid.*: 24, 53). He claims, for example, that in order to make sense of human behaviour, some understanding of strong evaluations is necessary, even if these judgements remain tacit and unformulated. (*ibid.*: 119). However, those who reject his view of moral life and selfhood would not agree that this was a necessary criterion of whether an explanation makes sense. All this might sound very subjective and woolly in comparison with the way natural scientists present and defend hypotheses and findings, but Taylor's whole point is that the comparison is invalid to begin with. In dealing with human affairs, a certain amount of undecidability is unavoidable. Aristotle's remarks on political science are apposite for the human sciences as a whole here. In the chapter referred to above, he also writes that:

> We must be content, then, in speaking of such subjects [that political science investigates] and with such premises to indicate the truth roughly and in outline, and in speaking about things which are only for the most part true and with premises of the same kind to reach conclusions that are no better. (Aristotle 1980: 1, iii)

One of the ways in which theories in the natural sciences have traditionally been held to demonstrate their validity is by yielding predictions, which presupposes an ability to extrapolate from one situation to the next. However, Taylor rejects this as a criterion for measuring the worth of theories in the human sciences: "prediction . . . cannot be a goal of social science as it is of natural science"

(1985b: 48). Two reasons inform this view. Firstly, and most fundamentally, there is the nature of human action and identity, its open-ended quality, which is related directly to the fact that self-interpretations can change. If a group or society change their self-interpretations in the future, then a modified or perhaps markedly different explanation of them will be required; new concepts and terminology will probably be needed to explain this changed vocabulary. Taylor holds, moreover, that it is impossible to predict what new vocabularies of self-understanding people will adopt and because these interpretations form part of the reality that is to be explained, and because their action might be influenced by these, there is no sure way of predicting the future (*ibid.*: 55–6). In the natural sciences it is assumed that terminology that accurately explains a phenomenon at one time will serve that purpose in the future. But when humans adopt a new language of self-description, their reality changes accordingly. Taylor conveys this fact of open-endedness in human affairs and its consequences for the ambition to predict them when he declares that:

> Really to be able to predict the future would be to have explicated so clearly the human condition that one would already have pre-empted all cultural innovation and transformation. This is hardly in the bounds of the possible. (*ibid.*: 57)

Secondly, prediction in any domain assumes either that one can identify which variables will remain constant and which will change, or that one can come up with enough combinations and permutations of change and stability to cover all the possible fluctuations in the system. But this is based on the idea of a closed system; it assumes that one can identify and anticipate what forces will be influential in the future and what their effects will be. In human affairs, by contrast, Taylor claims that it is difficult to delineate a comparably closed system and to identify what the salient variables will be and how they might interact and affect one another (*ibid.*: 55). Social scientists working in psychology, for example, cannot know if and how political forces might affect their subjects' behaviour in the future. Political scientists cannot predict what and how economic forces will affect political events, and so on. These problems of circumscribing a domain of study in human affairs are compounded by globalization, for it would be unwise to treat any country as if it were a bounded entity, let alone trying to extrapolate from the outside forces that currently influence a nation to what they will be in some future time. So rather than expecting accounts of human affairs to have predictive powers, Taylor endorses Hegel's observation that an understanding of human affairs can only be achieved *ex post facto*. Only when change has occurred and its participants or recipients have made sense of it can we hope to interpret its meaning (*ibid.*: 56–7; cf. 1979a: 122–3).

In "Interpretation and the Sciences of Man", Taylor nominates three thinkers who agree that understanding human affairs is an inescapably hermeneutical enterprise. They are Paul Ricoeur, Jürgen Habermas and Hans-Georg Gadamer (1985b: 15 n.1–3). In an essay written nearly 30 years later for inclusion in a *festschrift* to celebrate Gadamer's one hundredth birthday, Taylor elaborates upon just how influential Gadamer's thinking has been for his own on this topic (Forthcoming a. Gadamer's importance is also testified to in Taylor 1995a: 148). This essay also reprises some of the themes from "Interpretation and the Sciences of Man" as well as reiterating Taylor's continuing commitment to its basic argument that there are some ways in which the knowledge pursued in the social sciences must be qualitatively different from that sought by natural scientists.

In *Truth and Method*, first published in 1960, Gadamer argues that understanding an historical text that belongs to the reader's cultural tradition is a different sort of endeavour from scientific understanding. The appropriate model is not that of a subject's observation and explanation of an object in which he or she strives to neutralize his or her ordinary categories of interpretation but rather that of a conversation in which interlocutors aim for mutual understanding. This practice also relies on, rather than strives to eliminate, the pre-understandings that the inquirer brings to inquiry. Taylor extends Gadamer's insight to all inquiry into human affairs: for him it is not just the knowledge of one's own heritage that needs to be construed along the lines of a conversation but knowledge of other societies and other histories too. So in Taylor's work, Gadamer's reflections on method acquire a relevance not just for the study of history or literature but also for all the subjects that fall under the rubric of the human sciences: sociology, anthropology, comparative politics, comparative religion and so on. They help to explain what is involved in trying to comprehend things that are initially alien as well as those that are originally perceived as familiar.

Taylor identifies a number of factors involved in understanding humans that do not figure in understanding the objects of natural science. As indicated by the comparison with a conversation, understanding humans is a more dialogical process than understanding nature is. In the first process, the people being studied can have a view of the inquirer and of his or her findings; they can talk back and resist or endorse the interpretations of them. This is clearly not the case when one's objects of inquiry are genes, rocks, planets or quarks. Of course it could be objected that this difference only applies when the inquirer is studying living humans; the works of a dead writer or the members of medieval society cannot respond in the way that the subjects of anthropologist, sociologist or psychologist can. The inquirer's interpretations can never affect the dead as they can the living. However, Taylor would presumably respond to this by saying that on this axis the historian's work is still closer to the anthropologist's than to the natural scientist's. The historian of texts or societies can and should try to imagine what his subjects would say about his interpretation of them in a way that the natural scientist need not (Taylor 1988a). So the historian's work is still dialogical in a sense; although no actual exchange might occur between inquirer and subjects, the inquirer can construct an imaginary conversation in which he or she speculates about how the subjects would answer back. As Chapter 2 shows, Taylor's conception of dialogue is wide enough to encompass such imagined exchanges with internalized others.

Secondly, Taylor proposes that the final goal of knowledge in the human sciences differs from that in the natural sciences. In the former, inquirers should realize that ultimate, definitive knowledge of their subject is impossible, whereas natural scientists aspire with more justification to develop a theory that is adequate for explaining the object in all its future states. This is not to say that scientific theories are uncontestable, but rather that the ideal of finding a final vocabulary for explaining their objects is not inherently implausible. In the social sciences, by contrast, one's understandings of a society or group depend on who is being interpreted, and different members of a society will bring different perspectives to bear on their social reality, thus changing the inquirer's understanding of that society. Here Taylor is directly reiterating the point from "Interpretation and the Sciences of Man" that individuals' self-understandings change, so any understanding of them is necessarily temporary and provisional. A third difference between the two sorts of inquiry is that in the natural sciences the aim of understanding is instrumental; scientists believe that understanding the natural world better will help them to control it. Taylor maintains that this is not so in the human sciences: their goal is understanding so that the inquirer and the subjects can comprehend one another and function together. Taylor could, however, be charged with naïvety here by those persuaded by Michel Foucault's arguments about the implication of the humanities in the diffusion of the disciplinary society.

The final salient difference between the natural and the human sciences discussed in this recent essay comes in the role that the inquirer's perspective plays in the process of interpretation. As understanding humans is necessarily a hermeneutical affair, no two inquirers are likely to understand the same phenomenon in exactly the same way, just as no two readers are likely to interpret the same text in exactly the same way. So the knowledge gained in the human sciences is "party dependent": Taylor accepts Gadamer's point that the inquirer's own knowledge, beliefs and values cannot but shape his or her interpretation of a particular society, group or event. As Taylor says, "The terms of our best account will vary not only with the people studied, but also with the students. Our account of the Roman Empire will not and cannot be the same as that put forward in eighteenth century England" (Forthcoming a). Analogously, the language in which an anthropologist comes to understand a Sowetan neighbourhood, for example, will be inflected with his language of origin. No matter how immersed in and conversant with everyday life he becomes, he can never experience that society in just the same language and with just the same interpretations as its participants do (1985a: 280–81). A person from a different home culture would develop a slightly different language of interpreting the same Sowetan neighbourhood, and so on (Forthcoming a). In the natural sciences, by contrast, reliable knowledge is not meant to be party-dependent. Any person from any culture when equipped with the same information, tools and materials should in principle be able to conduct the same experiments and come up with the same findings.

One general way of expressing the differences between the human and the natural sciences, which is evident in the second and the final points above, is that social scientists must take culture seriously: they should treat this as an irreducible feature of human life and an indispensable facet of their inquiry. Culture is one of the things to be explained by the human sciences; it should be viewed as one of the primary properties of the phenomenon under investigation. Culture has, moreover, a dual role. The meanings people give to their situation must be taken into consideration in trying to explain that situation, and conversely the inquirer's own cultural heritage will play an important role in shaping his understanding of others. Taking culture seriously also means respecting its diversity across time and place, and abandoning any ambition to come up with universalizable, context-free and lawlike generalizations about human action (*ibid.*). Another way of expressing this difference is to say that whereas modern science has, from its beginnings, tried to understand the world in a way that diminishes its human meanings, this same reduction should be inconceivable in the human sciences. Taylor maintains that "bracketing out human meanings from human science means understanding nothing at all" (*ibid.*). Giving weight to people's self-interpretations in trying to explain them also militates against ethnocentrism, for it discourages the inquirer from simply assuming that his or her categories of understanding are necessarily applicable to others (1985b: 140).

Yet underscoring the role of culture and human significance in the social sciences in this way could simply be a licence for rampant subjectivism. If important aspects of my cultural background play a role in the way I interpret another society, and if a necessary feature of my study is their culture, which is notoriously hard to quantify because it both affects, and is interpreted by, different individuals differently, where is the science? Is disciplined inquiry possible in such a milieu? If so, what form would it take? Taylor suggests that Gadamer's image of the fusion of horizons offers a useful way of appreciating the sort of understanding the human sciences require. The fusion of horizons argument also limits the danger of unbridled subjectivism.[6]

Taylor interprets Gadamer's notion of the fusion of horizons in the following way: the horizon refers to the zone of meaning in which a person operates. As indicated in previous chapters, this is heavily influenced by the individual's culture and comprises many beliefs that are simply taken for granted and considered natural or incontrovertible. A person's horizon of meaning or significance does not have to be something of which they are fully cognizant. When a person encounters another in face-to-face conversation or reads a text for the first time or studies an historical era or event or engages with people from another culture, a different horizon is encountered. Ideally what results from this is a fusion of horizons. In encountering difference, the first person's zone or horizon of meaning soon finds itself challenged; there is something that party A expressly believes or takes for granted that party B does not, or *vice versa*. For example, the members of the Sowetan neighbourhood all believe in witches, although they do so in various forms and to differing degrees. The US anthropologist does not: it has long been an accepted part of his background that witches do not exist and that supernatural forces are a figment of atavistic imaginations. At first he cannot believe that the Sowetans really believe this either, so he questions them, watches them carefully, listens to their conversations and so on. In many ways he becomes absorbed by and part of their world; he develops friendly and loving relations with some of the people and minor or powerful aversions to others, but there is still this alien belief that distances him from them. So in merely encountering the Sowetans, let alone in trying to explain and understand them, the anthropologist has come into contact with a very different horizon of meaning from his own. The particularity of his own horizon is also revealed with surprising force; what he thought was obvious and taken-for-granted comes to light as a cultural peculiarity. He goes on trying to understand the Sowetans' belief in witches in a way that does not impose his own beliefs upon them, trying to see their beliefs from their point of view rather than dismiss them as irrational superstition. In so striving for an undistorted understanding of the other, he tries to minimize the imposition of his own outlook on them and to attain the fullest, most coherent account of theirs. He might never be persuaded that witches exist, but his horizon of meaning has shifted by its encounter with this other one. As this indicates, horizons are permeable; they can be broadened to take account of other people's meanings and beliefs, even without those meanings and beliefs being adopted.

When the quest for understanding in the human sciences involves this sort of fusion of horizons, the centrality of culture in human life is both respected and interrogated. An attempt is made to develop as undistorted as possible an account of alien beliefs, but only after subjecting them to scrutiny and trying to understand them. Unusual beliefs are seen as puzzles to be explained rather than being accepted as cultural difference *ab initio*. However, in puzzling through these unfamiliar views, the inquirer also achieves some estrangement from the things he or she has hitherto taken for granted and failed to question. So while his or her initial beliefs and values provide an enabling starting point for the inquiry, they are not left to operate unconstrained or unquestioned. In trying to understand the other point of view, the inquirer becomes more clairvoyant about his or her own point of view. On neither side are cultural beliefs and values left to float free from scrutiny. As Taylor says, "Understanding other societies ought to wrench us out of this [ethnocentricity]; it ought to alter our self-understanding" (1985b: 129; cf. 131). Another way to describe this process is to say that through this encounter with a quite different culture, a language of perspicuous contrasts can develop; one that is not wholly the interpreter's own nor that of the people being understood but one that enables the differences and convergences between the two worlds to be articulated (*ibid.*: 125–6).

This is, needless to say, a rather stark example of fusing horizons. In ordinary conversation where we have a difference of opinion with a friend, the matter in contention could be minute by contrast with the reality of witches. And the less there is to differ over, the more likely is agreement. I might end up agreeing with my friend that I really am still in love with my ex-husband, despite the fact that I denounce him wherever possible. Yet even this rather banal example illustrates a fusion of horizons; my understanding of myself and my world has been shifted through an engagement with a different one. But both these examples illustrate Taylor's point that coming to understand others changes our understanding of ourselves. And the cost or struggle involved in this exchange varies with the magnitude of the differences that appear when horizons clash. The US anthropologist returns to his university unconvinced that witches exist but with a different understanding of himself and a richer appreciation of other humans and cultural differences. His own horizon of meaning has both become clearer to him and expanded in the process of this encounter with a radically different worldview.

Of course, the fusion of horizons can only occur when the process is underpinned by a cluster of intellectual virtues or values. These include the genuine desire and willingness to know what is other, the ability not to dismiss things that seem strange as necessarily irrational, the respect for difference, the ability to change, the courage to question one's own assumptions and so on. Taylor does not enumerate these intellectual virtues, but something like this disposition is presupposed by his depiction of the fusion of horizons. And finally, as in "Interpretation and the Sciences of Man", Taylor again claims that it is possible to rank the different interpretations that come from these sorts of inquiries. Comprehensiveness is a key measure, for the more horizons an interpretation manages to account for, the more powerful an explanation it will be (Forthcoming a).

Yet even some of those who share Taylor's belief in the need for a hermeneutical approach to the human sciences have charged him with overstating the difference between the natural and the human sciences, or rather with reifying one difference and neglecting others as well as ignoring similarities between them. Clifford Geertz, for instance, suggests that Taylor constructs the relationship between the natural and the human sciences in an excessively binary way. As a consequence, the differences among the various natural sciences get eclipsed. Because Taylor proceeds with an ideal type of "the natural sciences", his approach lacks an awareness of their plurality and the particular developments within each. Rather than making global claims about the natural sciences as such, Geertz advocates awareness of their variety. The various natural sciences have different objects, methods, procedures, working assumptions, cultures and histories. As this suggests, Geertz accuses Taylor of taking an ahistorical approach to these sciences; he operates as if they have simply been unfolding the unitary logic laid down in the seventeenth century. Another unfortunate consequence of Taylor's excessively binary separation of the natural and the human sciences is his failure to acknowledge the impact that developments within different branches of the natural sciences have had on human self-interpretations (Geertz 1994: 83–95). Joseph Rouse (1991) also makes these criticisms of Taylor. He argues that appreciating the histories of the different natural sciences is essential to understanding what they are and how they differ from one another. From this sort of historically informed vantage point, the natural sciences cannot be treated as "a natural kind". Rouse too points out that Taylor neglects the impact that developments within the natural sciences have had on humans' self-interpretations. In this context he raises a further question about Taylor's dichotomizing of the natural and the human sciences: where is the dividing line to be drawn? Are biology and primatology not sciences that tell us anything about humans and their behaviour? This question seems especially apposite in the light of Taylor's demand that humans be understood as embodied beings (see below.)

Taylor concedes many of these points and clarifies just what he means by insisting on a separation between the natural and the human sciences. Firstly, he does not want the differences between these two domains to obscure the intramural heterogeneity within each camp. On the contrary, he has, as Rouse notes (Rouse 1991: 55–6), always claimed that the image of the unity of the natural sciences is a myth. Taylor confesses, though, that he has paid too little attention to the developments over time within the different branches of the natural sciences. Secondly, he does not want the distinction between the human and the natural sciences to imply a radical separation of humans from nature: on the contrary, his aim is to relocate humans within nature. However, for Taylor the crucial difference between the two domains of inquiry boils down to the criteria that measure success in each. As we have seen, for him successful human sciences must take account of their subjects' self-interpretations; successful natural sciences need not and indeed cannot (Taylor 1994d: 233–6).

Practical reason

In modern western culture there has been a tendency to think that scientific reasoning is the highest or only mode of reasoning available, and where its canons fail, reason can find no purchase. As Taylor describes it, "modern philosophy, and to some extent modern culture, has lost its grip on the proper patterns of practical reason. Moral argument is understood according to inappropriate models" (1995a: 59). He rejects this assimilation of all human reasoning power to the classical scientific style of reasoning, and delineates a field and function for what he calls practical reason. When it comes to conflicting views in areas like ethics, religion, culture and politics, practical reason offers the possibility of a rational arbitration of differences. As he sees it, "Either reason is powerless to criticise, even for consistency, and nothing 'hangs together' with anything; or else we have to admit that there may be substantive issues between world-views which are arbitrable by reasoned argument aiming at validity" (1990b: 262; cf. 1991a: 23, 41, 53, 73). He draws on elements of the hermeneutical tradition in elaborating this conception too, but whereas a fusion of horizons can result in a more perspicacious appreciation of the differences between the interlocutors, the goal of practical reason is to reach agreement between disputing positions. Such resolution might not always be achieved, but this is the aim. As such, practical reason provides an alternative to lapsing into subjectivism and relativism, on the grounds that there is no fair, rational or unbiased way of mediating these sorts of normative differences (1985a: 12; 1995a: 34, 38, 55).

Like the interpretative activities of social scientists, this style of reasoning proceeds along the lines of a conversation and, like the means of evaluating their activities, it draws on a circular way of arguing. This is because practical reason starts from something that is common to the two (or more) positions in dispute. This shared element might be explicit in both or tacit in both or explicit in one and tacit in the other (1995a: 50–51, 55). Either way, practical reason draws on what the antagonists can see themselves as agreeing on. Without some common starting point or area of convergence in their outlooks, practical reason is helpless (*ibid.*: 53; cf. 1995b: 18). It cannot proceed from some point beyond the antagonists. In dramatic contrast to the natural sciences, which try to adopt "the view from nowhere" (Nagel 1979: 208),[7] to give an account of the natural world that is not situated, interested or partial, practical reason always starts with the view from somewhere, and that somewhere must be a place that can be acknowledged by the parties to the dispute. This is why Taylor describes this style of reasoning as *ad hominem*: it is directed at the participants in conversation and at the things they posit or value rather than introducing a set of neutral, independent criteria from outside the positions of the parties (Taylor 1989a: 505). This might upset or disappoint those who want to model their normative reasoning along the lines of natural science, which encourages the quest for neutral criteria and independent standards by which different positions can be judged. As Taylor says, "the very notion of giving a reason smacks of offering some external considerations, not anchored in our moral intuitions" (*ibid.*: 75). He calls this latter mode of reasoning apodictic: proceeding from its independent starting ground and employing neutral procedures, it presses on to conclusions that are final and certain. But once again he sees it as a category error to use or expect this sort of reasoning in normative debates. While this mode of reasoning might work in some parts of the natural sciences, it cannot be transplanted into areas where the disputes are primarily ethical in nature (1995a: 36, 38, 40). Practical reasoning offers a different style of reasoning from that associated with the natural sciences, but Taylor sees this as inevitable, given the different areas of contention and issues at stake between the two.

In contrast with the apodictic style of reasoning, practical reason strives, through the comparison, questioning and re-articulation of views, either towards some reconciliation of difference or to persuading the interlocutors that they should come to agree that one position is better. The successful account might be the position held originally by one of the sides in the debate or it might synthesize views from both or all sides. Taylor describes practical reason as reasoning in transitions. It is an inherently comparative enterprise and proceeds in stages by showing why one position is stronger than the alternatives in terms that all the parties can be induced to accept. The movement to a stronger position might occur by showing how a contradiction or error in an earlier one is removed when the later one is adopted. Or it might transpire that one position reposes implicitly on a claim that is explicit in another. Or there might be some anomaly that the weaker position cannot resolve but that dissolves in the stronger one. Whatever the strategy employed, the argument progresses by one party making an "error-reducing move" that the other(s) cannot rationally repudiate or deny (*ibid.*: 15, 48, 50–51, 53–5).[8] As this reference to reducing error signals, the grounds for transition from a weaker to a stronger position are epistemic (1989a: 72). Hence Taylor's belief that this is an exercise of reason rather than rhetoric or power or obfuscation. As he says:

> we can give a convincing narrative account of the passage from the first to the second as an advance in knowledge, a step from a less good to a better understanding of the phenomena in question. This establishes an asymmetrical relation between them: a similarly plausible narrative of a possible transition from the second to the first couldn't be constructed . . . portraying it as a *loss* in understanding is not on.
>
> (1995a: 42, original emphasis)

However, even when such a stronger position is achieved and assented to by the parties, it yields only the "best account" rather than any final or definitive truth (1989a: 74). The outcome can only be the best account to date, because there is always the possibility that it may be superseded by a superior, more encompassing perspective in the future. In characterizing the products of practical reason as provisional, Taylor is drawing on the work of Alasdair MacIntyre, and in particular his claim that:

> we are never in a position to claim that we now possess the truth or now we are fully rational. The most that we can claim is that this is the best account which anyone has been able to give so far, and that our beliefs about what the marks of a "best account so far" are will themselves change in what are at present unpredictable way.
> (MacIntyre 1977: 455, quoted in Taylor 1995a: 54)[9]

So like the knowledge obtainable in the human sciences, practical reason is open-ended; because it too deals with human affairs, its results cannot aspire to some ultimate or definitive status. As Chapter 1 illustrates, Taylor puts this aspect of practical reasoning to work as a moral theorist when he defends his version of moral realism. It is argued below that it also provides the model for his approach to overcoming epistemology.

Underpinning Taylor's whole conception of practical reason is a definition of reason that goes beyond the usual formal requirements, such as the avoidance of contradiction, the need for consistency and so on. Drawing on the older Platonic notion of being rational as involving the ability to give an account of something, Taylor connects reason with articulation, with "being able to say clearly what the matter in question is" (Taylor 1985b: 136–8; cf. 1995a: 12). Of course giving a clear account of something usually involves avoiding contradiction and inconsistency in depicting a phenomenon, notwithstanding the fact that it is possible to give a clear account of contradictory or inconsistent behaviour or thinking. So the point here is not that Taylor excludes the formal characteristics usually associated with reason, but that his view of reason as articulation is wider than this.

The model of practical reason that Taylor advocates offends the traditional model of scientific reasoning in four important ways. Firstly, the belief that reason should be neutral and disengaged from the intuitions and commitments of ordinary ethical life makes the idea of directing one's arguments at a particular person or position's starting point seem illegitimate; it is too particular a way for reason to proceed. As Taylor notes, *ad hominem* arguments have been largely discredited by the apodictic style of reasoning, and while he is not trying to vindicate all uses of the *ad hominem*, when it comes to normative disputes he regards its redemption as essential. Secondly, practical reason employs criteria of evaluation that can be accepted by the parties to the dispute rather than appealing to external standards to judge a position in the way that scientific reasoning does. Thirdly, classical scientific reasoning sees itself as dealing with fully explicit positions, whose premises can be spelt out, examined and evaluated. Precisely because it might appeal to intuitions and implicit logics, practical reasoning can invoke claims and beliefs that lie unarticulated in a moral, political or spiritual outlook, but that are nevertheless essential to its coherence and credibility. In the process of reasoning about them, these tacit positions must become explicit, but the work of practical reasoning does not have to begin with fully expressed and explicit knowledge claims. And finally, the sort of outcomes are different for the two styles of reasoning. As noted, practical reasoning yields provisional, comparative, relatively stronger conclusions (1994f: 36), whereas traditional scientific reasoning aspires to conclusions that are absolute rather than relative assessments (1995a: 59–60).

Yet notwithstanding these notable differences between canonical scientific conceptions of reasoning and practical reason, some of the major innovations in scientific understanding seem to be illuminated by this model. The shift from pre- to post-Galilean science, for example, is better understood when construed as reasoning in transitions rather than by comparing two closed, seemingly incommensurable theories against independent criteria of evaluation. Perhaps this is because this sort of paradigm shift, as it has come to be known through the work of Thomas Kuhn, resembles a clash between two worldviews in the way that some normative disputes do (*ibid.*: 46–9). The reason why practical reasoning seems to furnish a way of arbitrating between different views of the natural world is also related directly to Taylor's realism. Although the model of practical reason is inspired by the hermeneutical tradition, it assumes that one account can emerge from this process as better than its rivals. When it comes to the natural sciences, Taylor is a more or less a traditional realist. He accepts that some accounts of natural phenomena are simply better or more correct than others. He is persuaded that "modern science represents a superior understanding of the universe, or if you like, the physical universe" and that "the superiority of modern science . . . has greatly advanced our understanding of the material world" (1985b: 148–9; cf. 150, 129; 1980a). When it comes to explaining the rise of modern science in purely epistemological terms, he suggests that this can be done by reference to the fact that it offers a better or truer account of the workings of the natural world than did its predecessors:

> a science which tried to explain inanimate nature in terms of the realization in different kinds of entity of their corresponding Forms has given way to a science which explains by efficient causation, mapped by mathematical formulae. Aristotle on this issue has been buried by Galileo and Newton, and there is no looking back. Certain views are unrecoverable; nobody can even get close to marshalling good grounds for believing them any more.   (1990b: 262; cf. 1994d: 221)

So when two scientific paradigms clash, the one that seems to afford the "best account" of the natural world can emerge as superior.

Taylor's realism impinges, in turn, on his position about the difference between the human and the natural sciences. As noted above, it has been argued that he exaggerates the differences between these two fields of inquiry. Another consequence of this is his failure to see that interpreting nature is also a hermeneutic enterprise (Rouse 1991; Kuhn 1991; Rorty 1994). Taylor would accept the claim that interpreting nature is such an enterprise, but the difference is that whereas natural science operates within one web of meaning, the social sciences involve two (Warnke 1985: 346). However, natural science needs to be seen as the sort of hermeneutic enterprise that practical reason is, where one interpretation can emerge as superior or more plausible than others; a "best account" of nature is attainable. As noted, Taylor thinks that the approach inaugurated in the seventeenth century, which strove for a non-anthropocentric account of the natural world, has proven itself superior to others, both in western and in non-western cultures. So, to use Kuhn's example, while different cultures might interpret "the heavens" differently, Taylor would contend that the account of the planetary system that has developed in western science is a truer and more accurate account than the others. While this analysis might not be compatible with all cultural understandings of the heavens, it can still be recognized as a better account of how this natural system operates. What is at stake here is not explaining how different cultures interpret the heavens – that would require a fusion of horizons – but rather determining which account gives a better explanation of the movements of these natural entities. Kuhn claims that:

> No more in the natural than in the human sciences is there some neutral, culture-independent, set of categories within which the population – whether of objects of or actions – can be described. (Kuhn 1991: 21)

But this seems to miss Taylor's point. The language of seventeenth-century science was not culture-independent or neutral; it did express a particular perspective on the natural world, but one that strove to imagine it in a disengaged way. This is a cultural achievement, not the absence of culture, and it is a particular, unusual and counterintuitive approach to nature that Taylor believes has proven to be immensely fruitful. So the difference between the human and the natural sciences is not that the former are hermeneutic and the latter not, for contending interpretations of the natural world can be arbitrated by a process like practical reasoning. Rather, the key point is that the human sciences must take account of the self-interpretations of their subjects. For Taylor, while it makes sense to strive for a perspective on nature that is shorn of its human meanings, this is lunacy when applied to society and human behaviour.[10]

To understand Taylor's views on natural science it is necessary to distinguish theoretical from atheoretical approaches. He notes that while being rational and being theoretical are closely connected in modern western culture, the two are not coextensive. This allows him to argue that cultures can be rational without being theoretical; an example he gives is the Azande culture with its belief in witchcraft. However, as illustrated by the discussion of practical reason, his concept of reason as involving clear articulation allows for comparative judgements about different reasonings: it does not enjoin the relativist acceptance that there are simply different ways of reasoning about things. If one culture gives a clearer account of something, such as the operations of the physical universe, we can say that it offers a more rational explanation of nature. Taylor believes that modern western science does offer a better account of the natural world, and so deems it a superior form of reasoning to the belief in witchcraft. As noted above, not all cultures have striven for this sort of disengaged, theoretical understanding of the world, and western culture itself has not always done so. The scientific revolution of the seventeenth century was a turning point in this development; prior to that Taylor claims that the aspiration to understand nature was bound up with the goal of being attuned to it (see Taylor 1985b: 128–9). What allowed modern science to achieve its superior, theoretical understanding of nature, which then had immense spin-offs in terms of the ability to control it via technology, was its ambition to formulate a disengaged perspective on the natural world.

The scientific revolution

In both of the major topics discussed so far – the nature of the human sciences and the nature and purpose of practical reason – Taylor is anxious to draw attention to and begin to roll back the hegemony of scientific models of reason on western thinking. To see why he believes this to be so necessary, appreciating his interpretation of the scientific revolution of the seventeenth century and its legacy is essential. For Taylor this period was a watershed in epistemology in particular and philosophy in general, and its impact went way beyond debates about truth, knowledge, method and procedure. He refers, for example, to "the tremendous hold of epistemology over modern culture" (1995a: 40), and to understand what he means by this it is necessary to see what he deems the distinctive features of the scientific revolution to be and how he explains their immense reach.

The foci of Taylor's interest in the scientific revolution of the seventeenth century are less the natural scientists than the philosophers of the new science: Descartes, Bacon, Hobbes and Locke. This can be explained by the fact that as a philosopher, he is concerned with the conceptions of reason, truth, knowledge and so on that were used to explain and justify these developments in the understanding of nature, and so it is to those who articulated the new science rather than those who practised it that he turns. Of course in many cases these were the same people: Descartes was a mathematician as well as a philosopher of science; Bacon was a natural scientist as well as a theorist of scientific method; Hobbes was a geometer as well as a political scientist. But in these cases, it is the interpretation and defence of what it means to engage in science that interests Taylor.

Taylor uses Max Weber's image of "the disenchantment of the world" to capture the wider background against which the epistemological innovations of the seventeenth century occurred and to which they, in turn, contributed. As noted in Chapter 2, what Taylor means by describing the modern world as disenchanted is that the cosmos was no longer held to harbour any final purposes or intrinsic moral value, and that consequently there was no need for humans to seek any preordained meaning or order in it (1985b: 256–60; 1989a: 18, 160, 395). Although influenced by older religious debates about voluntarism and nominalism, the erosion of belief in an inherently meaningful cosmos that bore prescriptions for human life began with the scientific revolution's mechanistic view of nature. Taylor claims that from this time onward, "the world was no longer seen as the reflection of a cosmic order to which man was essentially related, but as a domain of neutral, contingent fact, to be mapped by the tracing of correlations, and ultimately manipulated in the fulfilment of human purposes" (1975a: 539; cf. 7).

This change in worldview helps to explain one of the most influential developments in modern scientific thinking: the quest for disengaged, objective knowledge. This involved an attempt to understand the world devoid of its human meanings and significance. The ambition was to distil what the essential or primary properties of things were by distinguishing these from what humans bring to the process of knowing (1985b: 136, 143; 1995a: 65; Forthcoming a). Taylor describes this as trying to identify, and then neutralize, the anthropocentric aspects of human knowledge. Anthropocentric features such as colour became secondary properties; they were qualities that things acquired in the human beholding of or contact with them, but that were not essential to the things themselves (1980a: 48; 1985a: 2, 106; 1985c: 267–8; 1989a: 130; 1995a: 40, 148). This way of interpreting the world has, by Taylor's own admission, proven hugely beneficial in advancing knowledge in the natural sciences, but, as indicated above, he believes that it is wholly inappropriate when extended to the human sciences.

This new image of humans as detached from their world contributed to another distinctive feature of the epistemological innovations of the scientific revolution: representationalism. This is a conception of knowledge as occurring when humans form inner mental pictures or representations of the outside world. The truth or accuracy of the knowledge thus generated depends on how exact the fit is between the inner representations and the independent reality they portray (1985a: 200; 1995a: 3–4; Forthcoming b; Forthcoming c). While the representationalist approach to knowledge was obviously compatible with Cartesian dualism, for mind was seen as inner and the material body and the natural world as outer, Taylor does not see it as confined to dualism. In fact, he contends that the representationalist view of knowledge is broader than any one epistemological theory. The general representational outlook is that "knowledge is to be seen as correct representation of an independent reality" (1995a: 3; cf. 4; 1991c: 308; Forthcoming b).

However, congruence between the inner, mental representation and the outer reality is only part of the representationalist picture of knowledge, for there is always the risk that such agreement is born of chance. To have confidence in the reliability of one's knowledge it was necessary for it to be acquired via a dependable procedure. In this development, associated most famously with Descartes, the emphasis on correct knowing devolves on the process or method of knowing; there is a belief that only if knowledge is pursued in the correct way will its outcomes be reliable. Confidence that knowledge is reliable is therefore something that the mind can procure for itself by following the correct method and ordering its thoughts accordingly. This is related to the development of what Taylor calls radical reflexivity (Chapter 2) or "self-monitoring reason" (1996d: 6), whereby thinking becomes preoccupied with its own procedures. The mind must turn in on itself and its operations and scrutinize these carefully before it can have any faith in its ability to know the external world (1989a: 144; 1995a: 4–5; 64). Taylor deems this shift from substantive to procedural reason as a momentous one for western thinking. He describes it and compares it with the older view when he writes that with Descartes' epistemology:

rationality is no longer defined substantively, in terms of the order of being, but rather procedurally, in terms of the standards by which we construct orders in science and life. For Plato, to be rational we have to be right about the order of things. For Descartes rationality means thinking according to certain canons. The judgement now turns on properties of the activity of thinking rather than on the substantive beliefs which emerge from it ... Rationality is now an internal property of subjective thinking, rather than consisting in its vision of reality. In making this shift, Descartes is articulating what has become the standard modern view. In spite of the wide disagreements over the nature of the procedure ... the conception of reason remains procedural.

(1989a: 156; cf. 121; 1995a: 40)

As Taylor acknowledges, Descartes tried to demonstrate that when the correct procedure was correctly followed it would yield substantive truths. So this is more a shift in emphasis rather than the absolute privileging of procedure over substance (1989a: 156; 1994d: 214–19).

However, in this quest for true knowledge, the goal was not knowledge for its own sake. Instead, the scientific revolution was notable for the belief that one of the benefits of understanding the natural world correctly would be the ability to reorder and reorganize it. This instrumental approach to knowledge is especially evident in the work of Francis Bacon, who claimed that knowledge is power and who hoped that the progress of scientific learning would yield myriad improvements in ordinary life (1975a: 8; 1989a: 232). Moreover, the faith that there would be pay-offs from this new knowledge in terms of humans' capacity to control the world confirmed the value and correctness of this new knowledge, and of the disengaged stance towards the world that made it possible.

The final distinctive element of the approach to knowledge bequeathed from the seventeenth century is foundationalism. This has two dimensions: macro and micro. The first, macro dimension is adverted to at the beginning of this chapter, for it relegates epistemology to a primary position in philosophy. The belief is that in order to understand anything it is essential to get the epistemology right first; to have a correct understanding of the procedures that generate reliable knowledge. From this standpoint, the nature of knowledge is always the prior question. The second, micro aspect of foundationalism appears in the demand that knowledge claims be thoroughly scrutinized, which requires that they be stripped back to their irreducible, underlying bases. Once the foundations of knowledge are endorsed as solid and dependable, then by following the correct method a sound structure can be erected on them, one that will prove impervious to error. Taylor expresses this micro dimension of foundationalism when he writes that:

> The aim of foundationalism is to peel back all the layers of inference and interpretation, and get back to something genuinely prior to them all, a brute Given: then to build back up, checking all the links in the interpretive chain. Foundationalism involves this double move, stripping down to the unchallengeable, and building back up.
>
> (Forthcoming c; cf. 1995a: 2, 40)

So in Taylor's estimation, the major epistemological legacies from the scientific revolution are the aspiration to disengagement, objectivity and neutrality, representationalism, proceduralism, instrumentalism and foundationalism. As a realist, he has no particular objection to these as modes of knowledge in the natural sciences (1985a: 291). However, as the above reference to hegemony intimates, what he opposes and tries to explain is their encroachment from one domain of intellectual activity on to others. At one point he characterizes this expansion as a norm being transposed into a theory of knowledge. The representationalist norm is that:

> it is essential to our scientific practice, to what we understand as the correct search for knowledge, that we set ourselves the goal of making an accurate representation of things. And this has meant shaking ourselves free from earlier views in which the demands of connection, communion, or attunement with the cosmos were still intricated with those of attaining an adequate picture of the true state of affairs. (*ibid.*: 291)

However, this norm about how to proceed in the pursuit of scientific knowledge has expanded into a theory of all knowledge. A particular and limited approach to understanding has become normalized as the approach to knowledge. In a different formulation, Taylor describes this process as ontologizing the disengaged perspective by reading it into the constitution of the mind itself (1995a: 61, 66). Although the description is different, the point is the same: through this ontologizing step, one particular way of knowing becomes inflated into all knowing; one particular exercise of reason becomes synonymous with reason itself; one form of mental activity becomes co-extensive with intellectual activity itself.

Taylor posits several reasons why this transposition or ontologizing occurred. Because the sort of knowledge purveyed in the natural sciences promised the power to reorder things, it was aspired to by those inquiring into human affairs also (1985b: 130). Hobbes's writings about the science of politics provides a good illustration of such emulation of the natural sciences. Since the scientific revolution, the natural sciences have been hugely successful in interpreting and changing the world and great prestige attaches to this sort of knowledge. However, Taylor also claims that the appeal of this epistemology has come from more than simply its promise of power and instrumental control. A certain ethical conception of what it was to be human was woven into this way of knowing the world, and this too has proven attractive. There is, he proposes, a notion of disengaged freedom bound up with the disengaged approach to knowledge. The belief that humans inhabit a disenchanted world means, for example, that they are free to develop their own goals and purposes rather than having to bend to preordained ones. A belief in self-responsibility and a certain conception of human dignity also inhere in this approach to knowledge. Thus the immense attraction of what Taylor calls the epistemological model has several sources, and these prove to be mutually reinforcing, for once the image of human identity and agency that the epistemological model presupposes is accepted, then its approach to knowledge seems all the more plausible. Certain social institutions and practices entrench this view of the self, and so on (1975a: 9; 1985a: 5–6, 12; 1985b: 5–7; 1995a: 4, 7–8, 75). Describing this process of mutual reinforcement, Taylor writes that:

> In a given society at a given time, the dominant interpretations and practices may be so linked with a given model that it is, as it were, constantly projected for members as the way things obviously are. I think this is the case – both directly, and via its connection with influential modern understandings of the individual and his freedom and dignity – with the epistemological model. (1984a: 21)

Paradoxically then, the place of the epistemological model becomes so preponderant in the theoretical imaginary and its appeal so multifaceted that eventually ethical and other considerations seem to overwhelm epistemological ones. How else, Taylor leads us to wonder, could social scientists be inspired to apply methods and models so patently unsuited to their topic? The imbrication of epistemological and ethical motives that he sees as explaining the dominance of this approach to knowledge means that in order to really understand it, it is necessary to go beyond epistemology to the spiritual roots of this outlook, to the strong evaluations or background distinctions of worth that draw people to it. The power of epistemological arguments cannot be understood in epistemological terms alone (1980b). However, as Taylor freely acknowledges, conducting this sort of analysis requires drawing on the tacit background of this approach to knowledge, on the things that do not feature overtly in the epistemological claims but that are, none the less, essential to explaining their force.

Overcoming epistemology

Many contemporary philosophers share Taylor's conviction about the need to challenge the epistemological legacy of the scientific revolution. However, the consensus weakens once the discussion continues about just what this involves. For some, challenging this legacy means attacking foundationalism, but not all agree on what this means nor where to go from there.[11] For Taylor a broader critique is required, because, as indicated, his understanding of the epistemological model includes more than foundationalism (1995a: viii, 13, 15, 19; Forthcoming b). Moreover, the attack on foundationalism does not go to the heart of this model as Taylor sees it: for him the central feature is the representational construal of knowledge, its assumption of disengagement and the ethical outlook inherent within it.

Just as it is the hegemony of the epistemological model that Taylor criticizes, so his aim in overcoming epistemology is not to jettison this approach to knowledge outright but to restore it to its proper, limited place. He wants to resituate, rather than repudiate, the epistemological model. As he says:

the disengaged identity is far from being simply wrong and misguided, and besides, we are all too deeply imbued with it to be able really and authentically to repudiate it. The kind of critique we need is one that can free it of its illusory pretensions to define the totality of our lives as agents, without attempting the futile and ultimately self-destructive task of rejecting it altogether.   (1985a: 7; cf. 1994f: 21, 43)

In going about this work of relocation, he draws on three continental thinkers of the twentieth century: Martin Heidegger, Maurice Merleau-Ponty and the later writings of Ludwig Wittgenstein (1991c: 304; 1993c; 1995a: 9, 21, 61–78, 165–80; Forthcoming b). From them he derives the ideas of engaged, embodied agency and a sense of the importance of the tacit background. He argues that the epistemological model's approach to knowledge is actually embedded within this more prior ontology of engaged, embodied agency, from which it tries to abstract itself. As this suggests, whereas the modern scientific approach to knowledge tries to prescind from ordinary human ways of being in and coping with the world in order to attain "the view from nowhere", Taylor's approach to knowledge begins with the fact and significance of embodied, quotidian involvement. One of the lessons Taylor takes from Heidegger is that humans are:

at grips with a world of independent things, prior to any attempt on our part to represent them ... The framework understanding ... which Heidegger sometimes calls "pre-understanding", is not itself a representation of our position in the world. It is that against the background of which I frame my representations, and that in virtue of which I know that these are true or false because of the way things are.

(1990b: 270)[12]

With the idea of embodied, engaged agency, Taylor is drawing attention to the fact that in our ordinary ways of being in the world, humans are creatures with bodies who find ourselves in a world where we have to act and meet practical demands. This sounds like a statement of the obvious, but for Taylor these are some primordial features of human existence that have been clouded over by the epistemological model's hold on the theoretical imaginary. Because the representational view of knowledge understates and tries to transcend the role of engaged embodiment in knowing, it becomes necessary for him to issue reminders about its significance. This aspect of Taylor's epistemology owes a debt to Hegel too, for Taylor reads him as saying that embodiment is fundamental to subjectivity (1975a: 567, 571; 1979a: 162–4). Merleau-Ponty's influence is especially salient here too: Taylor says he vindicated the necessary role of the body in human knowledge of the world (1989e).

The fact of embodiment means that we experience the world in a qualitatively different way than a disembodied being would; the body is both an enabling and constraining feature in our knowledge. It limits, for example, the ways in which we can perceive the world. We are, moreover, always oriented in space by virtue of being embodied, so that spatial orientation is a vital component of human experience. An embodied agent is one who:

> acts to maintain equilibrium upright, who can deal with things close up immediately, and has to move to get things farther away, who can grasp certain kinds of things easily and others not, can remove certain obstacles and not others, can move to make a scene more perspicuous; and so on.
>
> (1995a: 62; cf. 1991c: 309)

Taylor's reminder about the embodied self's location in physical space represents the material counterpart of his claim that one of the ontological features of selfhood is the self's being situated in moral space. He posits that "Being a self is existing in a space of issues, to do with how one ought to be, or how one measures up against what is good, what is right, what is really worth doing. It is being able to find one's standpoint in this space, being able to occupy, to be a perspective in it" (1988c: 298; see Chapters 1 and 2). His claim that "topography is essential to our language of the self" (1988c: 301) applies as much to the material, as to the moral, aspects of personhood.

The embodied self's orientation in space is directly related to its ability to cope in the world around it. One of the symptoms of being disoriented, either because of illness or unfamiliar surroundings, is the feeling of not being able to function as well as one normally does, of having to work at things that can usually be accomplished effortlessly. In fact, as Taylor says, being able to cope is itself a form of orientation. He observes that:

what we think of as orientation is not a form of "knowing-that", but a kind of "know-how"; that is, its contents cannot be expressed in a list of facts known about the environment, but it is a more general capacity to get around, to go from any point to any point in the environment. (1964a: 165; cf. 1989a: 74–5)

Once learned, much of this coping becomes unreflective; in the usual course of events, we make our way around without thinking about what we are doing. There is a body of knowledge or know-how and an acquisition of skills embedded in this ordinary, practical activity that is so familiar that it has become forgotten; it slips into the background of our awareness. Only when it fails – when I trip over the curb or bang into a lampshade – am I reminded of how much ordinary knowledge and ability is taken for granted (1995a: 11–12; Forthcoming d). This sort of practical, everyday coping is, in turn, linked with intentionality. As we have seen in Chapter 2, Taylor sees humans as oriented toward the world as purposeful beings. Our everyday coping occurs as we set out to achieve our goals, and things show up for us against the wider background of daily life according to their relevance for our purposes (Forthcoming b; Forthcoming c. For a general picture of engaged, embodied agency see 1991a: 105–7; 1995a: 21–25, 61–3).

This picture of engaged embodied agency challenges not just the tendency towards minimizing the body's impact on ordinary ways of knowing but also the very possibility of an inner/outer separation that characterizes the representational approach to knowledge. The sort of know-how that expresses itself in everyday coping cannot be construed as something that resides in my head or even in my body alone. It manifests itself in a way of operating in and with the world, so any idea of separating the self from its world becomes forced and artificial. From this perspective, "The idea is deeply wrong that you can give a state description of the agent without any reference to his/her world (or a description of the world *qua* world without saying a lot about the agent)" (Forthcoming b; cf. 1995a: 26–7; Forthcoming c).

However, it is not just knowledge about the world that Taylor depicts in this way: self-knowledge and self-interpretations are also embodied. What this means is that the very way in which people hold themselves, the way in which they occupy and move through space, conveys something about their sense of who they are. Those who hold their head high and stride confidently through a crowd embody one sense of self. Those who lower their eyes as they scuttle past others embody a quite different sense of self, and so on. A great deal of subtle, cultural knowledge is also embedded and expressed in such embodiment. For example, Taylor argues that people hold themselves differently, or speak more readily, in the presence of equals than with those to whom they feel some deference is owed. These examples also point to the social situation of the embodied self; these various comportments communicate not just how the person feels about himself or herself but also something of how he or she sees himself or herself *vis-à-vis* others. In making this argument that modes of embodiment and comportment convey something about the individual's sense of his or her social relationships, Taylor finds Pierre Bourdieu's notion of habitus useful: "A bodily disposition is a habitus when it encodes a certain cultural understanding. The habitus in this sense always has an expressive dimension. It gives expression to certain meanings that things and people have for us" (1995a: 178; cf. 170–71).

What Taylor is sketching with his picture of engaged, embodied agency is clearly a different type of knowledge from that postulated by the epistemological model. But he wants to go further than simply adumbrating an alternative account of knowledge. For him, engaged, embodied identity is prior to, and indeed the precondition of, representational knowledge. Once the significance and normalcy of engaged, embodied identity is appreciated, the representational approach to knowledge must be seen as nested in this wider way of being in and knowing the world. The limited, disengaged approach to epistemology only becomes possible against the wider background of everyday being in the world and appears as an aberration when compared to this more usual way of being and doing. Taylor explains that:

> Grasping things as neutral objects is one of our possibilities only against the background of a way of being in the world in which things are disclosed as ready to hand. Grasping things neutrally requires modifying our stance to them, which primitively has to be one of involvement . . .. The comportment to things described in the disengaged view requires for its intelligibility to be situated within an enframing and continuing stance to the world that is antithetical to it – hence this comportment couldn't be original and fundamental. The very condition of its possibility forbids us to give this neutralizing

stance the paradigmatic place in our lives that the disengaged picture supposes.

(Taylor 1995a: 73; cf. 11–12, 21, 70; 1991c: 308; Forthcoming b; Forthcoming c)

Taylor suggests, moreover, that it is only by depicting knowledge as the epistemological model does that the project of artificial intelligence becomes credible (1995a: 4, 63, 67; Forthcoming b). When this sort of knowledge is seen as ensconced in, and made possible by, engaged agency and the tacit background, this project appears less compelling because an agent's knowledge cannot be programmed into a computer.

As the point about the importance of this sort of practical know-how being occluded by the representational outlook indicates, one of Taylor's aims in giving an account of engaged, embodied agency is to bring to light the tacit background of representational episte-mology. This approach to knowledge overlooks and obscures its own background conditions, its own conditions of possibility. However, Taylor's concern in criticizing representational episte-mology is not only to unearth its own enabling conditions that reside in a more ordinary way of knowing and doing, but also to draw attention to the concept of the tacit background itself. This double movement is necessary because representational episte-mology suppresses not only the awareness of the tacit background that makes it possible, but also of any notion of the background at all (1999c: 173).

The phrase "the tacit background" or sometimes just "the back-ground" refers to the often unarticulated, unacknowledged, but vitally important assumptions, abilities and practices that underlie any activity. In his critique of representationalism, Taylor is talking about the things that make reflective, conceptual under-standing possible. But all activities are underlain by this sort of tacit background – language is another example. As this reference to language signals, this aspect of Taylor's thinking has been powerfully shaped by his interpretation of Wittgenstein's later arguments, in particular those from his critique of scepticism in *On Certainty* (1972), his challenge to the idea of language as ostensive definition in *Philosophical Investigations* (1958) and his account of what it means to follow a rule (Taylor 1995a: 165–80). Michael Polanyi's argument about the tacit dimension has also influenced Taylor's thinking on this score (Taylor 1985a: 146 n.2; 1995a: 294

n.7; 1999c: 165). All knowing, and indeed all activity, takes place against, and draws on, a tacit background of assumptions, practices and abilities. The significance of any element – sign, word, deed, gesture, symbol or object – relies not just on its meaning but also on the background milieu against which it shows up.[13]

This enabling background typically works in an imperceptible way. Yet despite its usual status as unacknowledged, unreflective and untheorized, it is not doomed to perpetual obscurity. Certain elements of the background can at times be retrieved, made explicit, reflected on and problematized. However, it is impossible for the whole background to be made explicit at the same time: understandings and activities are always parasitic on some things that cannot be brought into the focus of awareness (1975a: 467; 1995a: 11, 69, 74–5; 1999c: 165). As Wittgenstein says, "the *questions* that we raise and our *doubts* depend on the fact that some propositions are exempt from doubt, are as it were like hinges on which those turn" (Wittgenstein 1972: #341 original emphasis; cf. #163, #167, #337, #344, #354, #519). Conversely, things that occupy part of the foreground of awareness can, over time, slip into the background. This is well illustrated when a new skill is being acquired: consider learning to drive a car. At first I have to focus intently on every thing I do, on when to change the gears, when to flash the indicator, how to change from the brake to the accelerator pedals and so on. But over time and with practice, many of the capacities so painstakingly acquired become automatic, and I can think about refining my driving skills or I can engage in the activity with very little thought and attention at all. Driving a different car for the first time, some of the things that have lapsed into the background of my awareness will command my attention again, but this is only until I have mastered the new car, and then they will resume their place in the tacit background.

When thinking about the relationship between the tacit background and reflective, theoretical knowing, Taylor proposes a continuum of knowledge that stretches from engaged embodiment and ordinary coping at one end to the highly abstracted, disengaged scientific theorizing at the other. What changes in the move along the continuum is the level of consciousness at which beliefs are held as well as the level of consciousness of the knowing activity itself. Disengaged knowledge is highly self-conscious and highly artificial; it strives for a particular sort of understanding that does not come readily. Engaged embodiment is the opposite;

most of its knowing expresses itself in a doing that is unreflective and unselfconscious. Yet however different they are, these two types of understanding are not necessarily at odds; rather, the disengaged model actually relies on engaged embodiment for its realization. While it strives to think of the world in a disembodied, disinterested way, it still reposes upon and relies on the ordinary abilities of coping in the world. Thinking about knowledge in this continuous way avoids the ontologizing error Taylor imputes to the epistemological model, for it shows disengaged theorizing as one, rather than the only, type of knowledge and acknowledges its dependence on a more primitive, ordinary way of being and doing in the world (Taylor Forthcoming b).

The representational approach always harboured the danger of solipsism and scepticism: How can I be sure that my picture of the outside world is really true? How can inner and outer be connected in a reliable way? How can I be sure that the outside world is really there? In contrast to these doubts, Taylor points to the unproblematic realism of embodied agency. This approach to knowledge is immune from the sort of fundamental uncertainties that plague representational epistemology, or rather there is an *a priori* presumption of reliable knowledge in the engaged, embodied outlook. As he puts it, "non-realism is itself one of the recurrently generated *aporiai* of the [epistemological] tradition . . . To get free of it is to come to an uncompromising realism" (1990b: 258). Of course, from this perspective particular parts of an agent's knowledge about the world remain amenable to doubt, error and correction: I can wonder if I turned the coffee pot off before leaving home or I can forget where I put my watch. But the fundamental realities that there is a world with which I am engaged as an intentional, embodied being cannot meaningfully be thrown into question.

> These [particular] doubts can only arise against the background of the world as the all-englobing locus of my involvements. I can't seriously doubt this without dissolving the very definition of my original worry which only made sense against this background. (Taylor Forthcoming b)

To continue the example, I can wonder if I really did put my watch on the table as I thought I had, or I can even wonder whether I simply dreamt this and whether my watch might have slipped off my wrist unknowingly. But I cannot meaningfully doubt that the table exists, or that I did once have a watch or even that I have a wrist. Taylor quotes Merleau-Ponty on the meaninglessness of these sorts of fundamental doubts in this context: "If you ask yourself if the world is real, you're not hearing what you're saying" (Merleau-Ponty quoted in Taylor Forthcoming b).[14]

Of course the fact that the locus of embodied involvements is a shared world and that others are engaged and embodied in different ways does provide the possibility for disputes and controversies. So when Taylor characterizes this sort of realism as unproblematic, he does not mean that there is no room for debates about "how it really is" or "what is truly the case" but rather that the fundamental reality of this world is never thrown into doubt. These debates and disputes are limited; they take place against the background of a taken-for-granted realism. Moreover, the fact of the shared world means that the parties to the dispute have a common reference point for their arguments. And because they have been practically engaged in the world as agents, no outlook can be thoroughly wrong; no grip on the world by an engaged participant can be totally deluded. Some can be distorted or erroneous in parts, and some more distorted or erroneous than others, but the fact that knowing is so intimately connected with doing means that I must engage in a dispute with another on the assumption that his perspective has some validity (Taylor Forthcoming b; Forthcoming c).

This principle of initial respect for another's take on the world also extends to other cultures, and provides a further basis for Taylor's argument about the fusion of horizons when trying to understand other ways of life and systems of belief. No matter how unusual some culture's practices might seem, the realization that its members are also engaged embodied agents trying to make their way around and make sense of their world provides a foundation for common understanding (Forthcoming b). Describing John McDowell's approach to epistemology, Taylor says that "human knowing [is] finite, situated, and social-sense making" (2000a: 249). Taylor could be recounting his own views here, and once we see this fact about humans, we have some basis for mutual understanding as well as for the perception of different understandings of the world.

While most of the thinkers who have shaped Taylor's ideas on epistemology wrote during the twentieth century, Immanuel Kant is also an important source. In fact, Taylor contends that these twentieth-century thinkers were influenced by Kant's example of an "argument from transcendental conditions" (1995a: 9; cf. Forthcoming b). This style of argument starts with what is taken to be a basic, indisputable feature of existence and infers backward from this robust starting point. The justification for the inference is a logical one; for example, the inference of B might based on the fact that B is a condition of A's possibility where A is an undeniable feature of existence (1979a: 32–4; 1995a: 20–21).[15] Kant puts this sort of argument to work in the service of epistemology by starting with the basic fact that subjects have particular sorts of experiences; of time and space, for example. He "retrojects" from this to infer something about the constitution of the knowing subjects who have this sort of experience. As Taylor sees it, Wittgenstein, Heidegger and Merleau-Ponty all start with what he calls the agent's knowledge of the world, and go on to draw conclusions about the world and the agent from this tough starting point. As we have seen, the salient features of agents here are that they are embodied, engaged and intentional. And the picture of the self and its knowledge of, and relationship to, the world that emerges from this is very different from that associated with representational epistemology (1995a: 10–11, 22, 72).

Ultimately though, the power of a transcendental argument depends on its starting point and how robust it really is; as Taylor observes, "the philosophical achievement is to define the issues properly" (*ibid.*: 11). If a picture of ordinary experience presented as indisputable is actually contentious, then the transcendental argument might never get off the ground or might generate false inferences. This style of argument stands and falls on how perspicacious and convincing an account it gives of this primary reality. As Taylor acknowledges, because these arguments are "grounded in the nature of experience, there remains an ultimate, ontological question they can't foreclose . . . they must articulate what is most difficult for us to articulate, and so are open to endless debate" (*ibid.*: 33). Of course the dominance of the epistemological tradition and its attempt to transcend the dimensions of ordinary experience mean that we are little used to formulating these starting points. However, this weakness can be mitigated by the unproblematic realism Taylor associates with his preferred approach to knowledge, for debate about the features of ordinary existence is something that can be widely and fruitfully pursued.

There is a strong convergence between Taylor's use of a Kantian-inspired transcendental deduction and his advocacy of the "best account" approach to knowledge, which obtains in his moral theory as well as his reflections on epistemology. In both cases, the centre of theoretical gravity is how ordinary life is lived and what concepts are useful in making sense of this. Taylor asserts that "Nothing can trump the best account of what we have to presuppose in order to get on with the business of living" (1988d: 57).

These considerations become crucial in weighing the value of a theory, be it of moral life or of knowledge. A theory can be deemed more or less useful to the extent that it illuminates the ways in which ordinary life is lived and shows whether these terms are indispensable or not. The links between the transcendental deductive style of argument and the best account are manifest in the following passage:

> Once we have established our best possible account of the questions we have to take seriously in order actually to live our lives, once we have clarified, in other words, what the ontological assumptions are that we can't help making in practice as we go about the business of living, where in heaven or earth could the epistemological arguments come from that should convince us that we are wrong? What considerations could possibly trump the best self-understanding of what is inseparable from and indispensable in practice? (*ibid.*: 56)

An important question to arise from Taylor's critique of the epistemological tradition is to what extent and in what sense is he really overcoming it? One possible rejoinder to his argument is that rather than overcoming the foundationalism of the epistemological model, he simply substitutes a different sort of foundationalism. Rather than his approach taking an "anti-foundational turn" (Forthcoming b), the fundaments of knowledge are now revealed to lie in engaged embodiment and ordinary coping. There is something to this claim, for Taylor *is* advocating a new way of grounding disengaged knowledge and indeed all human knowing. However, it differs from the foundationalism of the epistemological model at both the levels identified above. Unlike what I have called the micro-level of foundationalism, Taylor's approach does not advocate that knowledge claims be stripped back to their irreducible, underlying bases. He sees the aspiration to strip down to the unchallengeable bases of knowledge as chimerical, for any act of knowing must presuppose some things that cannot be known reflectively, that cannot be formulated. Some things must remain as part of the tacit, unproblematized background in order for others to come into the light of awareness and scrutiny. In foundationalism, by contrast, "there is a temptation . . . to a kind of self-possessing clarity" (1995a: viii; cf. 11–12).

In contrast to the macro-level of foundationalism, Taylor's approach to knowledge does not accord epistemology a primary position. In his preferred model, what matters primarily is not knowing about knowing, but knowing about being or doing: knowledge of ontology rather than of epistemology assumes priority. So while knowledge is still central, the nature of knowledge itself is no longer the most important question. This becomes a secondary issue, something to be dealt with once we have an appreciation of the way humans are in the world and what they are doing. As Taylor sees it, "The great vice of the tradition is that it allows epistemology to command ontology" (1990b: 264).[16] His approach does not share the fixation with method and procedure that marks the epistemological model; as indicated at the beginning of this chapter, questions of correct method are contingent upon the object under study; they cannot be determined in advance.

So Taylor is rejecting the proceduralism of the epistemological model, and its particular understandings of foundationalism. He also repudiates the inner/outer dichotomy associated with the representational approach in favour of one that posits embodied engagement in the world as primary. He challenges the conflation of disengaged knowledge with knowledge itself, and relocates disengaged knowledge as an unusual and dependent theoretical achievement. He sheds light on the importance of background practices and assumptions, which he believes is obscured or denied by the epistemological model. This renders the belief that knowledge can be fully explicit fanciful. As he says in a claim that emphasizes the finitude of human knowing, "Instead of . . . hoping to achieve total reflexive clarity about the bases of our beliefs, we would now conceive this self-understanding as awareness about the limits and conditions of our knowing" (1995a: 14).

What this amounts to is an overcoming of the epistemological tradition in an Hegelian sense; it does not seek to jettison every aspect of the epistemological legacy but tries to preserve whatever is valuable in it and move it forward into a better, more comprehensive understanding of knowledge. Taylor himself underlines the continuity involved in his way of thinking about knowledge by claiming that his approach furthers the quest for "self-clarity about our nature as knowing agents" (*ibid.*: 14; cf. 15, 17) that was one of the motivations of the epistemological model. Practitioners of the older model thought that this clarity would be enhanced by identifying and abstracting from those things that humans brought to the quest for knowledge, features that were not inherent in the things themselves. Taylor, by way of compensation, progresses this quest by encouraging a recognition and re-engagement with those same things and a reconceptualization of knowledge that goes along with it.

So the ambition that unites Taylor's epistemology with the traditional model is that of achieving greater clarity about knowledge; he wants to take "the modern project of reason a little farther" (*ibid.*: 15). This common denominator provides a basis for practical reasoning about the two approaches. In fact there are several ways in which Taylor's critique of the epistemological model puts into practice some of his own ideas about practical reasoning. He argues comparatively for the superiority of his approach to epistemology, trying to present it as a gain in understanding compared to the traditional one. He claims, for example, that his approach is more comprehensive than the traditional one; it can account for disengaged knowledge along with engaged, embodied agency as well as the relationship between them. The epistemological model, by contrast, only has eyes for disengaged and representational knowledge. There is also an *ad hominem* element in Taylor's argument, for he believes that he can elicit the motivations of the older model. He maintains that its epistemological precepts were bound up with particular construals of moral notions like reason, freedom, and dignity and with a certain atomistic conception of the person. This model also offered the attraction of greater instrumental control over nature. So, like practical reasoners, Taylor is digging into the tacit background of the opposing approach and trying to make sense of it by reference to things that usually remain implicit but that are actually important forces in its appeal. Finally, from Taylor's concession about the difficulty of formulating the starting point for his argument about engaged embodiment, we can infer that this approach represents a "best account" argument about epistemology. Were someone to develop more perspicacious formulations about ordinary experience that then lead to quite different inferences about knowledge and subjectivity, he would have to be amenable to these.

Language

"Man is above all the language animal" (1985a: 216). As this claim signals, and as previous chapters have illustrated, the importance of language in Taylor's philosophy goes beyond his arguments about epistemology, for the question of language percolates through his analyses of morality, personhood and politics. For example, language is never a wholly individual matter; it always reaches beyond the self to posit another in conversation. This dialogical perspective is central to Taylor's claim about selfhood and self-interpretation as well as to his analysis of the politics of recognition. In all of this he employs an expressivist view of language, and contrasts this with the older instrumental view that saw language as simply a means to the end of more efficient communication and mental organization (see Chapter 2). This instrumental view was, moreover, closely associated with representational epistemology, for the role it accorded language was that of representing as adequately as possible an independently existing external reality (1985a: 224–6, 252–5, 282). The expressivist approach does not see language as a medium for representing an independently existing reality but is aware of its power to shape and perhaps transform the things that come into its domain. This sense of the importance of articulating something for the first time or articulating it differently informs Taylor's arguments about the importance of articulation in moral life (see Chapter 1). The expressivist understanding of language as constitutive, not merely representative, of reality is also central to his analysis of the distinctively modern self and to his argument that self interpretations are partly productive of selfhood (Chapter 2).

As this chapter has shown, retrieving the tacit background of practices and assumptions assumes significance at several points in Taylor's understanding of knowledge. It appears in his depiction of how horizons are fused, in his description of how practical reason operates and in his appeal to engaged embodiment as a way of dethroning the representational view of knowledge. The importance of language for humans, and the understanding of language as a shared good, also emerge through this exercise of retrieval. Seeing language as central to all facets of human life threatens atomistic ontologies, for they are unable to account for language as an irreducibly shared force in human life (1995a: 77).

However, it is insufficient to say that Taylor's attention to the pivotal role played by background practices and assumptions brings to light the centrality of language in human life. In important ways, his analysis of the background is modelled on his theory of language. For example, he insists on the holism of both the tacit background and of language. When he talks about the holism of language, three features, listed here in the order of diminishing scope, need to be appreciated. Firstly, language is embedded in a culture or a form of life, so in order to really understand a language it is necessary to have some appreciation of the way of life that it both reflects and shapes. As Rouse puts it, for Taylor "Linguistic distinctions and ways of employing them are embedded in larger contexts of social practice, which in turn could not exist without the appropriate linguistic resources" (1991: 47). The link between language and a form of life or culture means that like language, the tacit background can not be understood in an atomist way. The background consists of a web of shared meanings that are created and reproduced inter-subjectively. This web is independent of any particular individual although it is only activated by and through individuals.

Secondly, Taylor uses something like the *langue / parole* distinction from Ferdinand de Saussure's influential analysis of language. What this refers to is the dialectical relationship between the structure of a language (*langue*) and its everyday use in particular instances by ordinary speakers (*parole*). Acts of *parole* take place, and indeed are only possible, against the wider background of *langue*: it underpins and is implicitly present in or pointed to by them. But this does not mean that *langue* determines *parole* entirely; through innovation, speakers can make contributions and modifications to the wider linguistic structure (Taylor 1985a: 233; 1995a: 134; Forthcoming b). What this points to is the interaction between the part and the whole; the part only shows up against the wider, implicit whole. As Taylor says:

> This is what the holism of meaning amounts to: individual words can be words only within the context of an articulated

language. Language is not something that can be built up one word at a time. Mature linguistic capacity just doesn't come like this, and couldn't, because each word supposes a whole of language to give it full force as a word. (1995a: 94)

Thirdly, there is the claim that particular words in a lexicon deriving their meaning from the differences that separate them. So meaning is relative and relational; a word derives its denotation not simply from its referent but also from the ways in which it resembles and differs from the other lexical elements.

Similar relationships between part and whole obtain in Taylor's depiction of the tacit background of embodied agency. While particular items of this whole show up according to individuals' purposes and intentions, they only do so against the wider background of the whole. So as I stumble out of bed in the morning, the particular things that command my attention are the coffee pot and the coffee. But properly understood, these things must be situated in their wider, relational context of the kitchen, and the cupboard, and the stove and so on. All these other things do not dominate my awareness because I can take them for granted; they slip into the background. But if one of them breaks down or goes missing, it becomes the focus of my attention or concern.

So Taylor's approach to language is marked by its holism and its expressivism. The holist and expressivist aspects of language come together in the work of Herder, who Taylor describes as a hinge figure in the philosophy of language. For Herder the holism of language had two dimensions; the way in which language operates and the fact that it is the property of the collective first and then individuals derivatively (*ibid.*: 79–99). Taylor argues that Herder changed the way in which language could be understood in important ways, ways that are still being worked through and debated today.

One thing to emerge clearly from this chapter is that, for Taylor, the debate about overcoming epistemology has consequences for more than matters of truth, knowledge, method and certainty. Arguments about these matters are knotted up with views about language, personhood, society and ethics. Understanding knowledge differently affects the ways in which we explain morality, interpret selfhood and theorize politics (*ibid.*: vii, 3, 15; Forthcoming b; Forthcoming c).

Chapter 5

Conclusion: sources of secularity

In April and May 1999, Charles Taylor delivered a course of ten lectures at the University of Edinburgh as part of the annual Gifford lecture series. The Gifford lectures aim to "promote and diffuse the study of Natural Theology in the widest sense of the term – in other words, the knowledge of God".[1] Taylor's predecessors include William James, Sir James Frazer, Alfred Whitehead, Arnold Toynbee, Paul Ricoeur and Iris Murdoch. The theme of Taylor's lectures was secularity: he tried to answer from several angles the question of what it means to live in a secular age. In what follows, I outline the major contours and arguments of the lectures and note some points of continuity with his published works. Because the lectures have not yet been published and because they represent a work in progress for Taylor, there must be a provisional and general quality to this account.[2] However, because the project is of comparable magnitude to *Sources of the Self*, it seems important to give some indication of it in these closing pages. Moreover, when dealing with a thinker as indefatigable as Taylor, it is fitting to "conclude" an overview of his work by pointing to its future directions.

The first question Taylor addresses is "what is secularity?" Standard answers refer to the decline of religious belief in western societies, the separation of church and state and the disappearance or diminution of God from the public realm. As Taylor observes in an earlier piece on this question:

> when people talk about "secularization", they can mean a host of different things. In one sense, the word designates the decline of religious belief and practice in the modern world, the declining numbers who enter church, or who declare themselves believers. In another, it can mean the retreat of religion from the public space, the steady transformation, of our institutions toward religious and ideological neutrality their shedding of a religious identity. (1997c: ix)

Neither of these depictions seems adequate to Taylor. With regard to the first point about diminishing religious faith, he argues that there is actually a plurality of religious and spiritual belief in western societies rather than any straightforward decline. His remarks in an earlier essay on religion apply here:

> Agnostics often present a picture of linear development, in which more and more people have gradually lost their religious beliefs, culminating in an eventual condition in which religious belief and practice will be a marginal phenomenon. But things do not seem to be turning out that way. For one thing, there seems to be a great deal of lapsing from churches in present-day society that is not matched with a loss of belief in God, in the afterlife, or in some spiritual principle. Deconfessionalization is a major phenomenon, but it by no means betokens simply unbelief. Religion does not decline because churches do. (1990a: 105)

While he is more willing to accept the second depiction of a secular society as one that separates religion from the public domain, it is still insufficient. One reason for this is that, at least in the USA, the separation of religion and the state was initially conceived of as a way of preventing any single faith being imposed on the different believers who made up society. The aim was not so much to drive religion out of the public realm as to protect its diversity. Religion's withdrawal from public life was not a necessary part of this vision. Here Taylor distinguishes the disestablishment of church and state from the privatization of religious faith. Part of the challenge of understanding secularity is to explain how the first became subsumed under the second and the distinction between them eclipsed (*ibid.*: 102–3, 104, 111). He suggests, moreover, that rather than the complete eradication of God from public life, what we have seen is more a change in his mode of involvement. Whereas in the past political power and authority were seen to be underwritten by the deity, these are now seen as created by the consent of the people for the furtherance of their individual ends. This does not preclude groups and individuals from appealing to God or religious values in political debates, but there is no longer a widespread consensus about exactly how God should figure in politics; this is now a matter for debate and deliberation.

Taylor proposes a third definition of secularity, which is not necessarily at odds with the second one but which takes a wider, cultural vista and focuses on the changed conditions of religious belief. From this perspective, the most notable feature of living in a secular age is that adherence to religious belief seems problematic to many, and even for those who are theists, their faith appears as one among several reasonable and possible alternatives. But non-theists exist in this situation of cross-pressures too: as Taylor says:

> It is impossible in our days to be a Christian, atheist, or anything else, without a degree of doubt. Our situation is characterised by this instability, much more than by the idea that secularism has swept away religion.   (1998b: 111)

The contemporary context of religious faith differs markedly from that in the pre-modern western world, where belief in God was simply part of the cultural furniture. So in trying to understand secularity, Taylor conducts a historical inquiry into what has changed in the years from 1500 to 2000, from a time when belief in God was part of the accepted background and foreground of western culture to one where it is now optional. He even contends that in some milieux, such as the academic world, theism is an embattled option, one that must always be on the defensive.

This marginalization of theism, its move from the taken-for-granted position to one among other options, is closely related to one of the singular features of the secular age: the power and influence of what Taylor calls exclusive or self-sufficient humanism.[3] This is a moral-cum-spiritual outlook that construes human flourishing solely in this-worldly terms, without any reference to God, divinity, transcendent goods or an after-life. Taylor is not claiming that the possibility of such a doctrine is unprecedented, for some of the ancient Epicurean outlook resembles this sort of exclusive humanism. Rather it is the pervasiveness of this outlook, its reach and dominance, that he finds remarkable. Human flourishing, understood in human and only human terms, is for many people life's ultimate goal. What this represents, conversely, for those who continue to believe in God and to prize goals that transcend the all-too-human, is a major change in the context of their spiritual outlook.

Explaining how this change occurred is no simple task; Taylor draws on many different, yet interwoven threads while acknowledging that even his rich and complicated exposition will be incomplete. Yet while cognizant of these limitations, he insists that reconstructing a history of the present is invaluable. One reason for this is his general agreement with Hegel that the present cannot be understood without a knowledge of history; the past is sedimented in the present. But an historical perspective on secularity is important for a more specific reason. Taylor suggests that many critics of theism script for themselves a sort of enlightenment narrative whereby freedom from theism counts as progress, where the overcoming of religious faith is a step forward in human rationality and maturation. Individuals or cultures that remain mired in theism are seen as backward. This tendency to interpret contemporary theism as a throwback to an earlier age represents a particular manifestation of some general points that Taylor has made before. For example, at the most general level he argues that this sort of contrastive self-understanding is inevitable for human beings, referring to "the universal human necessity of defining one set of possibilities by contrast with others" (1978b: 22). More particularly, he observes that in the modern world, the contrast has typically been with former times, with the ways of life and self-understandings of our predecessors:

> ours is a historical civilization, in the sense that we have defined ourselves by certain notions of progress, or development, or maturation relative to earlier civilizations. It is a central feature of our civilization that an important part of the contrasts in terms of which we define ourselves is historical. That is, we consider ourselves to be moderns who are rational, who have a certain ideal of autonomy, and we define this

partly by the contrast with earlier civilizations, which we believe to have lacked those notions in important ways.

(*ibid.*: 22; cf. 23; 1978a: 135–6)

Thirdly, Taylor's historical approach stems from his persistent concern with promoting cultural self-awareness in westerners. It follows from the second point above about the enlightenment narrative seeing freedom from theism as progress and individuals or cultures that retain theism as atavistic. In tracing the history of secularity, Taylor is showing that what is seen as natural and taken for granted is actually historical and particular. People have not always thought or lived in this way and many people still do not, so again he is suggesting that fuller self-knowledge will enhance the ability to appreciate and respect difference in others. But in telling the story of how theism moves from being part of the cultural landscape to an embattled option in western culture, Taylor is also dispelling any hopes that its former pre-eminence can be recaptured. He is acutely aware that secularity has changed the context of belief forever in western cultures. Irrespective of how embattled it might be in certain contexts, it is necessarily made more fragile by the plurality of alternatives spawned in the modern and postmodern eras.

From this sketch alone it is clear that Taylor's latest project complements the work of *Sources of the Self* in many ways. In fact, the current project can be seen as elaborating upon the passage in *Sources of the Self* where Taylor writes that:

> something important and irreversible did happen in the latter part of the nineteenth century with the rise of unbelief in Anglo-Saxon countries. It was then that they moved from a horizon in which belief in God in some form was virtually unchallengeable to our present predicament in which theism is one option among others. (1989a: 401; cf. 408)

Like *Sources of the Self*, the current work is concerned with a large-scale cultural shift in self-understandings and notions of morality, remembering that Taylor construes morality broadly, as encompassing what it is right to do as well as what it is good to be and what is worthy of love. Both projects also take an historical turn, contending that in order to understand contemporary culture it is necessary to be aware of its genesis, evolution and the outlooks and possibilities that have been marginalized along the way. In both cases, Taylor is adamant that modernity provides a new vision of the good rather than representing the mere loss of some older worldview and morality. And both projects emphasize the phenomenological: the aim is to understand how people experience modern selfhood or secularity rather than simply evaluating theories that purport to explain either phenomenon. The people whose experiences are interpreted in both projects are those who live in western societies, those who Taylor describes as living in the North Atlantic world, even though he would not want to exclude most of the inhabitants of places like Australia and New Zealand from his account. Nor does this geo-cultural focus deny that secularity has touched other parts of the world; rather it is intended to underscore the fact that the experience of those in western societies is qualitatively different from those in which religious belief is still part of the shared fabric of ordinary life. So the secular age that Taylor is trying to describe and interpret has no neat boundaries; its borders can only be drawn with a combination of geographical, social, cultural and temporal considerations in mind. And finally, both projects hope to engender greater cultural self-knowledge in their western readers.

Taylor identifies two dominant, alternative approaches to explaining secularity. The first links it with the rise of science in a sort of zero-sum equation: as scientific knowledge increased, so belief in God decreased. According to this line of argument:

> Science . . . has displaced religion, made the old creeds incredible, and that is what has transformed public life. The crisis felt by many believing Christians in the nineteenth century after the publication of Darwin's theories is taken as a paradigm expression of the process at work.   (1997c: x)

Taylor is dissatisfied with this approach for several reasons. The first is that there is no necessary contradiction between the natural sciences' account of nature's operations and all forms of theism. He explains the perception of such a conflict as deriving from a pre-existing moral sense that these outlooks are incompatible, rather than being a conclusion reached on its epistemic merits alone. He is convinced that "the obstacles to belief in Western modernity are primarily moral and spiritual, rather than epistemic" (1996d: 24–5).[4] Secondly, given his focus on the experience and self-understandings of people as believers or unbelievers, he cannot accept an explanation that trades only in arguments and theories. He maintains that if the meaning of this transformation is to be grasped, a different sort of account is needed, one that takes seriously the drawing power of the ideals associated with secularity. This points to another reason for Taylor's dissatisfaction with the standard account. When the growth of scientific knowledge is forwarded as an explanation of secularity, ethical ideals usually play an auxiliary role. The suggestion is that science presents people with epistemic gains in understanding the world, and a certain quantity of courage and integrity is needed to accept these. Erstwhile believers are faced with the challenge of whether they are strong and daring enough to accept the truths of the disenchanted world as disclosed by science. The assumption is that those armed with the right information and the requisite strength and perspicacity will cease being theists.

The conventional explanation of secularity as presented and questioned by Taylor sees the displacement of religion by modern humanism as the loss of old illusions and superstitions. Coupled with this is a particular psychology of religion, which attributes theism to childish needs and the lack of the capacity for a robust, unflinching view of reality. Underpinning this whole outlook is what Taylor calls "the subtraction thesis", which explains secularity primarily in terms of loss: loss of faith in God, loss of need for God, loss of old illusions and superstitions and the sloughing off of childish ways. While Taylor does not deny that this approach captures some of what is involved in the shift to secularity, on its own he deems it to be an inadequate account. His general reluctance to privilege epistemic accounts over moral ones manifests itself here, for his preferred explanation of secularity accentuates the moral rather than the intellectual attractions of the secular outlook. Making the sort of argument that appears in *Sources of the Self* about the appeal of the ideals that attend the ambition toward disengaged knowledge, he proposes that its promises of power, agency, self-possession and dignity drew followers. So rather than view the change primarily in terms of intellectual pay-offs, Taylor proposes that in the clash between the scientific worldview and the older view of nature, a different model of what was higher triumphed. He is not saying that changes in scientific understandings of nature were wholly irrelevant to the growth of secularity. On the contrary, he discusses how the theory of evolution added fuel to the new way of viewing the universe. Whereas the older view saw the cosmos as fixed, limited and unvarying, with the development of modern science from the seventeenth century onward, the world has come to be seen as vast, perhaps infinite and constantly evolving. So rather than saying that advances in scientific learning are nugatory, he argues that they do not provide a sufficient explanation of secularity (Taylor 1989a: 402–3).

The second dominant approach to explaining secularity was pioneered by the French sociologist Émile Durkheim. Whereas the first line of argument makes personal beliefs and the declining belief in God the engine that drives secularism, this one makes the decline in personal belief a response to the changing institutional place of religion in social life. The Durkeimian approach sees religion as:

> a pattern of practices that gives a certain shape to our social imaginary. Religion – or, as Durkheim liked to put it, the sense of the sacred – is the way we experience or belong to the larger social whole. Explicit religious doctrines offer an understanding of our place in the universe and among other human beings, because they reflect what it is like to live in this place. Religion, for Durkheim, was the very basis of society. Only by studying how society hangs together, and the changing modes of its cohesion in history, will we discover the dynamic of secularization. (Taylor 1997c: x)

As the previous depiction of Taylor's contrast between the contemporary context of religious faith and the pre-modern world where belief in God was part of the accepted cultural background (and foreground) intimates, he is much more sympathetic to the Durkheimian approach.

In forging his own explanation of the rise of secularity, and in particular of exclusive humanism, Taylor conducts an excursion into medieval times, and in particular into the later mediaeval period. This marks a major difference between his current project and *Sources of the Self*, for the latter paid minimal attention to the medieval period. By blinking one could miss it in the move from Augustinian to Cartesian accounts of inwardness (see Adeney 1991: 208). In his current work, Taylor nominates three features of the older society that made belief in God seem inevitable, that provided bulwarks for belief. They were: the view that God created the natural world; the way that he was implicated in politics and indeed the whole order and operation of society; and the faith that in an enchanted world, populated by spirits and other supernatural powers, God was a force for the good. Over time each of these bulwarks crumbled. In the contemporary world, nature is explained in the disengaged terms of science; religion has withdrawn from or resituated itself within public life; and the cosmos is disenchanted in the sense that science seeks to provide an exhaustively naturalistic account of its dynamics. Although appeals to magic or supernatural forces still echo in western cultures, they can be dismissed by many as superstitious nonsense in a manner unthinkable in an enchanted world.

In analysing the gradual disenchantment of the world, Taylor makes a claim that recurs throughout his exploration of secularity. He contends that the process of disenchantment began within a religious outlook. In a drive to rationalize religious faith, Christianity generated its own critique of church-controlled magic and of sacred sacramentals. To illustrate his thesis that many of the impulses that lead to exclusive humanism originated from religious motives and aspirations, much of Taylor's discussion is occupied with recounting drives to reform religious faith and practice within Catholicism and, after the Reformation, within Christianity. He attributes, for example, considerable significance to the pushes for reform within the Catholic Church that began in the eleventh century with Pope Gregory VII and then to the goal of the Fourth Laerten Council in 1215 to require annual confession and communion for all lay people. This represents another difference from *Sources of the Self*, for discussions of canonical philosophical works occupy a lesser role in the current project and more straightforwardly historical accounts play a correspondingly larger one. Taylor's contention that many of the impulses that lead to exclusive humanism originated from religious motives and aspirations also means that his narrative of secularity includes many tales of roads not taken and of unintended, unforeseen and even contradictory consequences (see Taylor 1997c: xi).

As the world became increasingly disenchanted, what Taylor calls "the buffered self" came into being. This denotes a view of the self as far less vulnerable to forces beyond its control than was the case in an enchanted world of spirits and demons. For the buffered self, the boundaries between self and world, inner and outer, seem far less permeable than they did to those living in an enchanted world. The phrase "the buffered self" captures a more clearly and tightly bounded notion of selfhood as well as one that is less hostage to the slings and arrows of fortunes that it cannot control. As Taylor puts it:

> In the enchanted world of 500 years ago ... the boundary around the mind was constitutionally porous. Things and agencies which are clearly extra-human could alter or shape our spiritual and emotional condition, and not just our physical state (and hence mediately our spiritual or emotional condition), but both together in one act. These agencies didn't simply operate from outside the "mind", they helped to constitute us emotionally and spiritually.   (Taylor in Gifford Lecture)

Another defining feature of secularity is its changed view of time. In this case it is literally so, for the term secular derives from "saeculum", meaning a century or an age. Taylor notes that, traditionally, living in secular time meant living an ordinary life, as compared to the lives of those who had devoted themselves to God and higher things and who strove to live within the time frame of eternity. So the term secular once denoted a contrast between what was ordinary and what was higher or eternal. Secular time differed from higher time in being regular and linear; it could be measured in fixed, uniform amounts and events succeeded one another in the way most westerners now regularly think of time. In higher time, by contrast, the dynamics of ordinary time were suspended. From this perspective, a certain date, such as Easter Sunday, could be seen as being closer in time to the day of Christ's resurrection than to a Sunday two months ago. The order of higher time was determined by the nature, significance and quality of its events rather than by any number of the sun's risings. These two time frames, secular and higher, were not, however, wholly independent. An event in secular time could take on new meaning depending on its relationship to higher time (Taylor 1998a: 31–2).

In contrast to this differentiated consciousness of time, contemporary western culture is dominated by a single, uniform conception of time, one that Taylor, following Walter Benjamin, calls "homogeneous, empty time". However, there is a sense in which Christianity prepared the way for the dominance of this linear approach to time, for it obscured the older, cyclical approach to time with its depiction of the relationship between ordinary and higher time. In the older, cyclical view, patterns and events were seen to recur like the seasons. The Christian belief in God's intervention in history meant that this approach to time was no longer appropriate: to take the example of the Incarnation, Christ's becoming human could not be conceived of as an event in a self-repeating cycle but was to be appreciated as unprecedented and uniterable (Taylor 1995a: 269–71; 1997b: 38; 1998a: 42).

Along with the disenchantment of the world and the homogenization of time, a third major ingredient of secularity has been a new conception of order. Taylor describes the social imaginary of secular societies as constituted by a picture of individuals cooperating for mutual benefit through exchanging goods and services, with a spontaneous order and harmony generated by this aggregated cooperation. This conception runs very deep, and shapes our image of society, economy and politics. It provides a view not only of what human interaction is like but also of how it should be. This social imaginary is obviously modelled on images of economic life that emerged in the eighteenth century, and in turn it accords economic transactions a paramount importance in human life. This view of self-sustaining social order and stability gradually eclipsed older conceptions of social cohesion based on hierarchy and command, and it also made God seem superfluous to the maintenance of peace and prosperity. In contrast with the medieval social imaginary that had seen God's power and beneficence implicated in many areas of social life, this new view focused on human beneficence or even just self-interest to reproduce order.

To understand the formation of this new social imaginary, Taylor contends that it is necessary to reach back into church history, and to see how certain movements within the church pressed for increased social order. From around 1500, groups within Christianity sought to break down the barriers between elite and mass and to make ordinary people's lives more civilized. This amounted to a dual project, for civilizing people meant remaking their lives at the personal level as well as reshaping society. Taylor sees these early attempts at creating order as laying the groundwork for the secular social imaginary because they were activist, interventionist, strove for uniformity and homogeneity and were rationalizing; they sought to enhance social order by the application of a coherent set of rules. In contrast to an older world view that had seen order and chaos as necessary complements in the wider scheme of things, the reform projects sought to expunge disorder from social life, firstly by removing members of the elite from riotous popular activities and then by winding down these activities altogether. Eventually the private realm became the only permissable site of transgression, or of what Taylor calls "anti-code" or "anti-structure" activity.

As this recourse to religious history indicates, attempts to civilize people's behaviour were often based on religious motives: there was a sense that making them more pious was a way of making them more civilized and *vice versa*. The ethic affirming ordinary life, for example, as traced by Taylor in *Sources of the Self* and other writings, plays an important role here too, for it aimed both to bridge the gap between mass and elite and to improve the ways in which the ordinary activities of daily life were practised. He does acknowledge, however, that another motive for this civilizing mission was to mobilize military and economic resources for the state. But in effect he is indicating that Christianity's civilizing mission began at home. In tracing this mission in the domestic realm and depicting the increasing imposition of order on society, Taylor goes where thinkers like Max Weber, Norbert Elias, Michel Foucault and Albert Hirschman have gone before. Eventually religious belief came to be associated with morality and morality in turn became associated with conduct, so it is not hard to see how what began as a religious mission gradually occluded God and the transcendent and came to concern itself entirely with human behaviour.

Another impetus for this way of thinking about humans which valorized discipline and self-reconstruction at individual and social levels came from the neo-Stoic tradition, and in particular the work of Justus Lipsius (Taylor 1988c: 308). Taylor discerns a new view of human agency developing, one that sees the self as able to reconfigure itself and its world in accordance with its will. This new view of agency builds on the idea of the buffered self, for as well as being less vulnerable to external forces beyond its control, the self also aspires to master its passions and desires. Taylor turns to the work of Descartes as exemplifying this new view of the self and its ambition to master the passions. In this whole process, the self becomes more tightly bounded, increasingly insulated from the world outside, and in some cases from the non-rational world inside too. Here Taylor's reading dovetails with that offered in *Sources of the Self* of the disengaged, punctual self for at the core of these developments is an emphasis on instrumental, rational self-control. In the current context, however, his concern is to show how this increasingly restricted conception of the self contributed to the development of exclusive humanism by isolating the self more and more from the surrounding world. This process of insulation was consolidated by the fact that civilizing people meant making taboo, or at least private, certain topics and behaviours that had once been shared openly. Here Taylor draws heavily on Elias's history, but focuses on the way that the demands of civilized behaviour limited intimacy and encouraged a certain distance and disengagement from one's own bodily functions and powerful emotions. In this process, an even tighter cordon was drawn around the buffered self.

In order for humans to be sole guarantors of order and good conduct in the world, they needed not just a view of their technical capacity to change themselves and their world but also an argument about motivation. This had to be painted as ultimately or potentially benign. Here Taylor traces the demise of what he calls the judicial-penal notion of religion with its emphases on humans' innate depravity and eschatological judgements and punishments. In its place came an affirmation of human innocence or goodness. In charting this development, he draws on arguments from *Sources of the Self* about the role of deism and then Romanticism in imputing an inherent benevolence to humans. Here again we see how a doctrine of human nature with religious beginnings and motivations contributed to the eventual supersession of religious faith, for if humans are fundamentally good to begin with, and can sustain this goodness in themselves and in their dealings with others, divine grace becomes less necessary in ordering society. That this view of human nature could become so credible and influential is, according to Taylor, testimony to the success of the civilizing mission.

The new views of selfhood and of society that contributed to the development of exclusive humanism were compounded by new conceptions of politics. In fact, along with the notion of the economy described above, and the increasing primacy it enjoyed as a significant area of human life, Taylor identifies a series of related developments that proved crucial to the creation of a secular age. The first was the notion of the public sphere as a meta-topical space and of civil society as an arena beyond the state where people could discuss and debate politics and the proper use of power. The second is the ethos of democratic self-rule and the third is the conception of humans as equal bearers of rights.[5] These changed understandings of politics furthered secularity in mutually reinforcing ways. The idea of the public sphere, for example, pointed to a realm beyond politics where the use of power could be scrutinized, criticized and evaluated by reason. What was new, compared to the medieval world, was the idea that this arena existed wholly within society; no recourse to the transcendent realm was needed to mount moral critiques of politics. The fact that both society and politics came to be seen as self-grounding and self-reproducing points to yet another way in which what was once transcendent – the source of social order – became immanent and secularity became further entrenched.

A way of capturing this new view of power and rule is to say that political relationships are now imagined in a primarily horizontal way as opposed to the traditional hierarchical, vertical conception. Of course this does not mean that all people are effectively equal, nor that some do not rule others; rather the idea is that the state is an instrument designed to serve individuals and in principle it should serve all equally. None should enjoy an *a priori* privilege in this. Drawing on the work of Craig Calhoun, Taylor characterizes this sort of politics as "direct-access". In principle at least, all members of the polity are equally placed *vis-à-vis* the state and all deal directly with it: their relationships are not mediated through some other stratum of society. In the medieval world, by contrast, peasants were linked to the monarch via their lord. The modern view of politics makes such intermediaries unnecessary; individuals, or at least adult ones, are linked directly to the state. In western societies, for example, the latest form of mediated access, that of women through men, has disappeared and as citizens women are, officially at least, now on an equal footing with men (see Taylor 1998a: 39).

It should now be clear why Taylor does not wholly reject the association of secularity with the separation of religion and politics, for this is part of what transpires in this new conception of politics. However, much more is going on than can be captured by the disestablishment of church from state; a new conception of radical human autonomy percolates through the political realm as through the social and through interpretations of selfhood. Increasingly in all these departments, God's presence and power come to be of reducing relevance, allowing anthropocentric outlooks to expand and fill the available space.

The grounds for Taylor's mistrust of the "subtraction thesis" account of secularity should also be clearer by now. He believes that secularity cannot be explained wholly in negative terms, by what was lost or the illusions that fell away. Many positive doctrines about the self, society and politics had to be formulated and to get a purchase before the idea of a world without God could be conceivable and attractive. It is not as if these more hopeful views were simply waiting at the ready to be marshalled when the reality of disenchantment dawned. However, even when the new humanist views contained strands of older doctrines, such as Stoicism, Taylor submits that they were inflected by certain Christian-inspired notions. One is the belief that the self and the world could be actively re-ordered for the better. Another is the commitment to, and moral resources for, doctrines of human universalism. However, Taylor also acknowledges the role that critiques of Christianity and organized religion played in fostering secularity. In the eighteenth and nineteenth centuries, there were expressions of anger at the legal-penal model of Christianity with its depiction of human corruption and punitive attitude toward the body and sensual pleasure in general. Figures like Voltaire, Marx and Nietzsche illustrate this sort of attack on religion, and suggest that the rise of secularity was fuelled by a mixture of religious and anti-religious motives.

The end of the eighteenth century saw the emergence of a doctrine of exclusive humanism as a viable alternative to Christianity, one that could give an account of human flourishing, of selfhood, society and politics without reference to God, the divine or transcendent concerns. This developed first among the intelligentsia and other social elites of western societies but was then disseminated more widely throughout society in the nineteenth and twentieth centuries. But its progress was not straightforward and linear. There have been significant variations among countries, regions and social strata, and some periods have even seen increases in religious practice. And of course not everyone adopted the outlook of exclusive humanism. None the less, the reach, appeal and plausibility of exclusive humanism meant that theists henceforth would be faced with a rival, secular account of human purposes and the meaning of life. The context of their belief had changed irrevocably.

Taylor does not, however, structure this new context in terms of a simple binary opposition between belief and unbelief. He argues instead that a profusion of different religious or spiritual positions and possibilities has been spawned and that many people wander among these rather than cleaving exclusively to one or none. This plurality of spiritual possibilities has been fostered by the ethic of authenticity which, as discussed in Chapter 2, encourages individuals to shape lives that are truly their own rather than simply conforming to existing, custom-made models. So rather than suggesting that there has been a straightforward decline in religious belief, Taylor depicts secularity in a different way.

> Secularity closes old, and opens new, avenues of faith. What it doesn't seem to allow, however, is a new "age of faith", that is a time of universal belief, where the undeniable common experiences that no-one can escape bespeak some commonly agreed spiritual reality. That seems no longer possible in a secular age. (Taylor in Gifford Lecture)

Nor has the understanding of exclusive humanism gone unchallenged. Taylor points to the spread of postmodern doctrines, which have perpetuated the anti-humanist and anti-religious aspects of Nietzsche's thought. Indeed, a whole counter-Enlightenment tradition emerged from the nineteenth century onward, which emphasized the darker, irrational, violent and transgressive forces in human existence and derided the humanist concern with securing and improving the conditions of ordinary life for all. Yet while posing a challenge to the Enlightenment's rationalist brand of humanism, it did not simply advocate a return to pre-Enlightenment beliefs. Taylor calls this the "immanent counter-Enlightenment" because it remains within the naturalist vista of humanism, repudiating any interest in theism and the transcendent realm. So rather than a simple binary opposition between theism and atheism, Taylor sees the contemporary scene as triangulated between exclusive humanism, the immanent counter-Enlightenment and a capacious theism, one that entertains a variety of ways of believing in God and practising spirituality. These different positions align themselves differently on different issues. In terms of compassion for human suffering, for example, exclusive humanism would find more in common with many spiritual outlooks than it would with the counter-Enlightenment. In terms of awareness of the significance of death in human existence, the counter-Enlightenment and spiritual outlooks would have more to say to one another than either would to exclusive humanism, and so on (see Taylor 1996d: 25–7; 1999a: 25–30; 2000b).

Taylor proposes that the persistence of theism and the immanent counter-Enlightenment point to some of the malaises that beset exclusive humanism with its aspiration to give a complete account of human meaning in human, all too human terms. He proposes that the human heart, or soul, yearns for something beyond itself, although this need not always be construed in religious terms. He interprets the nineteenth century's fascination with the sublime and the twentieth century's interest in wilderness as expressing the importance of going beyond anthropocentrism to make contact with a force greater than humans. The power and importance attached to art and the way people look to it for quasi-spiritual nourishment, is taken as another sign of the incompleteness of exclusive humanism. This argument about the inadequacy of exclusive humanism also appears in an earlier essay where he notes the way that many people turn to religious ideas or practices at critical or threshold times in their lives, such as births, deaths, marriages. Taylor takes this as evidence that:

> Unbelief for most people has not come to fill all the niches in their lives and answer all the questions that religious belief did formerly . . . Faced with questions about death, about the ultimate meaning of life, about the deepest sources of moral goodness, many people who otherwise think of themselves as secular or agnostic turn to the religion from which they or their family emerged. (Taylor 1990a: 106)

Anticipating the objection that these moments represent lapses into weakness, Taylor claims that this is not how the people involved interpret their turns, or returns, to religion. (Here we see again his emphasis on explaining action and experience in ways that the protagonists themselves could recognize.) At a more general level, he interprets the sense of flatness and loss of meaning that many experience in their lives as a symptom of this outlook's attempt to provide motivation and fulfilment in exclusively human terms. It is as if the question "Is that all there is?" underlies the experience of living within the confines of exclusive humanism.

As this indicates, Taylor's project includes a reading of what he calls "contemporary spiritual experience" which speaks to the "spiritual hungers and tensions of secular modernity". What seems to underpin this is a view of human nature as including a fixed need for contact with the transcendent as harbouring a permanent desire to go beyond the all-too-human. As he says in an earlier work, "From my perpsective, humans have an ineradicable bent to respond to something beyond life; denying this stifles" (1996d: 25). This means that another ontological property of selfhood can be inferred from his more recent work: that humans aspire to some form of transcendence. Some commentators might say that this represents nothing new in Taylor's thought, being closely connected to the foundational role of theism in his moral theory. However, it seems to me that what is only intimated in his previous writings acquires a firmer role in his analysis of secularity. As noted in the discussion in Chapter 1 of Taylor's falsifiable realism, in previous writings his claim has been that humans feel their strongly valued goods to be grounded in something more than individual choice. But this is presented as part of his "best account" of moral experience, and as something that could be disproved. The suggestion that humans need to surpass anthropocentrism does not enjoy the ontological status it seems to acquire in these later works.

This is no doubt connected to the fact that, as *A Catholic Modernity?* signals, Taylor's religious beliefs are assuming a more obvious presence in his more recent writings. He confesses that these beliefs have influenced his interest in and approach to the question of secularity. But even when he speaks as a believer, he does not do so from a position of smug self-certainty. He has, rather, a powerful sense of how fragile theism has become in a secular age and how it will remain subject to challenges and cross-pressures from the attractions of exclusive humanism. As Taylor says, for all of those who live it, believers and non-believers alike, life in a secular age "doesn't lend itself easily a comfortable resting place".

Notes

A note on sources

Three of Taylor's major works (1985a; 1985b; 1992c/1993; 1995a) are collections of essays previously published elsewhere (with the exception of Chapter 11 in 1985b and Chapter 13 in 1995a). For the convenience of readers, when essays from these collections are cited, the reference is to the essays in their collected form, rather than to the originals.

Introduction

1. Taylor's remarks about Paul Ricoeur apply equally to Taylor himself (1968a: 402).
2. This reference to "reconciling the solitudes" is borrowed from the title of Taylor's collection of essays on Canadian federalism edited by Guy Laforest (1992c/1993). This title, in turn, echoes that of a 1945 book about Canada by Hugh MacLennan entitled *Two Solitudes*.
3. I am grateful to Jean Bethke Elshtain for suggesting that this feature of Taylor's thought deserves emphasis.
4. These remarks are part of a very informative interview with Taylor (1989b).
5. Taylor's contribution to this commission is published as "The stakes of constitutional reform" in Laforest (ed.) (1992c/1993: 140–54).
6. As Hauerwas & Matzko write, "Active in the politics of Quebec, he brings to his work the passion of concrete political engagement" (1992: 286; cf. Birnbaum 1996: 39–41).

7. Expressivism is explored more fully in Chapter 2.
8. Reflecting on Taylor's impulse to mediate between seemingly rival outlooks, Ignatieff also suggests that Taylor's biography helps to explain this. Taylor is a thoroughly bilingual and bicultural Quebecer who grew up in a household with a Francophone mother and Anglophone father. Among the solitudes that Taylor tries to reconcile, Ignatieff singles out "Marxism and Catholicism, liberalism and socialism, English analytical philosophy and French and German metaphysics" (1985: 63).

Chapter 1: Explaining morality

1. Beiner interprets this as a crucial tension, and a crucial weakness, in *Sources of the Self*. He accuses Taylor of a sort of positivism; if something has come to be valued as good it is *ipso facto* worthy of affirmation. He uses this to explain the lack of radicalism and critique in Taylor's work and argues against this that social theory should concern itself not just with the understanding of social practices but also with their evaluation (1997: 156, 160, 166 n.12, 224).
2. See, for example, Williams (1985). Taylor refers to Williams's work in *Sources of the Self* (1989a: 64) and discusses it in more detail in "A Most Peculiar Institution" (1995b). In his later writings, Michel Foucault also distinguished morality from ethics in a similar way: morality was concerned with rules and codes governing relationships with others while ethics referred to the individual's personal comportment or orientation towards those rules. As such, ethics allowed greater scope for personal style and creativity (Foucault 1978–88, 1998).
3. As Smith observes, Taylor rejects "the neo-Kantian differentiation of the moral and the ethical domain" (1996: 107). But from the fact that both morality and ethics involve strong evaluation, it should not be inferred that strong evaluation is confined to moral or ethical judgements. While Taylor believes that all moral questions involve strong evaluation, other areas of inquiry can too: aesthetics is one example of a field of inquiry that can involve strong evaluation (1985a: 24n.7; 1985b: 236, 238–9; 1989a: 55; 1995b: 134).
4. Kingwell (1998: 378) also identifies Aristotle as a source for Taylor's pluralism. The influence of Aristotle on Taylor's thinking is evident from *The Explanation of Behaviour* onward. Given the importance Taylor attributes to Aristotle, it is curious, as O'Hagan notes, that no chapter of *Sources* is devoted to him (1993: 74).
5. See, for example, Berlin's essay on "The Originality of Machiavelli" in *Against the Current* (Berlin 1979).
6. This point recurs in the discussion of multiculturalism and the politics of recognition in Chapter 3 and in the depiction of practical reason in Chapter 4.
7. See Rosen (1991: 185), Weinstock (1994: 174); Anderson (1996: 18, 23); Flanagan (1996: 152–4); Smith (1996: 114); and Gutting (1999: 158). Edgar (1995) also takes strong evaluation to require reflection on and articulation of one's values, but he sees this as a virtue of the concept. He uses Taylor's notion of strong evaluation to criticize the way public

consultation over the allocation of health resources is conducted. He argues that this process would be improved if people were treated as strong evaluators who had to define and defend their qualitative judgements rather than being treated as weak evaluators who only have preferences to register.

8. Flanagan offers a different interpretation. He sees *Sources of the Self* as introducing a (welcome) equivocation in Taylor's conception of strong evaluation, one that relaxes the reflection and articulation requirement (1996: 158).

9. Fuller discussion of the role of the background appears in Chapter 4.

10. Yet while acknowledging that not all strong evaluators are reflectively aware of the value distinctions that underlie their judgements, Taylor confesses his sympathies for the Socratic belief in the value of the examined life (1989a: 92).

11. As Waldron writes, for Taylor "there are no unmixed blessings, since not all good things can be compatible" (1990: 328).

12. This is discussed more fully in Chapter 2.

13. For criticisms of the way Taylor depicts utilitarian thought, see Braybrooke (1994: 105–6) and Kymlicka (1991: 168ff).

14. He connects this in turn with the wider cultural developments in western thinking from the seventeenth century onwards, and in particular the influence of natural science and the disenchantment of the world (1985b: 230–31, 242–3). Chapter 4 discusses these developments.

15. As Williams says, "much of what he says about the character of our moral experience seems to me, up to this point, importantly true, and any adequate account of morality must try to explain it. From this strong base in experience, however, Taylor very rapidly moves uphill, metaphysically speaking" (1990: 46). Compare this with Schneewind's objection that "from Taylor's Frankfurtian view about how human identity involves second order desires capable of controlling first order desires, nothing follows about any need for highest order desires, for 'ultimate' sources of 'incomparably higher' value to give force to all the rest" (1991: 426). Similarly, from Smith's comparison of Taylor and Rorty, we can infer that while Rorty might accept the claim about the necessity for the higher/lower discrimination of strong evaluation, he could not accept the moral realism that underpins this (1996: 116–17).

16. MacIntyre (1996: 523). Even an interpreter as sympathetic to Taylor's program as Morgan can mistake his falsifiable realism for strong realism. According to Morgan, Taylor believes that "The constitutive goods that ground and direct our moral beliefs and that empower our moral judgements and choices are real. They are objective components of our moral universe" (1994: 52–3).

17. Chapter 4 contains a more detailed description of what the phrase "the best account" means.

18. Along with appreciating some of the goods of other religious traditions, Taylor also promotes pluralism within Catholicism. He proposes that "a Catholic principle . . . is no widening of the faith without an increase in the variety of devotions and spiritualities and liturgical forms and responses to Incarnation" (1999a: 15).

19. This is not to suggest that all theists would necessarily accept Taylor's moral theory. The claim would be that sharing his religious belief is a

necessary but not sufficient condition of accepting his moral theory. For criticisms in this vein, see Baier (1988), Schneewind (1991), Skinner (1991: 146), Lane (1992) and O'Hagan (1993).

20. The continuing problem of evil in the Christian worldview plays an important part in Hans Blumenberg's *The Legitimacy of the Modern Age* (1985). This is discussed, and contrasted with Taylor's approach, in Rosen (1991: 190–91).

21. Even some believers might challenge Taylor's claim here. Consider the Catholic novelist, Morris West, who is reported to have said, "Christianity is not always a comfort but a bleak acceptance of a dark mystery" (Obituary for Morris West, *New York Times*, 2 October 1999, B13).

22. Marsden congratulates Taylor for doing in that lecture what a Christian scholar should: reflect on "how their faith provides fresh perspectives for viewing contemporary issues" (1999: 83). However, Taylor also does the converse in this lecture, reflecting on how contemporary, or at least modern, conditions provide fresh perspectives on Catholicism.

23. A good illustration of the self in crisis comes in Kazuo Ishiguro's novel *The Remains of the Day*, in which the protaganist, the butler Stevens, is forced, because of changes in his life, to reflect on the values, ideals and sense of moral and social order that had given meaning to his life.

24. These examples come from newspapers.

25. See, for example, Calhoun (1991: 234, 241), Weinstock (1994: 173) and Gutting (1999: 150–51). Rorty even seems to read Taylor as saying that some hypergoods are there for all of us (1994: 20–21). See also Hittinger (1990: 125). However, the source Hittinger cites for this interpretation is one that I take as being more hypothetical; Taylor counsels that we should not be deterred from hypergoods "if these turn out to be really ineliminable from our best account" (1989a: 69).

26. When considered in this way, we can see how the rise of the modern novel in the eighteenth century both reflected and encouraged this tendency for individuals to give meaning to their lives in terms of a narrative.

27. One of the things Taylor discusses when reviewing *After Virtue* is MacIntyre's emphasis on narratives (1984b: 304; cf. 1994f: 34). On Ricoeur on narrative, see Taylor (1985f).

28. Appiah endorses both these points about the seminal role of narrative and the intersection between personal and collective stories. He writes that:

> crossculturally it matters to people that their lives have a certain narrative unity; they want to be able to tell a story of their lives that makes sense. The story – my story – should cohere in the way appropriate by the standards made available in my culture to a person of my identity. In telling the story, how I fit into the wider story of various collectivities is, for most of us, important.
>
> (1994: 160)

29. This is discussed in more detail in Chapter 4.

30. Flanagan posits the opposite relationship between moral crisis and reflection. He suggests that in Taylor's view, the crisis is a result of dissatisfaction with reflection's results:

> Normally, the scrutinizing of the framework engenders confidence in the framework ... It is only when reflective evaluation fails to engender such confidence that the agent is prone to an identity crisis. (1996: 159).

But he provides no evidence to support this reading of their relationship.

31. Contra Anderson's claim (1996), Taylor believes that it is possible to identify what moves people without being moved by it oneself. To use an analogy, we can see what is loveable about an individual without falling in love with him or her.
32. Beam (1997: 775) offers a good account of Taylor's rejection of "*a priori* relativism".
33. This phrase is explained in Chapter 2.
34. Many of these same goods converge in the defence of negative freedom, as discussed in Chapter 3.
35. A parallel point is made in Chapter 3 in the context of irreducibly social goods. Taylor argues that acknowledging these goods can strengthen them, just as failing to can enervate them.
36. I assume that a defunct moral system could be comprehensively articulated. There are obvious parallels here with outlining the workings of a living as opposed to a dead language.
37. While the contrast between constitutive goods and life goods is mentioned in Part I of *Sources of the Self* (1989a: 93, 122), it is only really put to work in Part IV (307–42). See also (1991d: 243; 1997a: 173) for discussions of this distinction.
38. Wood (1992), for example, suggests that there is a theistic bent to Taylor's conception of constitutive goods.
39. In the light of this discussion, Beiner's criticisms that Taylor does not treat religious unbelief as a moral source (1997: 160) and that he slights "the moral sensibilities of atheists" (*ibid.*: 162) seem misplaced. That Taylor is qualified to disinter the constitutive goods of secular outlooks is suggested in his claim that "I am a believer, and I also find spiritual greatness in the views of unbelievers" (1991d: 241).
40. As Clark says, "Platonism and Hebraic Christianity alike are founded on the recognition of 'constitutive goods', realities the love of which moves us to right action" (1991: 198).
41. Rorty makes a similar point about how returning to the original sources or articulations of a moral outlook can strengthen adherence to it. Discussing Christianity and Marxism, he argues that just because their predictions have not been realized, this:

> should not stop us from finding inspiration and encouragement in the New Testament and the [*Communist*] *Manifesto*. For both documents are expressions of the same hope: that someday we will be willing and able to treat the needs of all human beings with the respect and consideration with which we treat the needs of those closest to us, those whom we love. (1999: 217)

42. Williams is right to identify the belief that we can only understand human affairs by their history as one of Hegel's legacies for Taylor (1990: 45).

Chapter 2: Interpreting selfhood

1. Compare Cockburn (1991: 364) and Thiebaut (1993: 133). Kymlicka makes similar criticisms of *Sources of the Self*. He complains that Taylor's use of terms is idiosyncratic, it is hard to know exactly what he is saying, whom he is disagreeing with and why (1991: 159).
2. Note too the title of one of his articles: "What is *human* agency?" (emphasis added), which also provides the title of the first volume of his 1985 collection, *Philosophical Papers*. However, his reference to "our ordinary understanding of human agency, of a person or self" (1985a: 3) suggests that at other times he makes agency synonymous with these other terms rather than distinguishing it from them (cf. 1985b: 258).
3. This is discussed by Loew-Beer (1991) and contrasted with Taylor's approach.
4. This issue is discussed in more detail in Chapter 4.
5. Taylor nominates feminism as a force that has changed the way we interpret the actions of others (1988d: 53). My discussion gives this example a reflexive turn.
6. In this Taylor is, as he notes, following the work of Isaiah Berlin, who uses the term "expressionism" to discuss Herder's ideas. Taylor adapts this to "expressivism" (1975a: 13 n.1). This term has been applied to Taylor's own work. Loew-Beer characterizes Taylor's approach to morality as "hermenuetic expressivism". He also identifies other strands within expressivism: romantic, psychological and artistic (1991: 228, 236).
7. *Philosophical Papers I* (Taylor 1985a: 248–92) contains a more detailed comparison of these two approaches to language.
8. Some of this history is recounted in Taylor (1975a: 4).
9. For evidence of how powerfully this aspect of Taylor's thought has been informed by his reading of Hegel, see (1975a: 381) or (1979a: 87).
10. Wittgenstein's argument against the possibility of a private language is an important influence on Taylor's thinking here (1975a: 305; 1985a: 231 n.6; 1989a: 38; 1995a: 13, 133).
11. This point about the importance of the wider cultural background is revisited in Chapter 3.
12. Todorov (1984) provides a useful overview of some of Bakhtin's main arguments. The final chapter on philosophical anthropology is especially useful in the context of Taylor's work.
13. Chapter 4 contains a fuller discussion of this.
14. Todorov's description of Bakhtin's position is apposite for Taylor's too: "it is impossible to conceive of any being outside of the relations that link it to the other" (1984: 94). In a long footnote, Todorov acknowledges that Bakhtin was not the first to make this claim; rather the idea that the I–Thou relationship is constitutive of the self has been part of classical European philosophy since the eighteenth century (1984: 117–18). It seems probable then that Bakhtin's influence on Taylor's conceptualization of the self stems from his succinct way of expressing this – the dialogical – as well as from the variety of self–other relationships that he takes to be constitutive of selfhood.
15. Dauenhauer also raises this question about the moral and political

implications of Taylor's theory of selfhood (1992: 222). With the exception of (1985d), Taylor does not write on these topics. He sometimes refers to debates about abortion, however (1995a: 35; 1998a: 51).

16. Although *Hegel* is comparable in size, it is dedicated to the exposition of another thinker whereas *Sources of the Self* is a more original work.

17. Some of these limitations are mentioned by Nussbaum (1990: 32), although they pale by comparison with her praise for the book. See also Skinner (1991) and Shklar (1991: 108).

18. Interestingly the essay "Legitimation Crisis?" (1985b: 248–88) pays more attention to the role of social and economic relationships in shaping modern identity.

19. Consider some of his remarks on Alasdair MacIntyre's work. Reviewing *After Virtue*, Taylor comments on its author's one-sided view of the history of morality, his focus on the virtues and practices that have been lost. MacIntyre seems blind to the emergence of new virtues and practices in modernity, and this detracts from the equally important, but obverse task of the history of moral theory, which is "to discern and nurture the coherent moral visions of the good life" (Taylor 1984b: 306).

20. Other reviewers have made similar observations, but not necessarily as criticisms. Calhoun, for example, notes that Taylor pays little attention to the goods that have been lost over time (1991: 240), while Waldron describes *Sources of the Self* as "an optimistic, affirmative work" (1990: 325).

21. Nussbaum acknowledges this pivotal aspect of Taylor's position. As she says, "love proves to be, in the end, a more powerful source of motivation than hatred" (1990: 31).

22. Although it appears in a discussion of Taylor's theory of freedom, Flathman's insight that Taylor thinks of evil as absence or privation rather than as an independent force in its own right strikes me as a promising way of beginning this sort of examination (Flathman 1987: 79). This would be another sense in which Taylor is working within a Platonic/Augustinian tradition. Or rather, as Shklar's review rightly suggests, this is one strand of Augustinianism (1991: 106).

23. For an argument that Taylor has exaggerated the reach of such changes in the domain of family life, see Clark (1991: 202–3).

24. See Taylor (1992b: 1993b) The focus of the rest of this section is the most recent version of the argument as contained in (1999c).

25. He contrasts his approach with Foucault's, wondering how Foucault could give a history of modern society that neglected any sense of the goods that it offered, and with little sense of the past it was transforming. He sees this as actually being motivated by Foucault's admiration for radical autonomy (Forthcoming b).

26. Heidegger's influence on Taylor is manifest here.

27. See Chapter 5 for a fuller discussion of this.

28. For an overview and critique of Taylor's interpretation of Locke, see Wolterstorff (1996: 236–44)

29. This is discussed more fully in Chapter 4.

30. As Taylor suggests, there are strong parallels between his analysis and Max Weber's argument about the relationship between the protestant ethic and the growth of capitalism (1989a: 226). Weber's work is cited in note 26 of Chapter 13, "God Loveth Adverbs".

31. For a sample of feminist critiques of Marx, see O'Brien (1981) and MacKinnon (1989). As his treatise on *The Origin of the Family, Private Property and the State* indicates, Engels was more attuned to the role of the family in the production and reproduction of material life than Marx was, although in the *Economic and Philosophical Manuscripts* of 1844, there are some indications of Marx's interest in gender. There is also a large feminist literature on the ethic of care that takes up, from a non-Marxist perspective, the importance of domestic life and relationships.
32. This aspect of Stoicism has recently been revived by Nussbaum in her elaboration of a contemporary ethic of cosmopolitanism. See her opening essay in Nussbaum *et al.* (1996).
33. Taylor uses modern feminism as an illustration of the tension between the demands of authenticity and the commitments of family life. However, the fact that it is predominantly women who feel the need to loosen the bonds of marriage in order to realize themselves should make him suspect that it is not durable attachments *per se* that fetter the pursuit of authenticity but a particular sort of durable attachment – i.e. one that is perceived to be oppressive, exploitative or constraining.
34. See Chapter 1 for a fuller discussion of this.

Chapter 3: Theorizing politics

1. See Friedman (1994: 297), Miller (1995: 26), Kukathas (1996), Hampton (1997: 182–5), Mulhall & Swift (1997: 121, 162, *passim*) and Mouffe (1988: 197–202). Wallach is an interesting exception to this tendency to include Taylor in discussions of communitarian thinkers. However, it is only by failing to consider Taylor's contribution to the debate between liberals and communitarians that Wallach is able to claim that communitarian thinkers have neglected the political. Taylor could not be numbered among those who "make virtually no comments about any particular political arrangements they either abhor or endorse" (1987: 593; cf. 595, 601).
2. According to Friedman however, the community that most communitarians focus on is the state (1994: 298).
3. It has been argued that Internet use contributes to social isolation rather than to identification with community. But Etzioni has argued that "people do form very strong relations over the Internet, and many of them are relations they could not find any other way" (2000: 18).
4. As Kymlicka notes, many liberals "neglect the extent to which individual freedom and well-being is only possible within community" (1993: 369). He makes direct reference to Taylor's work when describing the "social thesis" of communitarianism, which contends that liberalism neglects the social conditions required for the exercise of individual autonomy. Mulhall & Swift (1997) also draw attention to this dimension of Taylor's work.
5. For a reading of Locke that emphasizes the place of community in his thought, see Tully (1980).
6. Hampton contends that communitarians advocate uncritical identifi-

cation with the community and recommends that they "develop their theory so that it can show us how we can take a morally critical attitude toward community, even while reconizing the importance of community. Otherwise, their theory gives them no critical moral distance from existing social practices" (1997: 188; cf. 190). Yet this misses Taylor's more fundamental argument that the very ideal of the critical, independent individual thinking against society is itself made possible by wider cultural forces. Flathman (1987: 76) also shows that Taylor's position does allow for social criticism.

7. As Kerr says, for Taylor "there is no way of affirming the value of personal freedom which does not include an equally basic affirmation of the obligation to belong" (1997: 138).

8. As Hampton observes, "Most . . . Western political theory has been highly individualistic in character: Hobbes and Locke begin their theories from individuals existing in prepolitical . . . states of nature. Modern consent-based theories of authority derive political authority from the actions of individuals" (1997: 169).

9. Buchanan, for example, argues that "In the market, individuals exchange apples for oranges; in politics, individuals exchange agreed-on shares in contributions toward the cost of that which is commonly desired, from the services of the local fire station to that of the judge" (1986; cf. 1972, 1979).

10. Aspects of Taylor's critique of this concept in his 1979 essay "What's wrong with negative liberty?" (1985b: 211–29) recur in "Liberal politics and the public sphere" (1995a: 257–87).

11. See Part II, "The notion of positive freedom". By the third paragraph Berlin has associated positive freedom with coercion of the individual by some larger entity: the tribe, race, church or state (Berlin 1969: 131–2).

12. However, in a footnote Berlin acknowledges that several criteria may be relevant in measuring the extent of negative liberty. One is "how important in my plan of life, given my character and circumstances, these possibilities are when compared with one another" (1969: 130 n.1). This seems to gesture towards the sort of qualitative discrimination that Taylor insists is central to the meaning of freedom. A stronger gesture appears toward the end of Berlin's essay: "To protest against the laws governing censorship or personal morals as intolerable infringements of personal liberty presupposes a belief that the activities which such laws forbid are fundamental needs of men as men, in a good (or indeed, any) society" (1969: 169). This latent exercise concept in Berlin's notion of negative freedom leads me to suspect that Taylor has him in mind when he writes of those who "abandon many of their own intuitions" to defend the cruder, opportunity concept of negative freedom. Fear of conceding any ground to totalitarianism leads them to support a less nuanced notion of negative freedom (Taylor 1985b: 215).

13. Berlin's own portrayal of Mill illustrates Taylor's point:

> Much of what he [Mill] says about his own reasons for desiring liberty – the value he puts on boldness and non-conformity, on the assertion of the individual's own values in the face of the prevailing opinion, on strong and self-reliant personalities free from the leading strings of the official law-givers and instructors of society –

> has little enough to do with his conception of freedom as non-interference but a great deal with the desire of men not to have their personalities set at too low a value, assumed to be incapable of autonomous, original, "authentic" behaviour.   (1969: 160)

This implies a connection between negative liberty and recognition of autonomy that can undermine Berlin's later insistence on their separation (see below.)

14. See Chapter 1 for a discussion of strong evaluation.

15. For a fuller discussion of this, see Pettit (1997: 35–41 and *passim*).

16. Aristotle defines the virtue of the citizen as free and equal participation in ruling and being ruled (1981: III iv 1277b7, xiii 1283b35) and associates politics with the common pursuit of the good life (*ibid.*: III ix 1280a–1281a2). One of the differences Berlin points to between his thought and Taylor's is the latter's belief that "human beings . . . have a basic purpose", which he links directly with Aristotelian thought (Berlin 1994: 1).

17. As noted by Pettit (1997: 7 n.1), who also sees his own work in this light (*ibid.*: 50).

18. Pettit challenges the traditional association of the republican conception of liberty with positive liberty. He argues instead that the republican tradition promotes participation in politics in order to protect negative liberty (1997: 21, 27–31, *passim*). He rejects, more generally, the binary approach to freedom and returns to the republican tradition of political thought for a third way of conceptualizing freedom. He distinguishes negative freedom as the absence of interference, positive freedom as self-mastery and republican freedom as the absence of domination (*ibid.*: 19, 21, *passim*).

19. However, as Kymlicka points out, much this tradition worked with an exclusive understanding of who could be a citizen. Women, workers, the property-less and foreigners have been excluded at some time or other (1993: 375). Pettit suggests that one reason for the demise of the republican tradition was precisely the difficulty of extending its ideal of freedom as non-domination to all individuals (1997: viii, 49). For republicanism to be a viable political ethic today, Taylor has to believe that the citizenry can be extended to include all these groups.

20. Kymlicka complains that Taylor's analysis offers little help in explaining why some nationalist movements take a liberal form (1997: 63–4). Feinberg (1997: 66–73) also criticizes Taylor's approach to nationalism.

21. Here Taylor is influenced by Alexis de Tocqueville, who feared that without the participation of citizens in their institutions democratic societies could descend into soft despotism (cf. Taylor 1993e).

22. This is the title of a 1990 essay (Taylor 1995a: 127–45). For a more general audience, Taylor uses the term "together-goods" (1999a: 112–13).

23. There are echoes of Aristotle's point that friendship only exists when people feel good will towards one another and know that they do; it requires mutual recognition of these good feelings (1980: VIII, ii.).

24. He thus endorses Sandel's view that "when politics goes well, we can know a good in common that we cannot know alone" (1982: 183). Compare this with Pettit's claims that republican freedom is a shared,

rather than an individual, good and should, therefore, appeal to communitarian thinkers (1997: 8, 120, 122, 126).

25. This mirrors de Tocqueville's fears of a vicious circle where citizen apathy and non-participation allow the rulers to disregard popular desires and interests. The realization that rulers are doing this further compounds a sense of helplessness, which results in non-participation in politics (Taylor 1995a: 282).

26. On the impact of Heidegger on Taylor's thinking here, see Taylor (1995a: 109–10, 112, 116).

27. The dangers that beset a democratic polity without this sort of collective identification are discussed in Taylor (1991a: 112–18).

28. This points, in turn, to another area of overlap between Taylor's thought and his interpretation of Ricoeur, for Taylor associates the latter's "careful, sensitive respect for diversity" with his Christian faith (cf. Taylor 1968a: 402–3).

29. Mulhall & Swift deny this advocacy aspect of Taylor's political thought. In their portrayal, he joins MacIntyre in challenging the philosophical bases of individualism, but not Sandel in defending "the importance of goods that are strongly communal in content" (1997: 122; cf. 158). Conversely, for Beiner, Taylor "is a communitarian and a liberal" because he tries to do justice to people's longing for community as well as to their aspirations toward individuality (1997: 157). But this sort of synthesis operates at the advocacy level only. I am suggesting that Taylor's blend of liberalism and communitarianism occurs at both levels.

30. Such a project of retrieval is anticipated as early as Taylor (1975a: 387). Taylor's work provides a good illustration of Wallach's general claim that "The debate between contemporary liberals and their communitarian critics has raised our understanding of the philosophical foundations of liberalism to new heights of theoretical sophistication" (1987: 582).

31. Taylor claims that practical wisdom is needed when "particular cases and predicaments are never exhaustively characterized in general rules" (1989a: 125; cf. 1994f: 28). Compare this with Berlin (1969: 119) on the sort of knowledge required for politics. Laforest describes Taylor's own political analyses as being imbued with "Aristotle's wisdom" (in Taylor 1992c [1993]: xiv).

32. Compare this with Gray's claim that:

> in some recent communitarian discourse, "community" figures in much the same way as "individual" or "person" does in standard liberal thinking – as a cipher, a disabling abstraction whose effect is to obscure the differences and conflicts in the midst of which we actually live. (1995: 17)

33. Waldron refers to the antipathy between communitarians and defenders of rights (1993: 582). Compare Kymlicka's claim that "communitarians argue [that] the liberal 'politics of rights' should be abandonned for a 'politics of the common good'" (1993: 369).

34. Compare this with Mulhall & Swift (1997: xii–iv). The internal plurality of liberalism is also emphasized by Ryan (1993). Another summary of some of the differences among adherents to the liberal tradition

comes in Hampton (1997: 170–82).

35. Canada is a federal system, and the provincial government in Quebec has passed laws with the aim of preserving and promoting the province's distinct culture. There are laws that limit parents' freedom to choose their children's schools, that oblige businesses with 50 employees or more to operate in French and that prohibit commercial signage in languages other than French (Taylor 1995a: 243–4). For a good discussion of the political background to Taylor's arguments, see Forbes (1997: 221–3).

36. As Laforest says, "Granting distinct treatment to a minority language group – in Quebec – . . . is not incompatible with the liberal tradition" (Taylor 1992c [1993]: x). This dimension of Taylor's political project has parallels with those of his late compatriot C. B. Macpherson, who explored the variety of forms democracy could take. (Macpherson 1966; 1977). That Taylor is aware of this comparison is suggested by his allusion to Macpherson and reference to the need for the USA to come to terms with "the real world of liberal democracy" that lies outside its borders (1995a: 203).

37. See the discussion of disengaged freedom in Chapter 2 for a fuller account of this.

38. "When we find we can't maximize both freedom and equality, for instance, we don't immediately conclude that one of these isn't a real good" (Taylor 1995a: 162).

39. Of course, in practice rights are often compromised. The right to abortion is often limited to a certain stage of the pregnancy; the right to medically assisted suicide is usually claimed only in extreme cases, such as painful terminal illness. Taylor would no doubt say that this contrast between absolute claims and compromise outcomes points to a tension between the pretensions of rights discourse and the actual demands of politics.

40. The remainder of this section summarizes the arguments of Taylor (1996b, 1999b).

41. The idea of fusing horizons, which Taylor takes from Gadamer, was mentioned in Chapter 2 in the context of individuals from different cultures being partners in dialogue. Here Taylor is using it to show how dialogue is possible among cultures. It is discussed more fully in Chapter 4.

42. I borrow this phrase from structuralist Marxist analyses that accord the state some relative autonomy from the economy.

43. Forbes (1997: 220–45) provides a good summary of this essay while also challenging Taylor's interpretation of Rousseau (*ibid.*: 228–39). For a fuller discussion of the interaction between the development of Taylor's political thought and political events in Canada, see Laforest (1994: 194–209).

44. Taylor describes Berlin as "an inspiring teacher and friend for many decades" (1994d: 213). It also seems appropriate to think of him as one of Taylor's internalized interlocutors, along the model of the dialogical self outlined in Chapter 2.

45. As Gray suggests, Berlin's recognition of insuperable value pluralism extends into his analysis of liberty. There are not just conflicts among values, but even within them (Gray 1993: 66). Interestingly, Taylor makes a similar point about justice (1994f: 38, 42).

46. At this point Berlin's legitimate ambition of identifying the specificity of freedom seems to become hair-splitting. As far as I can see, it would have been simpler to include the desire for recognition under the rubric of positive liberty by relating a group's desire for self-rule to the quest for self-mastery or self-direction. His unwillingness to do this seems to derive from the fact that at times his essay resembles an apology for negative freedom more than an analysis of freedom's different meanings. Treating the search for status as a component of positive freedom would have made it harder to discredit this type of freedom on the grounds that it posits a divided self, although towards the end of this section he does refer to this mechanism as being used by those who are imposing rule on others. Incorporating the quest for status into positive freedom would also have made it necessary to recognize the positive conception as very influential historically. As Berlin says, when the search for status is linked with the positive conception of freedom, it "is an ideal which is perhaps more prominent than any other in the world today" (1969: 160). Negative freedom, by contrast, has, by its defender's own admission, been demanded by only "a small minority of highly civilized and self-conscious human beings" (1969: 161).

47. Beiner criticizes Taylor for simply laying out the dynamics of the politics of recognition without offering any assessment of which identities are harmful and which benign, which are normatively defensible and which destructive (1997: 162–5). This illustrates his wider thesis about Taylor's conservative approach to social theory.

48. A fuller discussion of what Taylor means by the fusion of horizons appears in Chapter 4.

49. In the note accompanying this discussion, Taylor nominates Rawls, Kymlicka and Dworkin as proponents of the neutral state (1991a: 124 n.13).

50. The counter argument is that in promoting the ideal of non-discrimination, the state is simply protecting human rights, which is, from the liberal point of view, central to its *raison d'être*. But this raises the issue of the scope of human rights, which is beyond the present discussion.

51. The term secular here simply means the separation of church and state, or a situation where the state does not promote an official religion. See Chapter 5 for an account of Taylor's forthcoming work that considers the deeper meaning of living in a secular culture.

52. Taylor also echoes Locke's defence of toleration that is grounded in the pacifism of the gospels. As he puts it, "the gospel was always meant to stand out, unencumbered by arms" (1999a: 18).

53. A good example of this materialized in Australia when the government introduced a goods and services tax. Among the services to be taxed for the first time will be those of civil marriage celebrants. Couples who marry in churches will not face this tax because ministers of religion do not technically charge a fee for their services. The government's taxation regime will therefore, seemingly inadvertently, encourage church marriages over civil ones.

54. For further parallels between Taylor's political thought and Aristotle's see Laforest (1994: 206–8).

55. Neal (1997) makes a similar argument to Taylor's, albeit from a more straightforwardly liberal position.

56. Several of Taylor's interpreters point to the ways in which he transcends the simple liberal/communitarian opposition posited by Ryan. See Haldane (1993: 350), Hendley (1993: 297), Friedman (1994: 298), Mouffe (1988: 203) and Kingwell (1998: 377, 379–80). Forbes dubs Taylor a "communitarian liberal" (1997: 223; cf. 225, 239). This has limited utility, for while Taylor does try to give some traditionally liberal goods communitarian underpinnings, there are also aspects of the liberal tradition that he rejects. Huang's various descriptions of Taylor's position as "liberal communitarianism" (1998: 80), "radical liberal" (1998: 81) and "Platonic liberal" (1998: 87) exaggerate the extent to which Taylor defies the usual classifications.

Chapter 4: Understanding knowledge

1. As my distinction between epistemology and the epistemological model suggests, I do not share Smith's interpretation of Taylor's use of the term epistemology. For him, what Taylor means by epistemology is not "the sub-discipline of philosophy devoted to questions of knowledge and justification. It is more like a paradigm in which philosophical reflection is limited by constraints of legitimacy borrowed from the natural sciences" (Smith 1997: 132). I use the term epistemology to refer to the sub-discipline of philosophy that Smith describes. I use the phrase "the epistemological model" to refer to the view of epistemology that Taylor believes has dominated western philosophy since the seventeenth century. I think that Smith's account, while understandable in the light of Taylor's claims about overcoming epistemology, is wrong, and that in overcoming the epistemological model, Taylor is contributing to the sub-discipline of epistemology that stretches back in the western tradition to the pre-Socratics.
2. Rorty suggests that Taylor is conflating two things here: naturalism and reductionism. By reductionism he means the belief that all the things in nature can be encompassed by a single vocabulary. Rorty accepts naturalism, which he associates with premise 2, but rejects the reductionism of premise 1 and the conclusion (Rorty 1994: 30).
3. This seems to be the passage alluded to in Taylor (1985b: 57).
4. These arguments are also made in Taylor (1985b: 116–33). The arguments of "Interpretation and the Sciences of Man" are discussed in Bohman *et al.* (1991)
5. Warnke (1985) provides a good general account of Taylor's position and contrasts it with Rorty's.
6. The fusion of horizons is also discussed in Taylor (1985b: 126–6; 1995a: 148–51, 252).
7. See Taylor (1986g) for Taylor's review of this book.
8. Taylor notes the influence of Ernst Tugendhat's 1979 work *Selbstbewusstein und Selbstbestimmung*. See Taylor (1982a) for his review of this book.
9. Taylor's direct dependence on MacIntyre's formulation explains his bewilderment when MacIntyre criticizes him for this model of reasoning (see Taylor 1994c). Taylor gives a very concise account of practical reasoning (1994c: 205–6).

10. This is also relevant to one of Rouse's criticisms of Taylor. He quotes Mark Okrent's point that there is no logical need to take subjects' self-interpretations into account when trying to explain their behaviour (1991: 54). But Taylor is arguing here about what makes an account of human behaviour plausible, as well as what is logically demanded. Such an account is only plausible if it recognizes self-interpretations as a central part of social reality.

11. The debate between Taylor and Rorty on what it means to overcome epistemology is a good illustration of this (Taylor 1990b). Taylor accuses Rorty of being "in the thrall of a latter-day variant of this picture; and this fuels my desire to hurl at him the accusation we are constantly exchanging: of being still too much enmired in the bad old ways" (*ibid.*: 260; cf. 265; 1980b: 1466).

12. Taylor identifies Gareth Evans as another twentieth-century figure who is concerned to challenge the epistemological tradition. Evans was influenced by Wittgenstein, but not Heidegger or Merleau-Ponty (Taylor 1983b). Thanks to Sue Ashford for drawing my attention to the overlap between Taylor and Evans in this regard.

13. Although Taylor does not discuss him, John Dewey can also be numbered among the theorists of the background. He writes, for example, in a passage that is not an isolated one, that:

> The things which we take for granted without inquiry or reflection are just the things that determine our conscious thinking and determine our conclusions. And these habitudes which lie below the level of reflection are just those which have been formed in the constant give and take of relationships with others.   (1968: 110)

14. My translation of "Se demander si le monde est réel, ce n'est pas entendre ce que l'on dit".

15. Hoy (1977) provides a good discussion of transcendental arguments.

16. As Dunn puts this, Taylor "yearns to displace a philosophy dominated by epistemology with one in which ontology plays a far more prominent role" (1996: 26).

Chapter 5: Conclusion

1. The Gifford Lectureships were established under the will of Adam Lord Gifford, who died in 1887. They are held at the Universities of Edinburgh, Glasgow, Aberdeen and St Andrews in Scotland. This information is taken from the web site: www.faculty-office.arts.ed.ac.uk/ Gifford/Gifford_lectures.htm (accessed October 2000).

2. For this reason I rely as little as possible on quotations, resorting to them only when I cannot faithfully capture Taylor's position in my own words.

3. Henceforth I use the term "exclusive humanism" partly for the sake of economy and partly because this is the term Taylor uses when discussing this phenomenon in Taylor (1999a).

4. An opinion poll conducted by DYG Inc. in the USA found that 68 per cent of respondents found no conflict between accepting evolution and

believing in God; 1,500 people were interviewed, and there is a sampling error of plus or minus 2.6 per cent: "Survey Finds Support is Strong For Teaching 2 Origin Theories", *The New York Times*, 11 March, 2000: 1. The results of this poll also illustrate Taylor's point about the cross-pressures in contemporary society.

5. Most of Taylor's arguments on these topics, which are familiar from his published works, are summarized in Chapter 3.

Bibliography

Taylor's writings

1957a. Can Political Philosophy be Neutral? *Universities and Left Review* **1** (Spring), 68–70.

1957b. Socialism and the Intellectuals. *Universities and Left Review* **2** (Summer), 18–19.

1957c. The Politics of Emigration. *Universities and Left Review* **2** (Summer), 75–6.

1957d. Marxism and Humanism. *New Reasoner* **2** (Autumn), 92–8.

1957e. Review of *Les Democraties Populaires* and *La Tragedie Hongroise* by François Fejtö. *Universities and Left Review* **2** (Summer), 70–71.

1958a. (with M. Kullman) The Preobjective World. *Review of Metaphysics* **XII**(1), 108–23. Reprinted 1966 in *Essays in Phenomenology*, M. Nathanson (ed.), 116–36. The Hague: Martinus Nijhoff.

1958b. The Ambiguities of Marxist Doctrine. *The Student World* **2**, 157–66.

1958c. The Poverty of the Poverty of Historicism. *Universities and Left Review* **4** (Summer), 77–8.

1958d. Alienation and Community. *Universities and Left Review* **5** (Autumn), 11–18.

1959a. Ontology. *Philosophy* **XXXIV**, 125–41.

1959b. Phenomenology and Linguistic Analysis. *Proceedings of the Aristotelian Society, Supplementary Volume* **33**, 93–110

1960a. What's Wrong with Capitalism? *New Left Review* **2** (March/April), 5–11.

1960b. Changes of Quality. *New Left Review* **4** (July/August), 3–5.

1960c. Clericalism. *Downside Review* **78**, 167–80.

1962a. L'Etat et les partis politiques. In *Le Role de l'Etat*, A. Raynauld (ed.), 111–21. Montréal: Editions du Jour.

229

1962b. La bombe et le neutralisme. *Cité Libre* **13** (May), 11–16.

1962c. L'homme de gauche et les élections provinciales. *Cité Libre* **13** (November), 6–7, 21.

1962d. Review of *The Phenomenological Movement* by Herbert Spiegelberg. *Mind* **71**, 546–51.

1963a. Regina Revisited: Reply to Walter Young. *Canadian Forum* **43**, 150–51.

1963b. L'État et la laïcité. *Cité Libre* **14** (February), 3–6.

1963c. Le Canada, ouvrier de la paix. *Cité Libre* **14** (April), 13–17.

1964a. *The Explanation of Behavior*. London: Routledge & Kegan Paul.

1964b. Left Splits in Quebec. *Canadian Dimension* **1**(7) (July–August), 7–8.

1964c. La révolution futile: ou, les avatars de la pensée globale. *Cité Libre* **15** (August/September), 10–22.

1964d. Review of *La Philosophie Analytique, Cahiers de Royaumont. Philosophie IV*. *Philosophical Review* **73**, 132–5.

1965a. Nationalism and the Political Intelligentsia: A Case Study. *Queen's Quarterly* **LXXII**(1), 150–68.

1965b.What's Wrong with Canadian Politics? *Canadian Dimension* **2**(4) (May–June), 10–11, 20–21.

1965c. La planification fédérale-provinciale. *Cité Libre* **16** (April), 9–16.

1965d. Bâtir un nouveau Canada: Compte rendu de *Lament for a Nation* par George Grant. *Cité Libre* **16** (August), 10–14.

1966a. Marxism and Empiricism. In *British Analytical Philosophy*, B. Williams & A. Montefiore (eds), 227–46. London: Routledge & Kegan Paul.

1966b. Alternatives to Continentalism. *Canadian Dimension* **3**(5) (July–August), 12–15.

1966c. (with G. Horowitz) The End of Ideology or a New (Class) Politics? *Canadian Dimension* **4**(1) (November–December), 12–15.

1967a. Mind–Body Identity, a Side Issue? *Philosophical Review* **LXXVI**(2), 201–13. Reprinted 1970. In *The Mind/Brain Identity Theory*, C. V. Borst (ed.), 231–41. London: Macmillan.

1967b. Relations between Cause and Action. *Proceedings of the Seventh Inter-American Congress of Philosophy* Vol. 1. Sainte-Foy: Les Presses de l'Université Laval, 243–**55.**

1967c. Nationalism and Independence. *Canadian Dimension* **4**(3) (March–April), 4–12.

1967d. Review of *Signs* and *The Primacy of Perception* by Maurice Merleau-Ponty, *Philosophical Review* **76**, 113–17.

1967e. Teleological Explanation: A Reply to Denis Noble. *Analysis* **27**, 141–3.

1967f. Psychological Behaviourism. *Encyclopedia of Philosophy*, vol. 6. P. Edwards (ed.), 516–20. New York: Macmillan.

1968a. Review of *History and Truth: Essays by Paul Ricoeur*. *Journal of Philosophy* **65**(13), 401–3.

1968b. From Marxism to the Dialogue Society. In *From Culture to Revolution: The Slant Symposium*, T. Eagleton & B.Wicker (eds), 148–81. London: Sheed & Ward.

1968c. A Reply to Margolis. *Inquiry* **2**, 124–8.

1968d. René Lévesque's New Party: A View from Montreal. *Canadian Dimension* **5**(4) (April–May), 12–13.

1968e. Review of *Explanation and Human Action* by A. R. Louch. *Journal of Philosophy* **65**, 81–4.

1969a. Two Issues About Materialism: Review of *A Materialist Theory of Mind* by D. M. Armstrong. *Philosophical Quarterly* **19**, 73–9.

1969b. A Socialist Perspective on the 70s. *Canadian Dimension* **5**(8) (February), 36–43.

1969c. The 'America' Issue. *Canadian Dimension* **6**(6) (December/January), 6–7.

1969d. Platform: Either We Plan Our Own Economy – or We Become a Branch-Plant Satellite. *Maclean's Magazine* **82** (December), 77.

1969e. Sauf vot' respect, vive le Canada libre! *Le Magazine Maclean*, 9 December, 52.

1970a. *Pattern of Politics*. Toronto: McClelland & Stewart. Section reprinted 1971. In *Apex of Power*. T. A. Hockin (ed.). Scarborough: Prentice-Hall.

1970b. Explaining Action. *Inquiry* **13**, 54–89.

1970c. The Explanation of Purposive Behaviour. In *The Behavioural Sciences*, R. Borger & F. Cioffi (eds), 49–79. Cambridge: Cambridge University Press.

1970d. Marcuse's Authoritarian Utopia. *Canadian Dimension* **7**(3) (August/September), 49–53.

1970e. Behind the Kidnappings: Alienation Too Profound for the System. *Canadian Dimension* **7**(5) (December), 26–9.

1971a. The Agony of Economic Man. In *Essays on the Left*, L. Lapierre *et al.* (eds), 221–35. Toronto: McClelland & Stewart. Reprinted 1971. *Canadian Forum* (April–May), 43–9. Reprinted 1985. *Canadian Political Thought*, H. D. Forbes (ed.), 406–16. Toronto: Oxford University Press.

1971b. Les Cercles vicieux de l'alienation post-moderne. In *Le Quebec qui se fait*, C. Ryan (ed.) 161–5. Montreal: Hurtubise.

1971c. Review of *Psychological Explanation: An Introduction to the Philosophy of Psychology* by Jerry Fodor. *Philosophical Review* **80**, 108–13.

1972a. The Opening Arguments of *The Phenomenology*. In *Hegel: A Collection of Critical Essays*, A. MacIntyre (ed.), 151–87. New York: Doubleday.

1972b. Conditions for a Mechanistic Theory of Behaviour. In *Brain and Human Behavior*, A. G. Karczmar & J. C. Eccles (eds), 449–65. Berlin: Springer.

1972c. A Response to MacIntyre. *Philosophic Exchange* **1**, 15–20.

1972d. Is Marxism Alive and Well? *Listener* **87** (May 4), 583–5.

1974a. Socialism and *Weltanschauung*. In *The Socialist Idea: A Reappraisal*. L. Kolakowski & S. Hampshire (eds), 45–58. London: Weidenfeld & Nicolson.

1974b. The Canadian Dilemma. *Canadian Forum* (May/June), 28–31.

1975a. *Hegel*. Cambridge: Cambridge University Press.

1975b. Force et sens: les deux dimensions irréductibles d'une science de l'homme. In *Sense et Existence: En Homage à Paul Ricoeur*, G. Madison (ed.) 124–37. Paris: Editions du Seuil.

1975c. Neutrality in the University. *In Neutrality and Impartiality: The University and Political Commitment*, A. Montefiore (ed.), 128–48. London: Cambridge University Press.

1976a. Responsibility for Self. In *The Identities of Persons*, A. Rorty (ed.), 281–99. Berkeley: University of California Press.

1976b. The Politics of the Steady State. In *Beyond Industrial Growth*, A. Rotstein (ed.), 47–70. Toronto: University of Toronto Press.

1976c. Reply to Soll and Schmitz. *Journal of Philosophy* **73**, 723–5.

1977. On Social Justice: Review of *Understanding Rawls* by Robert Paul Wolff. *Canadian Journal of Political and Social Theory* **1**, 89–96.

1978a. Hegel's *Sittlichkeit* and the Crisis of Representative Institutions. In *Philosophy of History and Action*, Y. Yovel (ed.), 133–54. Dordrecht: Reidel.

1978b. Comments on Ricoeur's History and Hermeneutics. In *Philosophy of History and Action*, Y. Yovel (ed.), 21–5. Dordrecht: Reidel.

1978c. Contribution to Panel Discussion on Is a Philosophy of History Possible? In *Philosophy of History and Action*, Y. Yovel (ed.), 238–40. Dordrecht: Reidel.

1978d. Marxist Philosophy. In *Men of Ideas*, B. Magee (ed.), 42–58. New York: Viking Press.

1978e. Marxism: The Science of the Millennium. *Listener* (2 Feb), 138–40.

1978f. Feuerbach and Roots of Materialism: Review of *Feuerbach* by Marx Wartofsky. *Political Studies* **26**, 417–21.

1979a. *Hegel and Modern Society*. Cambridge: Cambridge University Press.

1979b. Action as Expression. In *Intention and Intentionality: Essays in Honour of G. E. M. Anscombe*, C. Diamond & J. Teichman (eds), 73–89. Ithaca, NY.: Cornell University Press.

1979c. Sense Data Revisited. In *Perception and Identity, Essays Presented to A. J. Ayer*, G. F. Macdonald (ed.), 99–112. Ithaca, NY: Cornell University Press.

1979d. There is a Hidden Psychic Cost Involved in Having Constantly to Play One's Part in a Systematic Lie. *New Statesman* (6 July), 13–14. Reprinted 1979 as Pall Over Prague: The Psychic Cost of Unremitting Repression. *Atlas* **26** (October), 64.

1980a. A Discussion: Rorty, Taylor and Dreyfus. *Review of Metaphysics* **34**, 47–55.

1980b. Minerva Through the Looking-glass: Review of *Philosophy and the Mirror of Nature* by Richard Rorty. *Times Literary Supplement* (26 Dec.), 1466.

1980c. The Philosophy of the Social Sciences. In *Political Theory and Political Education*, M. Richter (ed.), 76–93. Princeton: Princeton University Press.

1980d. (with A. Montefiore) From an analytical perspective. Preface to *Metacritique: The Philosophical Argument of Jürgen Habermas*, G. Kortian, 1–21. Cambridge: Cambridge University Press.

1980e. Understanding in Human Science. *Review of Metaphysics* **XXXIV**(1), 25–38.

1980f. Les Sciences de l'homme. *Critique* **36** (August–September), 839–49.

1980g. Leader du NDP-Quebec. In *Robert Cliche*, A. Rouleau (ed.). Montréal: Les Éditions Quinze.

1980h. Formal Theory in Social Science. *Inquiry* **23**, 139–44.

1980i. Le Centre du débat s'est déplacé. *Relations* **40** (May), 149–50.

1980j. A Voice for All in a Wider Labour Debate. *The Guardian* (17 Nov.), 9.

1980k. Review of *Karl Marx's Theory of History: A Defence* by G. A. Cohen, *Canadian Journal of Philosophy* **10**, 327–34.

1980l. Review of *Public and Private Morality*, S. Hampshire (ed.). *Mind* **30**, 623–8.

1980m. Review of *Linguistic Behaviour* by Johnathon Bennett. *Dialogue* **19**, 290–301.

1981a. Understanding and Explanation in the *Geisteswissenschaften*. In *Wittgenstein: To Follow a Rule*, S. Holtzman & C. Leich (eds), 191–210. London: Routledge.

1982a. Review of *Selbstbewusstein und Selbstbestimmung: Sprachanalytische Interpretationen* by Ernst Tugendhat. *Journal of Philosophy* **79**, 218–22.

1982b. Consciousness. In *Explaining Human Behavior*, P. F. Secord (ed.), 35–51. Beverly Hills: Sage.

1982c. Réponse à Jean-Marie Beyssade's *La Classification Cartesienne des passions*. *Revue Internationale de Philosophie* **37**, 288–92.

1982d. Table ronde sur Hegel. *Revue de l'Université d'Ottawa* **52** (October–December), 593–607.

1983a. *Social Theory As Practice*. Delhi: Oxford University Press. Reprinted in one section Taylor (1985a: 97–114) and as two sections of (1985b: 91–133).

1983b. Dwellers in Egocentric Space: Review of *The Varieties of Reference* by Gareth Evans. *Times Literary Supplement*, 11 March, 230.

1983c. The Significance of Significance: The Case of Cognitive Psychology. In *The Need for Interpretation*, S. Mitchell & M. Rosen (eds), 141–69. London: Athlone.

1983d. Political Theory and Practice. In *Social Theory and Political Practice*, C. Lloyd (ed.), 61–85. Oxford: The Clarendon Press.

1983e. Use and Abuse of Theory. In *Ideology, Philosophy and Politics*, A. Parel (ed.), 37–59. Waterloo: Wilfrid Laurier University Press.

1984a. Philosophy and Its History. In *Philosophy in History*, R. Rorty, J. B. Schneewind, Q. Skinner (eds), 17–30. Cambridge: Cambridge University Press.

1984b. Aristotle or Nietzsche: Review of *After Virtue* by Alasdair MacIntyre. *Partisan Review* **51**(2), 301–6.

1984c. Review of *Kant's Political Philosophy* by Howard L. Williams. *Bulletin of the Hegel Society of Great Britain* **9**, 44–7.

1985a. *Philosophical Papers I: Human Agency and Language*. Cambridge: Cambridge University Press.

1985b. *Philosophical Papers II: Philosophy and the Human Sciences*. Cambridge: Cambridge University Press.

1985c. The Person. In *The Category of the Person: Anthropology, Philosophy, History*, M. Carrithers, S. Collins, S. Lukes (eds), 257–81. New York: Cambridge University Press.

1985d. The Right to Live: Philosophical Considerations. In *Justice beyond Orwell*, R. S. Abella & M. J. Rothman (eds), 237–41. Montreal: Les Editions Yvon Blais.

1985e. Connolly, Foucault and Truth. *Political Theory* **13**, 377–85.

1985f. Table ronde sur temps et recit, vol. 1 par Paul Ricoeur. *Revue de l'Université d'Ottawa*, **55** (October–December), 311–16. English translation. 1991. Ricoeur on Narrative. In *On Paul Ricoeur: Narrative and Interpretation*, D. Wood (ed.), 174–9. New York: Routledge.

1985g. Humanismus und moderne Identität. In *Der Mensch in den modernen Wissenschaften*, K. Michalski (ed.), 117–70. Stuttgart: Klett-Cotta.

1986a. Human Rights: The Legal Culture. In *Philosophical Foundations of Human Rights*, P. Ricoeur (ed.), 49–57. Paris: UNESCO.

1986b. Leibliches Handeln. In *Leibhaftige Vernunft: Spuren von Merleau-Pontys Denken*, A. Metraux & B. Waldenfels (eds) 194–217. Munich: Fink-Verlag.

1986c. Zur Uberwindung der Erkenntnistheorie. In *Die Krise der Phenomenologie und die Pragmatik des Wissenschaftsfort-schritts*, M. Benedikt & R. Burger (eds). Vienna: Osterreichischen Staatsdruckerei.

1986d. Sprache und Gesellschaft. In *Kommunikatives Handeln: Beitrage zu Jurgen Habermas' Theorie des kommunikativen Handelns*, A. Honneth & H. Joas (eds) 35–52. Frankfurt: Suhrkamp. English Translation. 1991. Language and Society. In *Communicative Action*, Honneth A. & Joas H. (eds), 23–35. Cambridge: Polity Press.

1986e. Die Motive einer Verfahrensethik. In *Moralität und Sittlichkeit: Das Problem Hegels und die Diskursethik*, W. Kuhlmann (ed.), 101–35. Frankfurt: Suhrkamp. English translation. 1993. The Motivation Behind a Procedural Ethics. In *Kant and Political Philosophy: The Contemporary Legacy*, R. Beiner & W. J. Booth (eds), 337–60. Cambridge, MA: Harvard University Press.

1986f. Les pourquoi d'une philosophe. *L'Actualité* **11** (June), 13–14, 16–17.

1986g. Uncompromising Realist: Review of *The View from Nowhere* by Thomas Nagel. *Times Literary Supplement* (5 September), 962.

1986h. Lost Belonging on the Road to Progress. *Listener* (20 March), 16–17.

1987a. Dialektika segodnya ili struktura samootritsaniya. In *Philosophia Gegelya: Problemy dialektiki*, T. I. Oiserman & N. V. Motroshilova, (eds). Moscow; Nauka. Originally published in 1986 as Dialektik heute, oder: Strukturen der Selbsnegation. *Hegels Wissenschaft der Logik: Formation und Rekonstrucktion*, D. Henrich (ed.), 141–53. Stuttgart: Lett-Cotta.

1987b. Social Science in Relation to Practice. *Social Science* **72**, 110–12.

1988a. The Hermeneutics of Conflict. In *Meaning and Context: Quentin Skinner & His Critics*, J. Tully (ed.), 218–28. Cambridge: Polity.

1988b. Reply to de Sousa and Davis. *Canadian Journal of Philosophy* **18**, 449–58.

1988c. The Moral Topography of the Self. In *Hermeneutics and Psychological Theory*, S. B. Messer, L. Sass, R. L. Woolfolk (eds), 298–320. New Brunswick, NJ: Rutgers University Press.

1988d. Wittgenstein, Empiricism, and the Question of the "Inner": Commentary on Kenneth Gergen. In *Hermeneutics and Psychological Theory*, S. B. Messer, L. Sass, R. L. Woolfolk (eds), 52–8. New Brunswick, NJ: Rutgers University Press.

1988e. Critical Notice of *The Fragility of Goodness* by Martha Nussbaum. *Canadian Journal of Philosophy*, 805–14.

1988f. *Negative Freiheit: Zur Kritik des Neuzeitlichen Individualismus*. Frankfurt: Suhrkamp.

1988g. Algunas condiciones para una democracìa viable. In *Democracìa y Participaciòn*, R. Alvagay & C. Ruiz (eds). Santiago: Ediciones Melquiades.

1988h. Le Juste et le bien. *Revue de Métaphysique et de Morale* **93**(1), 33–56.

1988i. Review of *Logics of Disintegration: Post-Structuralist Thought and the Claims of Critical Theory* by Peter Dews. *New Left Review* **170** (July/August), 110–16.

1988j. Foreword to *Social Action and Human Nature*, A. Honneth & H. Joas, vii–ix. Cambridge: Cambridge University Press.

1989a. *Sources of the Self: The Making of the Modern Identity*. Cambridge, MA: Harvard University Press.

1989b. Balancing the Humours: Charles Taylor talks to the Editors. *The Idler Magazine* **26**, (November & December), 21–9.

1989c. Marxism and Socialist Humanism. In *Out of Apathy: Voices of the New Left Thirty Years On*, R. Archer *et al.* (eds), 59–78. London: Verso.

1989d. The Rushdie Controversy. *Public Culture* **2**(1), 118–22.

1989e. Embodied Agency. In *Merleau-Ponty: Critical Essays*, H. Pietersma (ed.) Washington, D.C.: University Press of America.

1989f. Taylor and Foucault on Power and Freedom: a Reply. *Political Studies* **37**, 277–81.

1989g. Où est le danger? *Liberté* **31**(3), 13–16.

1990a. Religion in a Free Society. In *Articles of Faith, Articles of Peace*, J. Davison Hunter & O. Guinness (eds), 93–113. Washington, D.C.: The Brookings Institution.

1990b. Rorty in the Epistemological Tradition. In *Reading Rorty*, A. Malachowski (ed.), 257–75. Oxford: Blackwell .

1990c. Modes of Civil Society. *Public Culture* **3**(1), 95–118.

1990d. Exploring 'l'humaine condition'. In *Fermentum Massae Mundi: Jackowi Wozniakowskiemuw Disdem Sziesata*, R. Urodzin, N. Cieslinska, P. Rudzinski (eds), 199–207. Warsaw: Agora.

1990e. Our Therapeutic Age. *Compass* **8** (November), 6–10.

1990f. A Free, Independent Quebec in a Strong, United Canada: Review of *The Challenge to English Canada – Le Défi Québécois*, Christian Dufour. *Compass* **8** (May), 46–8.

1991a. *The Malaise of Modernity*. Concord: Ontario. Reprinted 1992 as *The Ethics of Authenticity*. Cambridge, MA: Harvard University Press.

1991b. Civil Society in the Western Tradition. In *The Notion of Tolerance and Human Rights*, E. Groffier & M. Paradis (eds), 117–36. Ottawa: Carleton University Press.

1991c. The Dialogical Self. In *The Interpretive Turn: Philosophy, Science,*

Culture, J. Bohman, D. Hiley, R. Shusterman (eds), 304–14. Ithaca, NY: Cornell University Press.

1991d. Comments and Replies. *Inquiry* **34**, 237–54.

1991e. Hegel's Ambiguous Legacy for Modern Liberalism. In *Hegel and Legal Theory*, D. Cornell, M. Rosenfeld, D. Gray Carlson (eds), 64–77. New York: Routledge. Originally published 1989. *Cardozo Law Review* **10**(5–6), 857–70.

1991f. Comprendre la culture politique. In *L'Engagement intellectuel: Mélanges en honneur de Léon Dion*, R. Hudon & R. Pelletier (eds), 193–207. Sainte Foy: Les Presses de L'Université Laval.

1991g. Philosophical Gadfly: The Original Socrates and Plato's Version. Review of *Socrates: Ironist and Moral Philosopher* by Gregory Vlastos. *Times Literary Supplement* (7 June), 3–4.

1991h. N. Halmer. *Von der Macht der Sprache: Interview mit Charles Taylor*. *Mesotes* **1**, 85–7.

1991i. Die Beschwörung der Civil Society. In *Europa und die Civil Society*, K. Michalski (ed.) 52–83. Stuttgart: Klett-Cotta.

1992a. *Multiculturalism and The Politics of Recognition*. A. Gutman (ed.). Princeton, NJ: Princeton University Press.

1992b. Inwardness and the Culture of Modernity. In *Philosophical Interventions in the Unfinished Project of the Enlightenment*, A. Honneth, T. McCarthy, C. Offe, A. Wellmer (eds), 88–110. Cambridge, MA: MIT Press. German Original. 1988. In *Zwischenbetrachtungen: Im Prozess der Aufklärung*, Honneth *et al.* (eds), 601–23. Frankfurt: Suhrkamp.

1992c. *Rapprocher les solitudes: Écrits sur le fédéralisme et le nationalisme au Canada*, G. Laforest (ed.). Sainte-Foy: Les Presses de l'Université Laval. English translation: 1993. *Reconciling the Solitudes: Essays in Canadian Federalism and Nationalism*, G. Laforest (ed.). Montreal & Kingston: McGill-Queen's University Press.

1992d. Quel principe d'identité collective? In *L'Europe au soir du siècle*, J. Lenoble & N. Dewandre (eds), 59–66. Paris: Éditions Esprit.

1992e. Can Canada Survive the Charter? *Alberta Law Review* **XXX**(2), 427–47.

1992f. Review of *Ideals and Illusions: On Reconstruction and Deconstruction in Contemporary Critical Theory* by Thomas A. McCarthy. *Ethics* **102**, 856–8.

1992g. Un choix de somnambules. *L'Actualité* **17** (1 May), 3.

1993a. Hegel and the Philosophy of Action. In *Selected Essays on G. W. F. Hegel*, L. Stepelevich (ed.), 168–86. New York: Humanities Press.

1993b. Modernity and the Rise of the Public Sphere. In *The Tanner Lectures on Human Values*, G. B. Peterson (ed.), 203–60. Salt Lake City: University of Utah Press.

1993c. Embodied Agency and Background in Heidegger. In *The Cambridge Companion to Heidegger*, C. Guignon (ed.), 317–36. Cambridge: Cambridge University Press.

1993d. The deep challenge of dualism. In *Quebec: State and Society*, A. Gagnon (ed.), 82–95. Toronto: Nelson.

1993e. The Dangers of Soft Despotism. *The Responsive Community* **3**, 22–31. Reprinted 1994 as Between Democracy and Despotism: The Dangers of Soft Despotism. *Current* **359** (January), 36–9.

1993f. Nietzsche's Legacy. *Lonergan Review* **2**, 171–87.

1993g. Wieviel Gemeinschaft braucht die Demokratie? *Transit* **5** (Winter), 5–20.

1993h. Der Begriff der 'Bürgerlichen Gesellschaft' im politischen Denken des Westens. In *Gemeinschaft und Gerechtigkeit*, M. Brumlik & H. Brunkhorst (eds), 117–48. Frankfurt: Fischer.

1993i. *Liberale Politik und Öffentlichkeit*. In *Die Liberale Gesellschaft*, K. Michalski (ed.), 21–67. Stuttgart: Klett Cotta.

1993j. It is Strange and Wonderful that We Exist. *Compass* **11** (September/ October), 21–2.

1994a. Reply to Braybrooke and de Sousa. *Dialogue* **33**, 125–31.

1994b. Can Liberalism Be Communitarian? *Critical Review* **8**, 257–62.

1994c. Précis & Reply to Commentators in Symposium on *Sources of the Self*. *Philosophy and Phenomenological Research* **LIV**(I), 185–6, 203–13.

1994d. Reply and Rearticulation. In *Philosophy in an Age of Pluralism: The Philosophy of Charles Taylor in Question*, J. Tully & D. Weinstock (eds), 213–57. Cambridge: Cambridge University Press.

1994e. Philosophical Reflections on Caring Practices. In *The Crisis of Care*, S. B. Phillips & P. Benner (eds), 174–87. Washington: Georgetown University Press.

1994f. Justice After Virtue. In *After MacIntyre: Critical Perspectives on the Work of Alasdair MacIntyre*, J. Horton & S. Mendus (eds), 16–43. Cambridge: Polity Press.

1994g. Canadian Reality, a Little at a Time. *Compass* **14**, 47–8, 52.

1994h. Human Rights, Human Differences. *Compass* **12**, 18–19.

1994i. *Ne pas choisir: construire un Québec français et liberal*. *Nuit Blanches* (June/August), 48–50.

1995a. *Philosophical Arguments*. Cambridge, MA: Harvard University Press.

1995b. A Most Peculiar Institution. In *World, Mind and Ethics: Essays on the Ethical Philosophy of Bernard Williams*, J. E. J. Altham & R. Harrison (eds), 132–55. Cambridge: Cambridge University Press.

1995c. Response to Bromwich's "Culturalism, The Euthanasia of Liberalism". *Dissent* **42** (Winter) 103–4.

1995d. On "Disclosing New Worlds". *Inquiry* **38**, 119–22.

1995e. Federations and Nations: Living Among Others. In *States of Mind: Dialogues with Contemporary Thinkers*, R. Kearney (ed.), 23–32. New York: New York University Press.

1995f. Nationalismus und Moderne. *Transit* **9** (Summer), 177–98

1995g. *Identitet, Frihet och Gemenskap*. Göteborg: Daidalos.

1996a. Why Democracy Needs Patriotism. In *For Love of Country*, M. Nussbaum, J. Cohen (ed.), 119–21. Boston: Beacon Press.

1996b. A World Consensus on Human Rights? *Dissent* **43** (Summer), 15–21.

1996c. Communitarianism, Taylor-made: An Interview with Charles Taylor (with R. Abbey). *Australian Quarterly* **68**(1), 1–10.

1996d. Iris Murdoch and Moral Philosophy. In *Iris Murdoch and the Search for Human Goodness*, M. Antonaccio & W. Schweiker (eds), 3–28. Chicago, IL: University of Chicago Press.

1996e. Sharing Identity Space. In *Quebec-Canada: What is the Path Ahead?* J. Trent, R. Young, G. Lachapelle (eds), 121–4. Ottawa: University of Ottawa Press.

1996f. Deep Diversity and the Future of Canada. In *Can Canada Survive? Under What Terms and Conditions?* Transactions of the Royal Society of Canada, sixth series, vol. 7. Reprinted. 1997. In *Can Canada Survive? / Le Canada peut-il survivre?*, D. Hayne (ed.), 29–36. Toronto: University of Toronto Press.

1996g. Drei Formen des Säkularismus. In *Das Europa der Rligionen*, O. Kallscheuer (ed.), 217–46. Frankfurt: Fischer.

1996h. L'interiorità e la cultura della modernità. *Fenomenologia e Società* **XIX**(1–2), 4–24.

1996i. Spirituality of Life – and Its Shadow. *Compass* **14** (May/June), 10–13.

1996j. Les Sources de l'identité moderne. In *Les Frontières de l'identité: modernité et postmodernisme au Québec*, M. Elbaz, A. Fortin, G. Laforest (eds), 347–64. Sainte Foy: Les Presses de L'Université Laval.

1996k. Der Trend zur politischen Fragmentarisierung: Bedeutungsverlust demokratischer Entscheidungen. In *Demokratie am Wendepunkt: Die demokratische Frage als Projekt des 21. Jahrhunderts*, W. Weidenfeld (ed.), 254–73. Berlin: Siedler.

1996l. Introduction to *Qu'est-ce qu'une nation? / What Is a Nation?* Ernest Renan. W. R. Taylor (trans.). Toronto: Tapir Press.

1996m. Review of *Multicultural Citizenship* by Will Kymlicka, *American Political Science Review*, **90** (1996), 408.

1996n. *De politieke Cultur van de Moderniteit*. The Hague: Kok Agora, Kampen.

1997a. Leading a Life. In *Incommensurability, Incomparability, and Practical Reasoning* R.Chang (ed.), 170–83. Cambridge, MA: Harvard University Press.

1997b. Nationalism and Modernity. In *The Morality of Nationalism*, R. McKim & J. McMahan, (eds), 31–55. Oxford: Oxford University Press. Reprinted in a modified version. 1988. In *The State of the Nation*, J. Hall (ed.), 191–218. Cambridge: Cambridge University Press. Reprinted 1999. In *Theorizing Nationalism,* R. Beiner (ed.), 219–46. Albany, NY: State University of New York Press.

1997c. Foreword to *The Disenchantment of the World: A Political History of Religion*, M. Gauchet, ix–xv. Princeton, NJ: Princeton University Press.

1997d. Identity and Modernity. Paper presented to the conference "Twenty-five years: Social Science and Social Change", Institute for Advanced Study, Princeton, NJ, May 8–11.

1997e. The Distance between Citizen and State. (in Chinese translation). In *Twenty-first Century*, **40** (April), 4–20.

1997f. Was ist Liberalismus? *Hegelpreis 1997*, 25–54. Frankfurt: Suhrkamp.

1997g. Demokratie und Ausgrenzung. *Transit* (Winter), 81–97.

1997h. Die immanente Gegenaufklärung. In *Aufklärung Heute*, K. Michalski (ed.), 54–74. Stuttgart: Klett Kotta.

1997i. *La Liberté des Modernes*. Paris: PUF.

1998a. Modes of Secularism. In *Secularism and its Critics*, R. Bhargava (ed.), 31–53. Delhi: Oxford University Press.

1998b. From Philosophical Anthropology to the Politics of Recognition: An Interview with Philippe de Lara. *Thesis Eleven*, **52** (February), 103–12.

1998c. The Dynamics of Democratic Exclusion. *Journal of Democracy*, (October) 143–56.

1998d. Interview with Professor Charles Taylor, M. Ancelovici & F. Dupuis-Deri. *Citizenship Studies* 2(2), 247–56.

1998e. Globalization and the Future of Canada. *Queen's Quarterly* **105**(3), 331–42.

1998f. Living With Difference. In *Debating Democracy's Discontent: Essays on American Politics, Law, and Public Philosophy*, A. L. Allen & M. C. Regan (eds), 212–26. Oxford: Oxford University Press.

1998g. Le Fondamental dans l'Histoire. In *Charles Taylor et l'interprétation de l'identité moderne*, G. Laforest & P. de Lara (eds), 35–49. Sainte Foy: Les Presses de l'Université Laval.

1998h. Le redresseur de tordus. *L'Actualité* (July), 18–20.

1999a. *A Catholic Modernity?* J. L. Heft (ed.). New York: Oxford University Press.

1999b. Conditions of an Unforced Consensus on Human Rights. In *The East Asian Challenge to Human Rights* , J. R. Bauer & D. A. Bell (eds), 124–44. New York: Cambridge University Press.

1999c. Two Theories of Modernity. *Public Culture* 11(1), 153–74.

1999d. Democratic Exclusion (and its Remedies?). In *Multiculturalism, Liberalism and Democracy*, R. Bhargava, A. K. Bagchi, R. Sudarshan (eds), 138–63. New Delhi: Oxford University Press.

1999e. Comment on Jürgen Habermas's "From Kant to Hegel and Back Again". *European Journal of Philosophy* **2**, 152–7.

2000a. McDowell on Value and Knowledge: Review of *Mind, Value and Reality* and *Meaning* and *Knowledge and Reality*. *Philosophical Quarterly* **50**(199), 242–9.

2000b. The Immanent Counter-Enlightenment. In *Canadian Political Philosophy at the Turn of the Century: Exemplary Essays*, R. Beiner & W. Norman (eds), 583–603. Oxford: Oxford University Press. Projected publication date 2000.

Forthcoming a. Gadamer and the Human Sciences. Contribution to a *Festschrift* for Gadamer's 100th birthday, U. Arnswald (ed.).

Forthcoming b. An End to Mediational Epistemology. *Heidegger, Coping and Cognitive Science: Essays in Honor of Hubery L. Dreyfus*, vol. 2, M. Wrathall & J. Malpas (eds). Boston, MA: MIT Press.

Forthcoming c. Review of John McDowell's *Mind and World*. In *Reading McDowell: On Mind and World*, N. H. Smith (ed.). London: Routledge. Projected publication date 2001.

An updated list of Taylor's writings is kept by William Hughes and is available at the website: www.netidea.com/~whughes/taylor.html

References

Abbey, R. 1999. Charles Taylor's Politics of Recognition: A Reply to Jonathan Seglow. *Political Studies* **XLVII**, 710–14.

Adeney, F. S. 1991. Review of *Sources of the Self*. *Theology Today* **48**, 204–10.

Anderson, J. 1996. The Personal Lives of Strong Evaluators: Identity, Pluralism and Ontology in Charles Taylor's Value Theory. *Constellations* **3**(1), 17–38.

Appiah, K. A. 1994. Identity, Authenticity, Survival: Multicultural Societies and Social Reproduction. See Gutman (1994), 149–63.

Aristotle 1981 *The Politics*, T. A. Sinclair (trans.). London: Penguin.

Aristotle 1980. *Nicomachean Ethics*, D. Ross (trans.). Oxford: Oxford University Press.

Baier, A. 1988. Critical Notice of C. Taylor *Philosophy and the Human Sciences: Philosophical Papers*, vol. II. *Canadian Journal of Philosophy* **18**, 589–94.

Beam, C. 1997. The Clash of Paradigms: Taylor vs. Narveson on the Foundations of Ethics. *Dialogue* **36**, 771–81.

Beiner, R. 1997. *Philosophy in a Time of Lost Spirit: Essays on Contemporary Theory*. Toronto: Toronto University Press.

Berlin, I. 1969. *Four Essays on Liberty*. Oxford: Oxford University Press.

Berlin, I. 1979. *Against the Current*. London: Hogarth Press.

Berlin, I. 1994. Introduction. See Tully & Weinstock (1994), 1–3.

Birnbaum, P. 1996. From Multiculturalism to Nationalism. *Political Theory* **24**, 33–45.

Blumenberg, H. 1985. *The Legitimacy of the Modern Age*. Boston, MA: MIT Press.

Blum, L. A. 1994. Multiculturalism, Racial Justice, and Community: Reflections on Charles Taylor's "Politics of Recognition". In *Defending Diversity: Contemporary Philosophical Perspectives on Pluralism and Multiculturalism,* L. Foster & P. Herzog (eds), 175–205. Amherst: University of Massachusetts Press.

Bohman, J., Hiley, D. & Shusterman, R. (eds) 1991. *The Interpretive Turn: Philosophy, Science, Culture*. Ithaca, NY: Cornell University Press.

Braybrooke, D. 1994. Inward and Outward with the Modern Self. *Dialogue* **XXXIII**, 101–8.

Buchanan, J. 1972. Before Public Choice. In *Explorations in the Theory of Anarchy*, G. Tullock (ed.), 27–37. Blacksburg, VA: Center for Study of Public Choice.

Buchanan, J. 1979. Politics Without Romance. *HIS Journal Zeitschrift des Instituts fuer Hoehere Studien* **3**, 1–11.

Buchanan, J. 1986. The Constitution of Economic Policy. *Le Prix Noble*. 334–43. Stockholm: Almquist & Wicksell International.

Calhoun, C. 1991. Morality, Identity, and Historical Explanation: Charles Taylor on the *Sources of the Self*. *Sociological Theory* **9**, 232–64.

Clark, S. 1991. Taylor's Waking Dream: No One's Reply. *Inquiry* **34**, 195–215.

Cockburn, D. 1991. Review of *Sources of the Self*. *Philosophical Investigations* **14**, 360–64.

Connolly, W. 1996. Review of Tully (ed.) *American Political Science Review* **90**(1), 181.

Cooke, M. 1997. Authenticity and Autonomy: Taylor, Habermas and the Politics of Recognition. *Political Theory* **25**(2), 258–88.

Dauenhauer, B. 1992. Taylor and Ricoeur on the Self. *Man and World* **25**, 211–25.

De Sousa, R. 1994. Bashing the Enlightenment: A Discussion of Charles Taylor's *Sources of the Self*. *Dialogue* **XXXIII**, 109–23.

Dewey. J. Philosophy in Education. In *John Dewey: His Contribution to the American Tradition*, I. Edmain (ed.), 90–210. New York: Greenwood Press.

Dumm, T. L. 1994. Strangers and Liberals. *Political Theory* **22**(1), 167–75.

Dunn, J. 1996. Balancing Acts in a Nervous Age: Review of *Philosophical Arguments*. *The Times Higher Education Supplement*, 2 February, 26–7.

Edgar, A. 1995. Weighting Health States and Strong Evaluation. *Bioethics* **9**(3–4), 240–51.

Etzioni, A. 2000. A newer, lonelier crowd emerges in internet study. *New York Times* 16 February, 18.

Feinberg, W. 1997. Nationalism in a Comparative Mode: A Response to Charles Taylor. See McKinn & McMahan (1997), 66–73.

Flanagan, O. 1996. *Self Expressions: Mind, Morals and the Meaning of Life*. New York: Oxford University Press.

Flathman, R. E. 1987. *The Philosophy and Politics of Freedom*. Chicago, IL: University of Chicago Press.

Forbes, H. D. 1997. Rousseau, Ethnicity, and Difference. In *The Legacy of Rousseau*, C. Orwin & N. Tarcov (eds), 220–45. Chicago, IL: University of Chicago Press.

Foucault, M. 1978–1988. *History of Sexuality*, vols 2–3, R. Hurley (trans.). New York: Pantheon Books.

Foucault, M. 1998. An Aesthetics of Existence. In *Politics, Philosophy, Culture: Interviews and Other Writings, 1977–1984*, L. Kritzman (ed.), 47–53. London: Routledge.

Frankfurt, H. 1971. Freedom of the Will and the Concept of a Person. *Journal of Philosophy* **68**(1), 5–20.

Friedman, J. 1994. The Politics of Communitarianism. *Critical Review* **8**, 297–340.

Geertz, C. 1994. The Strange Estrangement: Taylor and the Natural Sciences. See Tully & Weinstock (1994), 83–95.

Goodin, R. & Pettit, P. (eds) 1993. *A Companion to Contemporary Political Philosophy*. Oxford: Blackwell.

Gray, J. 1993. *Post-liberalism: Studies in Political Thought*. New York: Routledge.

Gray, J. 1995. Vive la différence. *The Times HigherEducation Supplement*. 13 October, 17.

Guignon, C. B. 1991. Pragmatism or Hermeneutics? Epistemology after Foundationalism. See Bohman *et al.* (1991), 81–101.

Gutman, A. (ed.) 1994. *Multiculturalism: Examining the Politics of Recognition*. Princeton, NJ: Princeton University Press; expanded edition of a 1992 book of the same name.

Gutting, G. 1999. *Pragmatic Liberalism and the Critique of Modernity.* New York: Cambridge University Press.

Haakonssen, K. 1993. Entry in Goodin & Pettit (1993), 568–74.

Haldane, J. 1993. Review of *Multiculturalism and "The Politics of Recognition". European Journal of Philosophy* 1, 347–50.

Hampton, J. 1997. *Political Philosophy.* Boulder, CO: Westview Press.

Hauerwas S. & Matzko D. 1992. The Sources of Charles Taylor: Review of *Sources of the Self. Religious Studies Review* 18, 286–9.

Heidegger, M. 1962. *Being and Time*, J. Macquarie & E. Robinson (trans.). New York: Harper Row.

Hendley, S. 1993. Liberalism, Communitarianism and the Conflictual Grounds of Democratic Pluralism. *Philosophy and Social Criticism* 19, 293–316.

Hittinger, R. 1990. Review of *Sources of the Self. Review of Metaphysics* 44, 111–30.

Hobbes, T. 1974. *Leviathan*. J. Plamenatz (ed.). Glasgow: Collins/Fontana.

Hoy, D. C. 1977. Hegel, Taylor-Made. *Dialogue* 16, 715–32.

Huang, Y. 1998. Charles Taylor's Transcendental Arguments for Liberal Communitarianism. *Philosophy & Social Criticism* 24, 79–106.

Ignatieff, M. 1985. Of Human Interest. *Saturday Night Magazine* (December), 63–6.

James, S. 1994. Internal and External in the Work of Descartes. See Tully & Weinstock (1994), 7–19.

Kerr, F. 1997. *Immortal Longings*. London: SPCK.

Kingwell, M. 1998. Two Concepts of Pluralism: Critical Notice of *Philosophy in an Age of Pluralism: The Philosophy of Charles Taylor in Question*, James Tully (ed.). *Dialogue* 37, 375–86.

Kuhn, T. 1991. The Natural and the Human Sciences. 1991c. The Dialogical Self. See Bohman *et al.* (1991), 17–24.

Kukathas, C. 1996. Liberalism, Communitarianism and Political Community. *Social Philosophy and Policy* 13(1), 80–104.

Kymlicka, W. 1991. The Ethics of Inarticulacy. *Inquiry* 34, 155–82.

Kymlicka, W. 1993. Community. See Goodin & Pettit (1993), 366–78.

Kymlicka, W. 1997. The Sources of Nationalism: Commentary on Taylor. See McKinn & McMahan (1997), 56–65.

Laforest. G. 1994. Philosophy and Political Judgement in a Multinational Federation. See Tully & Weinstock (1994), 194–209.

Lane, M. 1992. God or Orienteering? A Critical Study of Charles Taylor's *Sources of the Self. Ratio* 5, 46–56.

Larmore, C. 1991. Review of *Sources of the Self. Ethics* (October), 158–62.

Laslett, P. (ed.) 1949 *Patriarcha and Other Political Works*. Oxford: Blackwell.

Locke, J. 1960. *Two Treatises of Government,* P. Laslett (ed.). New York: Cambridge University Press.

Locke, J. 1990. *A Letter Concerning Toleration.* Buffalo, NY: Prometheus Books.

Loew-Beer, M. 1991. Living a Life and the Problem of Existential Impossibility. *Inquiry* 34, 217–36.

MacIntryre, A. 1977. Epistemological Crises, Dramatic Narrative and the Philosophy of Science. *The Monist* 60, 453–72.

MacIntyre, A. 1996. Review of *Philosophy in an Age of Pluralism: the Philosophy of Charles Taylor in Question*. *Philosophical Quarterly* **46**, 522–4.

MacKinnon, C. A. 1989. *Toward a Feminist Theory of the State*. Cambridge, MA: Harvard University Press.

Macpherson, C. B. 1966. *The Real World of Democracy*. Oxford: Oxford University Press.

Macpherson, C. B. 1977. *The Life and Times of Liberal Democracy*. Oxford: Oxford University Press.

Marsden, G. 1999. Matteo Ricci and the Prodigal Culture. In *A Catholic Modernity?*, J. L. Heft (ed.), 83–93. New York: Oxford University Press.

McKinn, R. & McMahan, J. (eds) 1997. *The Morality of Nationalism*. New York: Oxford University Press.

Mill, J. S. 1980. *On Liberty*, G. Himmelfarb (ed.). Middlesex: Penguin Books.

Miller, D. 1995. What Holds Us Together: Review of *Philosophical Arguments* and *Philosophy in an Age of Pluralism: The Philosophy of Charles Taylor in Question*, J. Tully (ed.). *Times Literary Supplement* 15 December, 26.

Morgan, M. 1994. Religion, History and Moral Discourse. See Tully & Weinstock (1994), 49–66.

Mouffe, C. 1988. American Liberalism and Its Critics: Rawls, Taylor, Sandel and Walzer. *Praxis International* **8**, 193–206.

Mulhall, S. & Swift, A. 1997. *Liberals and Communitarians*. 2nd edn. Oxford: Basil Blackwell.

Nagel, T. 1979. *Mortal Questions*. Cambridge: Cambridge University Press.

Neal, P. 1997. *Liberalism and its Discontents*. New York: New York University Press.

Nietzsche, F. 1968. *The Will to Power*, W. Kaufmann & R. J. Hollingdale (eds). New York: Vintage Books.

Nietzsche, F. 1974. *The Gay Science*, W. Kaufman (ed.). New York: Vintage Books.

Nozick, R. 1974. *Anarchy, State and Utopia*. New York: Basic Books.

Nussbaum, M. 1990. Our Pasts, Ourselves. *The New Republic* 9 April, 27–34.

Nussbaum, M. 1996. *For Love of Country*, J. Cohen (ed.). Boston, MA: Beacon Press.

O'Brien. M. 1981. *The Politics of Reproduction*. London: Routledge & Kegan Paul.

O'Hagan, T. 1993. Charles Taylor's Hidden God. *Ratio* **6** (June), 72–81.

Oksenberg Rorty, A. 1994. The Hidden Politics of Cultural Identification. *Political Theory* **22**(1), 152–66.

Olafson, F. A. 1994. Comments on *The Sources of the Self*. *Philosophy and Phenomenological Research* **LIV**(I), 191–6.

Parfit, D. 1989. *Reasons and Persons*. Oxford: Clarendon Press.

Pettit, P. 1997. *Republicanism: A Theory of Freedom and Government*. Oxford: Oxford University Press.

Rawls, J. 1971. *A Theory of Justice*. Cambridge, MA: Harvard University Press.

Rawls, J. 1993. *Political Liberalism*. Cambridge, MA: Harvard University Press.

Rorty, R. 1994. Taylor on Truth. See Tully & Weinstock (1994), 20–33.

Rorty, R. 1999. Failed Prophecies, Glorious Hopes. *Constellations* **6**(2), 216–21.

Rosa, H. 1995. Goods and Life-forms: Relativism in Charles Taylor's Political Philosophy. *Radical Philosophy* **71** (May/June), 20–26.

Rosen, M. 1991. Must We Return to Moral Realism? *Inquiry* **34**, 183–94.

Rouse, J. 1991. Interpretation in Natural and Human Science. See Bohman *et al.* (1991), 42–56.

Ryan. A. 1993. Liberalism. See Goodin & Pettit (1993), 291–311.

Sandel, M. 1982. *Liberalism and the Limits of Justice* Cambridge & New York: Cambridge University Press.

Schneewind, J. B. 1991. Review of *Sources of the Self*. *Journal of Philosophy* **88**(8), 422–6.

Scialabba, G. 1990. Review of *Sources of the Self*. *Dissent* **37**, 534–7.

Seglow, J. 1998. Universals and Particulars: the Case of Liberal Cultural Nationalism. *Political Studies* **46**(5), 963–77.

Shklar, J. 1991. Review of *Sources of the Self*. *Political Theory* **19**(1), 105–9.

Skinner, Q. 1991. Who are "We"? Ambiguities of the Modern Self. *Inquiry* **34**, 133–53.

Smith, N. 1996. Contingency and Self-Identity: Taylor's Hermeneutics vs Rorty's Postmodernism. *Theory, Culture and Society* **13**(2), 105–20.

Smith, N. 1997. Reason after Meaning: Review of *Philosophical Arguments*. *Philosophy and Social Criticism* **23**(1), 33–42.

Thiebaut, C. 1993. Charles Taylor: On the Improvement of Our Moral Portrait: Moral Realism, History of Subjectivity and Expressivist Language. *Praxis International* **13,** 126–53.

Todorov, T. 1984. *Mikhail Bakhtin: The Dialogical Principle*, W. Godzich (trans.). Minneapolis, MN: University of Minnesota Press.

Tully, J. 1980. *A Discourse on Property: John Locke and his Adversaries*. Cambridge: Cambridge University Press.

Tully, J. & D. Weinstock (eds) 1994. *Philosophy in an Age of Pluralism: The Philosophy of Charles Taylor in Question*. Cambridge: Cambridge University Press.

Waldron, J. 1990. How We Learn to be Good: Review of *Sources of the Self*. *Times Literary Supplement* (23–29 March), 325–6.

Waldron, J. 1993. See Goodin & Pettit (1993), 575–85.

Wallach, J. R. 1987. Liberals, Communitarians, and the Tasks of Political Theory. *Political Theory* **15**(4), 581–611.

Warnke, G. 1985. Hermeneutics and the Social Sciences: A Gadamerian Critique of Rorty. *Inquiry* **28**, 339–57.

Weinstock, D. 1994. The Political Theory of Strong Evaluation. See Tully & Weinstock (1994), 171–93.

Wihl, G. 1994. Charles Taylor on Situatedness, Incommensurability and Symbolic Language. In *The Contingency of Theory: Pragmatism, Expressivism and Deconstruction*, 39–65. New Haven, CT: Yale University Press.

Williams, B. 1985. *Ethics and the Limits of Philosophy*. London: Fontana.

Williams, B. 1990. Republican and Galilean: Review of *Sources of the Self*. *The New York Review of Books* **37** (8 November), 45–7.

Wittgenstein, L. 1958. *Philosophical Investigations*. Oxford: Basil Blackwell.

Wittgenstein, L. 1972. *On Certainty*, G. E. M Anscome & G. H. von Wright (eds). New York: Harper & Row.

Wolf, S. 1994. Comment. See Gutman (1994), 75–85.

Wolterstorff, N. 1996. *John Locke and the Ethics of Belief*. New York: Cambridge University Press.

Wood, A. 1992. Review of *Sources of the Self*. *Philosophical Review* **101**, 621–6.

A comprehensive current list of writings *about* Taylor is kept by William Hughes and is available at the website: http://www.netidea.com/ ~whughes/taylor3.html

Index